Postconventional Moral Thinking

A Neo-Kohlbergian Approach

Postconventional Moral Thinking

A Neo-Kohlbergian Approach

James Rest
Darcia Narvaez
Muriel J. Bebeau
Stephen J. Thoma
Center for the Study of Ethical Development
University of Minnesota

LEA
1999

LAWRENCE ERLBAUM ASSOCIATES, PUBLISHERS
Mahwah, New Jersey   London

Lawrence Erlbaum Associates, Inc., Publishers
10 Industrial Avenue
Mahwah, NJ 07430

Cover design by Kathryn Houghtaling Lacey

Library of Congress Cataloging-in-Publication Data

Postconventional moral thinking : a Neo-Kohlbergian
approach / by James Rest, Darcia Narvaez, Muriel J.
Bebeau, Stephen J. Thoma.
    p. cm.
Includes bibliographical references and index.
ISBN 0-8058-3285-8 (hardcover : alk. paper).
1. Moral development. 2. Kohlberg, Lawrence, I. Rest,
James R. II. Narvaez, Darcia. III. Bebeau, Muriel J. IV.
Thoma, Stephen J.
  BF723.M54P675 1999
    155.2'5—dc21   98-43690
                                      CIP

Printed in the United States of America
10   9   8   7   6   5   4   3   2   1

Contents

ᐄ   ◆   ᐅ

Preface

৪৩ ✦ ৫৪

For decades, Lawrence Kohlberg provided major ideas for psychological research in morality. Yet these days some critics regard his work as outmoded, beyond repair, and too faulty for anybody to take seriously. These critics suggest that research would advance more profitably by taking a different approach. In this book, we acknowledge particular philosophical and psychological problems with Kohlberg's theory and methodology, but propose a reformulation, as a "neo-Kohlbergian" approach. Employing core ideas from Kohlberg's theory and method, research with the Defining Issues Test (hereafter, the DIT) has produced a large body of findings—reported by hundreds of researchers—attesting to the fruitfulness of his ideas.

In the first chapter, we briefly give an overview of what we mean by a *neo*-Kohlbergian approach. Then, in chapter 2, we discuss major criticisms of Kohlberg's approach made over the past 25 years by psychologists and philosophers. We group the criticisms under four headings:

1. *Psychological*: Criticisms from psychologists that require changes in both method and theory.
2. *Philosophical*: Criticisms from moral philosophers on Kohlberg's formalist, deontological normative theory.
3. *Limits*: Criticisms that Kohlberg's approach didn't cover aspects of the psychology of morality.
4. *Unwarranted*: Criticisms that we think are mistaken, not requiring any change in a Kohlbergian approach.

With these criticisms in mind, our theoretical reformulation into a neo-Kohlbergian approach is presented in chapter 3. Our theoretical solutions in chapter 3 are empirically reviewed in chapter 4, presenting data gathered over the past 25 years on the validity and reliability of the DIT. Other, independent researchers have also produced remarkably consistent validity findings—we cite over 400 published reports on the DIT. In Chapter 5, we summarize new questions that DIT research has addressed, new theoretical formulations that we have advanced, and some of the findings of this ongoing enterprise. In chapter 6, we discuss the relation of DIT research to American cognitive psychology—in particular, to schema theory in social cognition—and our reconceptualization of how the DIT works. In sum, chapters 3 through 6 focus on the DIT; and, of these, chapter 4 focuses on validity evidence of the DIT.

Chapters 7 and 8 attempt to integrate our neo-Kohlbergian approach with two alternative approaches: Turiel's domain theory and Shweder's cultural psychology approach. Chapter 9 summarizes the major points of the book. Readers who want to know where this book is headed may want to read the first and last chapters before reading the others.

This book is intended to give a coherent theoretical overview for hundreds of studies that have used the DIT. We propose reformulations in the underlying psychological and philosophical theories. This book attempts to pull together the analysis of criticisms of a Kohlbergian approach, a rationale for DIT research, new theoretical ideas, and new research—doing this theoretical work while simultaneously reviewing the existing body of DIT research. The logical flow of the book can be glimpsed from the major questions that each chapter considers:

Chapter 1: What is our neo-Kohlbergian approach (briefly)?
Chapter 2: What are the problems with the "classic" Kohlbergian approach?
Chapter 3: How can we deal with these problems in DIT research?
Chapter 4: What is the validity of the DIT?
Chapter 5: What new lines of research has the DIT fostered?
Chapter 6: How does schema theory help ?
Chapter 7: How can our neo-Kohlbergian approach be integrated with Domain theory?
Chapter 8: How can our neo-Kohlbergian approach be integrated with cultural psychology?
Chapter 9: Summary of major supporting arguments.

DIT research has flourished because it can be easily used by others who independently frame their research questions, collect data, and contribute to the research enterprise. Our thanks to the many researchers who have used the DIT, shared their findings with us, and contributed to this literature. We thank especially the following researchers for use of their data in this book: DeWitt Baldwin, Mark Davison, Deborah Deemer, Laura Duckett, Jean Evens, Irene Getz, Steve McNeel, William Penn, Donnie Self, and Muriel Ryden.

Writing this book has been a community project, involving many people who responded to many drafts. We wish every scholar could have the kind of feedback and encouragement that we have had. Many times, on many points, we were persuaded to change direction. Of course, we still might not have things right, and no one else is to blame. Nevertheless, with thanks, we merely list those who gave us significant feedback: Judy Andre, Mary Lou Arnold, Mary Brabeck, Marvin Berkowitz, Augusto Blasi, Dwight Boyd, Deborah Deemer, Lynn Edwards, John Gibbs, Uwe Gielen, Lisa Kuhmerker, Orlando Lourenço, Larry Nucci, Michael Pritchard, Bill Puka, Donald Reed, John Snarey, John Sullivan, Laura Lee (Dolly) Swisher, Lawrence Walker, Members of the Moral Cognition Research group at the University of Minnesota and Members of the Bioethics Reading Group, Affiliates of the Center for Bioethics, University of Minnesota: Mila Aroskar, Bill Doherty, Laura Duckett, Jeffrey Kahn, and Susan Wolf. Also, thanks to Christyan Mitchell, who provided help with the formidable job of compiling references, and who has been "running the shop" of the DIT Scoring Service at the center in recent years.

It is no coincidence that the first and last words of this text are "Lawrence Kohlberg." He died over 10 years ago, but his significance to the field of moral psychology endures.

1

⽧ ◆ ⽣

Overview of Our
Neo-Kohlbergian Approach

There have been numerous suggestions in the academic literature that
Kohlberg's approach to morality was so fundamentally wrong-headed
and flawed that researchers in morality are better off starting anew.
We disagree. Our neo-Kohlbergian approach contends that
Kohlberg's theory is still fruitful—although some problems warrant
modification. In chapter 1, we present a condensed overview of our
neo-Kohlbergian approach without developing the arguments for the
points, and without citing evidence. The development of our argument is the burden of this whole book; in this chapter, we only present
the gist of our approach.

Several core ideas of Kohlberg's have guided our research:

- *Emphasis on cognition.* Kohlberg contended that the developing
  child was like a moral philosopher (Kohlberg, 1968) in trying to
  make conceptual sense of social experience, particularly in developing concepts of how it is possible to organize cooperation on a
  societywide level. In order to understand moral behavior,
  Kohlberg argued that we have to understand how the person is
  making sense of the world.
- *The individual's construction of moral epistemology.* Kohlberg proposed that the basic categories of morality (such as "justice," "duty,"
  "rights," and "social order") are self-constructed by the individual.
  This is to attribute activity in meaning-making to the individual, not
  viewing the individual as simply passively absorbing the ideology of
  one's culture.

- *Development*. Kohlberg proposed that it is possible to talk about "advance," whereby one set of concepts was more developed (higher is normatively "better"). All of the differences among people aren't all equally defensible; some of the differences among people represent more comprehensive, more coherent, more elaborated—more developed—concepts. Furthermore, in broad terms (at least for a large number of people) the course of moral judgment development can be described as evolving from simpler ideas to more complex ideas.
- *The shift from conventional to postconventional thinking*. Kohlberg proposed that one of the major social cognitive developments in adolescence and young adulthood is the growing awareness of how people interrelate to each other through laws, rules, roles, and institutions—the "system" of a society. Furthermore, there develops a concern with the system's morality. He described development in terms of conventional moral thinking (the morality of maintaining social norms because they are the way we do things) shifting to postconventional thinking (the morality that rules, roles, laws, and institutions must serve some shareable ideal of cooperation).

It is useful to see Kohlberg's theory as primarily addressed to the formal structures of society (laws, roles, institutions, general practices) instead of to personal, face-to-face relationships in particular, everyday dealings with people. Just as in the field of economics a distinction is made between *macro*economics and *micro*economics, so also it is useful to distinguish levels of phenomena in "macromorality" and "micromorality." Macromorality concerns the formal structures of society that are involved in making cooperation possible at a society level (in which not just kin, friends, and long-known acquaintances are interrelated, but strangers, competitors, and diverse clans, ethnic groups, and religions are as well). Examples of the special concerns of macromorality include the rights and responsibilities of free speech, due-process rights of the accused, nondiscriminatory work practices, freedom of religion, and equity in economic and educational opportunity.

On the other hand, micromorality concerns developing relationships with particular others, and with an individual's creating consistent virtues within him- or herself throughout everyday life. Examples of micromorality include displaying courtesy and helpfulness to those with whom one personally interacts; caring in intimate relationships; observing birthdays and other personal events of friends and family; being courteous while driving a car; being punctual for appointments; and generally acting in a decent, responsible, empathic way in one's daily dealings with others (in contrast to being cantankerous, displaying road rage, being incommunicable, not carrying your share, being unreliable, and acting like a jerk).

In micromoral issues, what is praiseworthy is characterized in terms of unswerving loyalty, dedication, and partisan caring to special others. On the other hand, in macromorality, the praiseworthy response is characterized in terms of impartiality and acting on principle, instead of partisanship, favoritism, or tribalism. Both macro- and micromorality concern ways of constructing and enriching the web of relationships—one through the structures of society, and the other through personal, face-to-face relationships. To be sure, there is a tension between macromorality and micromorality, and there are many interconnections between the two. Our view is that Kohlberg's theory is more illuminating of macroissues than of microissues.

Consider the context of the 1960s, when Kohlberg's work became popular. At that time many young people were challenging the moral basis of American society, finding it too repressive at home and too imperialistic abroad. In addition, American society was purportedly materialistic, sexist, and racist. Many young people experimented with alternative lifestyles, including new work roles, alternative schools, self-supporting communes, and disdain for material goods. Hippies dramatized the question "Is society moral?" by answering it in the negative and advocating that people "drop out." They said that American society was too corrupt to be worth joining.

Recall, too, that in the 1960s the issues that dominated the front pages of newspapers were macromoral ones: the Civil Rights movement, the student protests for free speech, the antiwar protests, and later, the Black Power and the women's movements. Additionally, the United States had just gone through a period of ferocious anti-Communist McCarthyism in the 1950s. All these events made it important to understand what the ideal of social justice entailed, and thus made the focus of Kohlberg's work relevant.

For instance, in the 1960s a highly controversial figure, Martin Luther King, Jr., was deliberately disobeying the law by marching in illegal places, sitting in illegal places, and eating in illegal places. George Wallace, then governor of Alabama, gained national attention by calling King a lawbreaker, just like other lawbreakers. Wallace argued that if the United States was a country of law and order, then King should be treated like others who break the law, such as bank robbers or purse snatchers. Entering the debate of King and Wallace, Kohlberg proposed that development in moral judgment was sequenced into three main levels: preconventional, conventional, and postconventional. Kohlberg said that King was to be distinguished from common criminals because he represented Postconventional morality, whereas George Wallace's thinking was conventional (i.e., "law and order"). To many people, both in academic psychology and in the society at large, such a way of looking at the issues of social justice made sense. This book describes research with the Defining Issues Test (hereafter referred to as the DIT) that directly bears on Kohlberg's theory. The viability of Kohlberg's position depends on there being such a thing as a law-and-order orientation (in which conventionality defines what is moral), and evidence that there is a developmental progression from Conventionality to Postconventionality.

The DIT began life humbly in the 1970s as a "quick and dirty" multiple-choice alternative to Kohlberg's time-consuming and complicated interview procedure. Since the 1970s, over 400 studies have been published (cited in chaps. 3 and 4). As findings accumulated, we began to reconsider some of Kohlberg's theoretical points. Among the first to be modified was Kohlberg's notion of "Piagetian hard stages" based on the staircase metaphor as the model of development. Instead, we argue for a model of development that represents upward movement in terms of gradually shifting distributions of the use and preference for more developed thinking. For us, development is not change one step at a time, but instead is the gradual increase of higher over lower forms of thinking.

Second, over the years many moral philosophers (e.g., Beauchamp & Childress, 1994; Walzer, 1983—the list could go on and on) have cast doubt on defining the developmental endpoint of morality in terms of the individual's mental operations (and therefore have also cast doubt on Kohlberg's definition of Stage 6 as "moral musical chairs"). Philosophical critics object to the view that the most advanced form of moral thinking was the *individual's* cognitions, reflecting on his or her own mind, apart from the other people who may also be involved in the moral decision. Consider, for instance, the development of medical ethical guidelines for the discontinuance of life support systems in the case of Karen Quinlan. (Recall that Karen Quinlan was a young woman who had been in a tragic accident, was brain dead for years, and had been artificially kept alive in a hospital on life-support systems, without ever regaining consciousness.) Here, the peculiarities of institutional and societal circumstance—and the formation of consensus by medical, philosophical, legal, and political authorities—determine the "ethics" of such cases.

There has been a move within moral philosophy toward viewing morality as an inherently *social* phenomenon, embedded in the particular experiences and deliberations of a community. (The notion of an evolving "common morality" of a community entails this *social* character.) This view has implications for Kohlberg's structure-content distinction, for the definition of postconventionality (and Stage 6 and Principled Morality), for the claim of cross-cultural universality, and for the place of debate and deliberation in a moral society. The social construction of morality is more consistent with Kohlberg's discussions of the "just community" approach to moral education than with his discussions of the six-stage model of moral judgment development.

Third, we began to specify the limitations of a Kohlbergian theory—which aspects of morality it did not address. The distinction between macro- and micromorality has already been mentioned, with our neo-Kohlbergian theory applying more to macro- than to micromorality. Critics of Kohlberg claim that his stage sequence favors abstract, impartial principles over loyalty, friendship, and close relationships. Critics can cite the fact that Kohlberg's Stage 3, defined in terms of seeking interpersonal concordance, is portrayed as developmentally primitive in contrast to Stage 6, which is defined in terms of abstract, impartial principles. Contrasts between Stage 3 and Stage 6 have been interpreted as implying that Kohlberg advocates loyalty to abstractions over loyalty to persons, noncommitment to personal relationship, and "being a rat" whenever pressured (e.g., Gates, 1998).

However, we interpret this as a consequence of the particular emphasis of his theory on macromorality issues. This is our interpretation: The conditions for establishing a societywide system of cooperation (cooperation among strangers, not only among friends) require impartiality and acting on shared ideals, not acting on behalf of our friends and kin. For instance, judges must act impartially, not giving favorable verdicts to kin and friends; an educational system that is supported by public money ought to benefit all the children (not only one's favorites); in the health care system, decisions about who receives an organ donation must be governed by fairness principles, not favoritism. When seeking solutions to macromorality problems, Stage 3 interpersonal concordance is primitive. Favoritism to kin or friends, tribalism, and ethnic particularism are enemies of a state system of cooperation. The devastating ethnic/tribal warfare of Africa, Bosnia, and Ireland are examples of the insufficiency of Stage 3 concepts to solve problems of macromorality. Thus, we affirm that Stage 3 thinking is a primitive way of solving problems in macromorality; at the same time, we admit that Kohlbergian theory does not adequately cover micromorality issues.

Another limitation of Kohlberg's six-stage theory is that it is cast at a very broad-gauge level of abstraction. For instance, the many issues that are the focus of discussions of professional ethics (e.g., confidentiality, due process, paternalism, informed consent, patient autonomy, surrogate decision making) are more concrete and specific than are Kohlbergian stages. And these concepts and issues are intermediate to the even more concrete codes of ethics that prescribe specific acts for professionals. Therefore, one must recognize that there are different levels of abstraction in moral reasoning, that Kohlberg's characterizations deal with the broad level of society and institutions within it, and that a full representation of moral decision making must include more than Kohlbergian stages.

Furthermore, one must recognize that there is much more to the psychology of morality than moral judgment or Kohlbergian moral reasoning. For example, we refer to moral sensitivity, judgment, motivation, and character as four components in producing moral behavior. Different components are the starting points for different approaches to morality (psychoanalytic, social learning, various social psychology approaches; Rest, 1983). Although most researchers would agree that there is much diversity of constructs, processes, phenomena, and starting points for the psychology of morality, the greater challenge is to formulate how all these different parts fit together.

Fourth, we have found that schema theory—as used in contemporary social cognition research—offers many advantages over Kohlberg's version of Piagetian stage theory. The moral judgment interview method has been assumed to provide a clear window into the moral mind. Contrary to assuming the face validity of interviews, researchers in cognitive science and social cognition contend that self-reported explanations of one's own cognitive process have severe limitations. There is now a greater regard for the importance of implicit processes and tacit knowledge on human decision making that is outside the awareness of the cognizer and beyond the subject's ability to verbally articulate. Schema theory is helpful in understanding how the DIT works. Because the DIT has produced reliable empirical findings, we can ask why it does work.

This is our current view: The DIT is a device for activating moral schemas (to the extent that a person has developed them) and for assessing them in terms of importance judgments. The DIT has dilemmas and standard items; the subject's task is to rate and rank the items in terms of their moral importance. As the subject encounters an item that both makes sense and taps into his or her preferred schema, that item is rated and ranked as highly important. Alternatively, when the subject encounters an item that either doesn't make sense or seems simplistic and unconvincing, the item receives a low rating and is passed over for the next item. The items of the DIT balance "bottom-up" processing (stating just enough of a line of argument to activate a schema) with "top-down" processing (stating not too much of a line of argument such that the subject has to fill in the meaning from schema already in the subject's head). In the DIT, we are interested in knowing which schemas the subject brings to the task (are already in his or her head). Presumably, those are the schemas that structure and guide the subject's thinking in decision making beyond the test situation.

Of what importance to our world today is research in moral judgment? It is no longer the 1960s, and Hippies have passed from the current scene.

To give a short answer to an involved question, ruminate on this example: Some writers consider the greatest ideological clash since the cessation of the Cold War to be the polarization between fundamentalism and secular modernism. Marty and Appleby (1993) emphasized the international side of this ideological clash, stating that ideological disputes lead "to sectarian strife and violent ethnic particularisms, to skirmishes spilling over into border disputes, civil wars, and battles of secession" (p. 1). James D. Hunter, in his book Culture Wars: The Struggle to Define America (1991), described the ideological divide within the United States. Hunter used the terms *orthodoxy* and *progressivism* to define differences in ideologies that have very different conceptions of moral authority in society. Our research combines DIT scores with measures of political identification and religious attitudes to produce a measure of orthodoxy/progressivism. This combined score accounts for about two thirds of the variance of positions on divisive public policy issues (e.g., abortion, religion in public schools, rights of homosexuals, women's roles, and free speech). We argue that understanding the development of moral judgment is crucial to understanding the great ideological divide between orthodoxy and progressivism.

In conclusion, this book summarizes a great body of empirical research (chaps. 3 and 4 cite over 400 published reports using the DIT), but is not simply a compilation of a huge and sprawling literature. Our aim goes beyond summarizing existing research studies. First, we take stock of the problems in Kohlberg's own approach (noting them, analyzing them, and developing solutions to the problems). Then, in the course of working out solutions to these problems, we consider new theoretical reformulations (ranging from the stage concept itself and the definition of development to methodological issues) and propose modifications to the theory and methods. Third, we keep this theoretical work consistent with the vast number of research findings from DIT research collected by many people over 25 years. Doing all of these things simultaneously is the purpose of this book. The ensuing pages attempt to clarify the issues, present supporting arguments for our positions, integrate our perspective with existing psychological and philosophical views, and cite and summarize empirical findings.

Lest the reader get the wrong impression about our "reifying" the DIT, our intention is not to advocate the DIT as the ultimate solution to morality research. The constant references to DIT research are made in the service of having a consistent reference point and comparable database for a full cycle of research. Completing a full cycle has taken us much longer than anticipated (in the 1970s, we thought it would take a few years). However, having now completed a full cycle of research, we have better ideas for next steps. Now, various new areas are being studied (e.g., "intermediate concepts," moral sensitivity, and comprehension of moral texts). A new DIT is now being piloted (DIT2): The new instrument updates the dilemmas and items (Heinz is retired from active duty; the Vietnam War is no longer referred to as a current event; long hair in high school is not an issue; and Asian-Americans are not referred to as "Orientals"). The instructions are streamlined and the new test is shorter than the original DIT. The new test is less stringent in purging unreliable subjects, allowing more subjects to survive the subject-reliability checks, and thus permitting experimenters to retain larger samples. The new test also uses our new method of indexing, the N2 index. Most important, however, DIT2 appears to be more valid, producing better trends than did the original DIT. There is much to be done with DIT2 (in part, checking out DIT2 in studies similar to those conducted with the original DIT), but the research with new instruments attests to our expectation of an ongoing and changing research program, not fixed on any one instrument.

2

⋙ ◆ ⋘

Psychological and Philosophical
Challenges to Kohlberg's Approach

Kohlberg has had many critics, and he did try to reconcile his theory with many of its criticisms. Over his lifetime he made gigantic changes in his approach (see, especially, Kohlberg, 1984; 1986a; Kohlberg, Boyd, & Levine, 1990). Notably, he reformulated the stage definitions and his method of scoring; shifted his approach to moral education from a focus on individual cognitive growth through dilemma discussion to the focus on the formation of "just communities"; and narrowed the parameters of his six-stage theory, from all of moral reasoning to "the rational reconstruction of the ontogenesis of justice thinking" (Kohlberg, 1984, p. 217). Critics complain of the complexity in his later theory as compared to the relative simplicity of the early theory (e.g., Shweder, Mahapatra, & Miller, 1987), but complexity is often the price of trying to respond to one's critics.

LIMITS TO KOHLBERG'S APPROACH

Kohlberg acknowledged many limitations to his approach, and that there were other processes and constructs in the psychology of morality.[1] These

---

[1]Kohlberg stated:

"The research programme of myself and my Harvard colleagues has moved from restricting the study of morality to the study of moral development to restricting it to the study of moral judgment (and its correspondence with action) to restricting it to the form or cognitive-structural stage of moral judgment as embodied in judgments of justice. Obviously these successive restrictions on the moral domain do not mean that this is the only way to define and psychologically research the moral domain. . . . The restricted range of the moral domain as we have now come to define it for our own theory or research programme does not imply that these restrictions should guide all fruitful moral psychology research. The moral domain is large and varied, and no one approach to its conceptualization and measurement will exhaust or explain the variance in it. (Kohlberg, 1986a, pp. 499–500) limits hold true for the DIT as well. As is discussed in chapters 5, 7, and 8, identifying what the theory does not address helps in the programmatic exploration of other constructs and phenomena. Nevertheless, Kohlberg contended that any theory or approach must make initial assumptions (see Kohlberg, 1984). In disputing Kohlberg's approach, many critics argue for starting points and assumptions different from Kohlberg's (e.g., Shweder, Gilligan, Bandura), but their starting points are delimited too, making assumptions and focusing on some phenomena and not on others. We comment on four limitations in Kohlberg's approach: (a) moral judgment as only one psychological component amid other psychological processes that determine behavior; (b) the global nature of Kohlberg's life span developmental markers, and the need for intermediate-level concepts in depicting a full decision-making model; (c) the limits of "justice-structures" (i.e., "justice" is not the only issue or concept in moral philosophy); and (d) the limits of Kohlberg's dilemmas in not representing the whole moral domain.

Moral Judgment as One Component

As mentioned earlier, Kohlberg's six-stage theory addresses only one process in the psychology of morality (namely, moral judgment), not the entire ensemble of processes. Kohlberg discussed various component processes in the psychology of morality, dividing up morality mainly into judgments about justice, individual responsibility, and outward behavior (Kohlberg & Candee, 1984). Some critics have said that Kohlberg's theory (dealing with moral judgment) is too cerebral, that it misses the "heart" of morality (e.g., Gilligan, 1982). But the special function of the construct of moral judgment is to provide conceptual guidance for action choice in situations in which moral claims conflict. In contrast, there are other constructs that deal with the agony of divided loyalties, with the amount of compassion and emotional energy involved in moral conflict, and with the acceptance of responsibility and the motivation (or lack of it) to do the right thing ("right" as defined by moral judgment). Later, we present our conception of what is involved in the psychology of morality, moral judgment being just one of the processes. Briefly, we conceptualize the entire domain of moral psychology to include at least four major internal component processes that lead to moral behavior: moral sensitivity, moral judgment, moral motivation, and moral character (Bebeau, 1994b; Bebeau, Rest, & Narvaez, in press; Narvaez & Rest, 1995; Rest, 1983; Thoma, 1994a).

Need for Intermediate Constructs

There are different levels of abstraction in describing moral cognition. Kohlbergian stages are gross, highly abstract markers of life span development that deal with the overall justification of a moral system. Kohlberg's six stages are like describing general epochs in history (e.g., Stone Age, Bronze Age, Middle Ages, Industrial Age, Information Age), not fine-grained descriptions (e.g., month-day-year). The limits of the highly abstract nature of Kohlbergian stages were stated in a particularly succinct way by Kenneth Strike (1982) in regard to the moral decision making of teachers:

> Even if these views [Kohlberg's theory] are essentially correct, they do not provide an adequate basis for teaching teachers about ethics. The essential problem is that the emphasis is on the development of abstract principles of moral reasoning instead of instruction in the more concrete ethical principles that should inform the daily activities of the practicing teacher. It is no doubt desirable that teachers acquire sophisticated and abstract principles of moral reasoning. . . . But a teacher who has a good grasp of abstract moral principles may nevertheless lack an adequate grasp of specific moral concepts, such as due process. (p. 213)

The abstractness of Kohlberg's theory is comparable to the abstractness of Piaget's theory of cognitive development. Even attaining the highest stage of formal operations in Piaget's theory is not sufficient for carrying out the daily activities of the practicing scientist. For instance, having formal operations does not provide knowledge for building a bridge or operating a computer. In addition to formal operations, the practitioner needs intermediate-level concepts. This is not to deny the possibility of abstract markers of life-span development (such as Piaget's stages); rather, we are saying that abstract markers are not sufficient representations of all levels of cognition that are involved in making a moral decision. For example, ethics courses for professionals are often organized around intermediate-level concepts, such as due process, informed consent, paternalism, whistle blowing, punishment, and intellectual freedom (e.g., Beauchamp & Childress, 1994; Callahan, 1988).

At a third level of abstraction, even more concrete than either Kohlberg's stages or intermediate-level concepts, are codes of ethics. Various professional groups (lawyers, physicians, nurses, psychologists, engineers, etc., see Callahan, 1988) have adopted professional codes of ethics that are essentially brief lists of specific prescriptions and prohibitions, with little rationale or explanation from moral theory. In sum, there are three levels of abstraction: the justification for a moral system in society (i.e., Kohlberg stages), intermediate-level concepts that provide the rationale for certain kinds of decision making (e.g., informed consent, due process), and specific codes of ethics (e.g., psychologists should respect the confidentiality of information about clients). It is important to keep in mind the differences in level of abstraction, because some of the confusion in the field arises from not distinguishing among these different levels and from assuming that everything has to be at one level. For instance, the term *moral code* is sometimes used to refer to specific prescriptions (e.g., widows shouldn't eat fish) but at other times to refer to the general rationale behind a whole moral orientation (e.g., the "duty-based orientation").

Note that in saying that the Kohlbergian level of abstraction is very general and that other levels of abstraction are more specific, we are not invalidating the more general level or making it obsolete. The more general level can exist alongside the more specific. For instance, in our perception of people, we can have a very general impression of a person—we like that person or we don't. At a more specific level of person perception, one might note certain attributions or traits of the person. But the more specific level of person perception does not replace or invalidate the more general level. Likewise, when we refer to society, one can have a notion about its moral goodness at a very general level, and at the same time one can have more specific information about its parts and subaspects. The general level of abstraction (the Kohlbergian characterizations) is useful for explaining phenomena like the Hippies' rejection of American society, by American society's zealous support of McCarthyism's fierce anti-Communism, the law and order orientation, and the culture wars of orthodoxy versus progressivism. Just because Kohlberg's theory is very coarse-grained does not render it useless.

In discussing our neo-Kohlbergian view, we propose to reformulate Kohlberg's six stages into three basic schemas. This is an even more coarse-grained framework for analyzing the developmental sequence of moral judgment than Kohlberg's. We propose only three schemas because the empirical findings from the DIT clearly support only three. Perhaps a more refined instrument would provide evidence for six stages and Kohlberg's A and B substages, or more refined discriminations in Kohlberg's theory. In any event, the three schemas are not proposed to represent a full decision-making model of moral judgment (a full representation would include the schemas, plus the intermediate concepts used by a person, and specific codes). In other words, we agree with Strike's criticism: We don't suppose that the schemas portray all the cognition that is necessary for a practitioner to make decisions about actual moral dilemmas. The schemas, however, enable us to describe the *developmental* aspect of moral judgment, and the individual's construction of basic moral concepts. We do not know yet whether or not intermediate concepts—the second level of representation—follow a general developmental sequence. Nor do we make the claim that the most concrete level (e.g., knowledge about specific professional codes) follows a developmental sequence.

Emphasizing "Justice" in Macromoral Issues

At first, Kohlberg seems to have regarded his six stages as applicable to all kinds of moral problems, but, in his debate with Gilligan (1982), he changed his position. In Kohlberg's later writings, he acknowledged that his stages are limited to the scope of "justice" (1984): "Our moral dilemmas and scoring system were limited in the sense that they did not deal with dilemmas . . . of special relationships and obligations [including] . . . special relationships to family, friends, and to groups of which the self is a member" (pp. 228).

Still later (Kohlberg et al., 1990), Kohlberg redefined the Stage 6 principle to be "respect for persons," in which he attempted to include the principle of benevolence along with the principle of justice. The later move was intended to broaden the scope of morality covered by his six stages. Regardless of the reformulations, many moral philosophers still do not regard Kohlberg's dilemmas, his scoring system, or definitions of the stages as encompassing the whole spectrum of moral problems that a comprehensive moral theory needs to address (e.g., Blasi, 1990; Habermas, 1990; Locke, 1986; Puka, 1990; Vine, 1986). Michael Pritchard (1991) wrote a particularly lucid account of how "justice" does not cover all of morality. Pritchard made this argument clear in a detailed analysis of Kohlberg's "Heinz" dilemma, pointing out how Heinz's reason for stealing for his wife need not be "justice" but "care," and that care does not reduce to justice:

> It might be thought that justice is relevant to the question of whether Heinz should steal the drug for his wife. However, even if one is inclined to say that Heinz should steal the drug for her, it is implausible to ground this claim in justice. Certainly the vow of marriage, or even a written contract of marriage, is not sufficient to show that Heinz would be unjust to his wife if he were not to steal for her. Even if it is acknowledged that certain moral obligations flow from marriage vows or a contract of marriage, neither stipulates or implies that the marriage partners are morally obligated to steal for one another. The history of the relationship between Heinz and his wife might well make intelligible Heinz's conviction that he must steal the drug, but this conviction is more likely an expression of his love for his wife than his sense of justice. The upshot is that, ironically, if one is convinced that Heinz should steal the drug for a stranger, what one should really advocate is a broadening of Gilligan's ethic of care to include strangers as well as intimates. Contrary to Kohlberg, it is not a higher level of justice reasoning which is required. It is an extension of care. (p. 152)

Pritchard's interpretation of the Heinz dilemma underscores the point that "justice" is not the only principle in moral philosophy.

By our agreeing that there is more to moral thinking than justice issues, we are *not* suggesting (as, e.g., Gilligan, 1982, suggested) that "care" and "justice" are alternative sequences that develop along different pathways with different endpoints—"justice" being one, "care" being another—and that people favor one pathway or another. Rather, we are saying that although justice issues are a large part of any totally comprehensive set of moral problems and must be part of any comprehensive theory of morality, they do not cover the gamut of moral issues.

The scope and limitation of moral problems addressed by Kohlberg's theory is similar to Rawls' theory (1971): "For us the primary subject of justice is the basic structure of society, or more exactly, the way in which the major social institutions distribute fundamental rights and duties and determine the division of advantages from social cooperation" (p. 7). This formulation is not meant to portray how all people throughout the ages have thought of morality. There are other aspects of morality (e.g., What is the good life? How can a person cultivate deeply meaningful relationships? What is human excellence and how is virtue cultivated?) Like Rawls, Kohlberg's emphasis on what he called "justice" is more political than some other definitions. It is based primarily on the concept of "right" rather than on the concept of "good," based less on individual standards of personal perfection or virtue or theology. More recently, Rawls (1993) stated that his theory of justice has a more limited scope of application, as a "political philosophy" (i.e., a theory of justification for the basic institutions of society). For instance, Rawls stated "In *Theory* [*of Justice*, 1971] a moral doctrine of justice general in scope is not distinguished from a strictly political conception of justice" (1993, p. xvii). The same limitations as Rawls admits for his theory apply to Kohlberg's and to our neo-Kohlbergian theory: The special focus is the morality of society, of people interacting within a societywide system of cooperation.

Lawrence Blum (1980) made a similar distinction between a morality of impartiality and a morality of friendship: "Institutional roles and positions are an obvious arena of life in which a certain kind of impartiality between the interests of all, including those to whom we are personally connected and attracted, is demanded of us. Equally obvious is the fact that situations covered by such roles are very untypical of those in which we interact with and benefit our friends" (p. 48).

Blum's interest was to explicate the morality of friendship, arguing that it is not subsumed under the Kantian morality of impartiality; our interest is the opposite—to explicate the morality of impartiality and formal social structure, arguing that it is not subsumable under the morality of friendship (or "care").

Recall from chapter 1 our distinction between macro- and micromorality. Both macro- and micromorality are concerned with establishing webs of interdependence among participants for cooperation and enriching relationships. Macromorality focuses on the formal structures of society (laws, roles, institutions, general practices), whereas micromorality focuses on the personal, face-to-face relationships in everyday dealings. Of course, macro- and micromorality have many areas of overlap and tension. Both are important. Friendship (micromoral relationships) is one of life's greatest social goods. However, the possibility of establishing a system of cooperation at a societywide level (among strangers and competitors, not just among kin and friends) calls for impartiality, generalizable norms, and "a level playing field" among diverse ethnic, religious, and racial groups. Typically in adolescence there is the dawning awareness that there is something beyond the personal, face-to-face level of everyday dealings with people—that there is a "system" in society, a macro level of morality. Kohlberg's theory illuminates the first solution (conventional moral thinking) to the problem of macro-morality (how to organize cooperation among strangers and competitors in a state system); and then describes how the second solution (postconventional thinking) evolves. At the same time, Kohlberg's theory does not illuminate the phenomena of micromorality.

Theories can start with different assumptions and contribute to different aspects of understanding morality. For instance, feminist theories give special attention to the morality of intimate relationships (e.g., Okin, 1989); virtue-based theories attend to the morality of exemplary character (e.g., Pence, 1980); and communitarian theories show how "common morality" is embedded in communal living in the context of particular historical traditions and instituted practices (e.g., Walzer, 1983).

Limits to a Few Hypothetical Dilemmas

A related issue to the limits of Kohlbergian theory just discussed is that the moral dilemmas that Kohlbergians use do not adequately sample the entire range of the moral domain. This is a point well made by Eisenberg (1986); Krebs, Vermeulen, Carpendale, and Denton (1991); Walker, deVries, and Trevethan (1987); and Walker, Pitts, Henning, and Matsuba (1995). The problem remains, however, that no one yet has provided a satisfactory map of the whole moral domain. Many studies point out that this or that was neglected in the Kohlberg dilemmas, but their suggestions for inclusion are piecemeal. Despite many suggestions, we still do not know how to devise a set of dilemmas that adequately represents all portions of the moral domain in a balanced fashion. Furthermore, it is one thing to criticize the Kohlbergian dilemmas for being hypothetical, or restricted (which they are), and quite another thing to demonstrate that some specific other data-gathering procedures have greater validity or usefulness in explaining the broad array of phenomena. To date, we know of no alternative dilemmas or method of information collection that has demonstrated superiority over the Kohlberg dilemmas regarding macromorality phenomena. In the meantime, we may add dilemmas piecemeal to cover some missing aspects, but must realize that any general characterizations of how people think (stemming from responses to our newly expanded set of dilemmas) must be understood as still having unknown generalizability to the whole moral domain.

Acknowledging that the set of dilemmas on Kohlberg's interview (and on the DIT) do not adequately sample the full range of moral dilemmas and realizing the difficulty in verifying that one has fully covered all areas of morality, as DIT researchers we have made the decision to continue with an avowedly partial set of dilemmas in order to complete a cycle of research (thereby gathering evidence on multiple criteria for the validity of a single standardized measure of moral judgment). Success with such a circumscribed enterprise would encourage repeating the research cycle with a more complete set of dilemmas. The main alternative to this decision was to change the DIT to include every new aspect of morality that came to attention, and each time to start over with a new program of research. Going through one cycle of studies ("freezing" the DIT so that comparability could be argued across studies) has taken far longer than we expected. In the 1970s, we thought that it would take only a few years. Now, after 25 years, we are ready to begin a new cycle (to change the DIT; Rest, Narvaez, Bebeau, & Thoma, 1998).

PSYCHOLOGICAL CRITICISMS
THAT REQUIRE CHANGES

In the previous section, limitations to Kohlberg's approach were acknowledged. Many disputes are matters of choosing to start research at different points, with different assumptions. Acknowledging the possibility of different starting points does not necessarily require changes in the approach. In the previous section, the critical question is one of the fruitfulness of using certain starting points in which one asks, "In choosing to start where you did, what have you learned?"

Some disputes with Kohlberg are not questions of research priorities (starting with some aspects and working up to a comprehensive theory); they are questions of making false claims and being in error. We consider the crux of Kohlberg's difficulties to be the overextension of the psychology of Piaget and the philosophy of John Rawls. From Piaget, Kohlberg derived the idea of cognitive operations that define stages of development; Kohlberg based his methodology on Piaget's "clinical interview," asking subjects to explain their thinking. From Rawls (via Kant), Kohlberg derived the concept of constructing a moral point of view solely from rational imagination. This particular amalgam of Piaget and Rawls is the troublesome part of Kohlberg's theory. Simply put: Kohlberg was too Piagetian and too Rawlsian.

Problems with the "Stage" Concept

Kohlberg advocated a particularly strong version of the "stage" concept (Rest, 1979). The underlying metaphor for his notion of development was the staircase: Development consists of moving up the staircase one step at a time. Kohlberg contended that subjects were "in" one stage or another (i.e., on one "step" or another). Every subject would show stepwise, irreversible, upward progression in the stage sequence in longitudinal studies, with no stage skipping or reversals (one moves up the staircase one step at a time, and always forward). His own 20-year longitudinal study (Colby, Kohlberg, Gibbs, & Lieberman, 1983) gave support to that view. In contrast, current advocates of Piaget's theory (e.g., Lourenço & Machado, 1996) do not argue for as strong a stage concept as Kohlberg did. For instance, Lourenço & Machado said that Piaget did not imply by his stage concept that all the features of a stage occur in synchrony (the notion *of structure d'ensemble* does not entail that a stage appear all at once in holistic fashion; Lourenço & Machado, 1996). Furthermore, according to current Piagetians, Piaget himself held that "development could follow psychogenetic paths different from the one [Piaget] had identified" (Lourenço & Machado, 1996, p. 151). In short, stages of cognitive development need not be universal. Furthermore, Piagetians admit that there is a problem with assessment techniques of cognitive structures that rely too much on language (Lourenço & Machado, 1996). Kohlberg argued for a stronger version of the stage concept than current Piagetian advocates would claim for Piaget, and placed greater reliance on subjects' verbalization than did Piaget.

From Piaget, Kohlberg adopted the cognitive developmental approach in general (i.e., that one attempts to analyze the epistemology of how people make sense of the world, and that there is a progressive order of change in constructing these meanings). More specifically, Kohlberg was impressed by the particular way Piaget contrasted more advanced thinking with less advanced thinking: The higher levels of thinking were said to use cognitive *operations* that the lower stages did not have. Piaget modeled the way thinking is supposed to advance on the logicomathematical structures depicted by logicians. One of these structures used by Piaget is called the "INRC four-group." INRC stands for the four logical transformations of identity, negation, reciprocal, and correlative (see Flavell, 1963). We need not go into detail about these logical models here, except to say that Piaget attempted to depict the developing capabilities of people's thinking in terms of the acquisition of these abstract, formal operations (i.e., higher stages performed cognitive operations that the lower stages did not).

Kohlberg seemed to have been especially impressed by this type of explanation of cognitive development, and he sought to explain the development of moral stages in terms of "justice operations"—suggesting similarities to Piaget's use of INRC operations (e.g., Kohlberg, 1984, pp. 245, 246, 271, 304ff). Kohlberg maintained that moral Stage 6 was the culmination of the justice operations, characterized in terms of the operations of "ideal reversibility" (1984). He used the notion of cognitive operations to distinguish form (true structure) from content (surface appearance). Furthermore, Kohlberg claimed to have defined Piagetian "hard stages" of justice thinking in completely formalistic terms—that is, in terms of operations, not content.

Kohlberg merged this Piagetian model of stage development ("hard" Piagetian stages defined by justice operations) with a Rawlsian philosophy of morality. Rawls' philosophy (1971) invited psychologizing. Rawls proposed that his reader conduct a thought experiment in order to explain his philosophical concept of justice: Rawls asked the reader to understand his meaning of justice by imaginatively constructing a hypothetical social contract in which the participants meet together to decide the organizing principles for society. The participants enter these negotiations under special conditions. Each person is ignorant of his or her special interests in society. Not knowing whether any particular arrangement would benefit or penalize his or her interests, the reader must therefore be impartial or fair. Rawls contended that the outcome of such a social contract in the original position under a veil of ignorance would be an agreement on the principles of justice (1971).

Kohlberg substituted the features of Rawls' thought experiment with the psychological notion of justice operations. Kohlberg's Stage 6—and the notions of ideal reversibility or "moral musical chairs"—became the imaginative construction of a moral point of view described in terms of "justice operations," thus accomplishing the same end as Rawls' thought experiment. Kohlberg's conception of Stage 6, and the five stages leading to it, became simultaneously a developmental stage theory (a psychological theory of change over time) and also a normative theory of ethics (a philosophical theory, why higher is better; see Kohlberg, 1981). Furthermore, Kohlberg claimed that Stage 6 would produce moral consensus: At Stage 6, people would agree on substantive issues (e.g., 1984, pp. 246,

248, 259, 272, 285, 294, 299). In addition, this formalistic theory allowed Kohlberg to argue for a type of moral education in public schools that seemed to steer between the shoals of indoctrination (prohibited by the latest interpretation of the American Constitution) and moral relativism (skepticism that moral discourse was anything more than personal preference or unreflective conformity to group practice, leading either to an "anything goes" morality or a mindless conformity). Thus, Kohlberg formulated a psychological theory of development that at the same time was a philosophical theory of normative ethics.

In the 1950s and 1960s, designing a psychological theory on Piaget's model seemed like a good idea. However, since then scholars have questioned Piaget's model on several grounds: his portrayal of advanced thinking in terms of logicomathematical models (e.g., Flavell & Wohlwill, 1969), whether cognitive development actually happens as Piaget depicted it (e.g., Flavell, 1985; Gelman & Baillargeon, 1983), and problems with the staircase metaphor for development (e.g., Rest, 1979; Siegler, 1997).

Kohlberg portrayed development in an especially bold way: (a) that development is a matter of qualitative differences, not quantitative; (b) that the thinking of subjects displays a "structured wholeness" using only one (or sometimes two) stages of thinking at one period in time; and (c) that development occurs one step at a time, without reversals or stage skipping (see Rest, 1979, for citations from Kohlberg that document his views on these matters). Siegler (1997, p. 95) is especially succinct with what is wrong about the "hard" stage model:

1. In all areas of cognitive development, children typically have multiple ways of thinking about most phenomena.
2. Cognitive-developmental change involves shifts in the frequency with which children rely on these ways of thinking, as well as the introduction of novel ways of thinking; change is better depicted as a series of overlapping waves than as a staircase progression.

The challenge, therefore, is to find a way to portray development without invoking what Kohlberg called the "hard stage" model (variously called "the simple stage" model by Rest, 1979; or the "staircase" model by Siegler, 1997).

Problems With Interview Data

Another point of serious criticism of Kohlberg made by psychologists is the reliance on purely verbal methods for assessing moral judgment (i.e., the exclusive use of verbal productions of subjects reporting justifications for their moral judgments in interviews). Shweder put the matter vividly: "[Kohlberg used] a verbal production task that places a high premium on the ability to generate arguments, verbally represent complex concepts, and talk like a moral philosopher. . . . [But] people know more than they can tell. A distinction is needed between implicit, tacit, or intuitive knowledge of a concept and the ability to state explicitly the knowledge one has" (Shweder et al., 1987, p. 16).

Early in his career, Piaget favored assessing a person's stage of cognitive development by interviewing subjects with a semistructured interview, *la méthode clinique*. This method asks subjects to explain their own thinking. A subject who explains his or her own thinking in his or her own words has "face validity," in that the interpretation of cognitive process does not require complex chains of interpretation by the experimenter; the burden of explanation falls on the subject. Especially articulate subjects are often quoted in psychological reports. But later in his career, Piaget deemphasized the assessment of cognitive structure solely in terms of the verbal articulations of subjects in explaining their own cognitive process (see Lourenço & Machado, 1996).

In the 1970s, Kohlberg argued that the verbal productions of subjects in interviews could be regarded as direct, straightforward indicators of cognitive process. Ask a person how his or her mind operates and the person can provide the experimenter with sufficient information to determine what program is operating in the subject's mind that produces the judgment. Kohlberg (1976) wrote: "The claim we make is that anyone who interviewed children about moral dilemmas and who followed them longitudinally in time would come to our six stages and no others" (p. 47). He also noted that "[Moral justifications by subjects in interview productions are] theoretically the most valid method of scoring, since it is instrument free . . ." (p. 45). Kohlberg's scoring system of interview data is "relatively error-free" (p. 47). Accordingly, the psychologist's job was simply to ask a subject to report his or her mental process, and then classify the subject's report in terms of one of the six stages. Kohlberg's view seemed to assume that what subjects say is a straightforward readout of the internal program operating that produces their moral judgment.

In the 1970s, many psychologists pointed to the limits of verbalized explanation as a valid method for attributing cognitive structure to someone (e.g., Braine, 1959; Brainerd, 1973, 1977; Bruner, 1964; Gelman 1972; see Flavell, 1970, for many references). Over the years, psychologists have increasingly demonstrated the severe limitations of self-reported explanations of one's own cognitive process (e.g., Nisbett & Wilson, 1977; Uleman & Bargh, 1989). There is a greater regard for the impact that implicit processes and tacit knowledge have on human decision making, outside the awareness of the cognizer (Bargh, 1989; Holyoak, 1994) and beyond the subject's ability to verbally articulate. A lack of introspective access has been documented in a wide range of phenomena, including attribution studies (e.g., Lewicki, 1986), word recognition (Tulving, Schacter, & Stark, 1982), and conceptual priming (Schacter, 1996). This research calls into question the privileged place of interview data (as in interviews) over recognition data (as in the DIT).

On reviewing several research literatures, Nisbett and Wilson (1977, p. 233) stated:

> The accuracy of subjective reports is so poor as to suggest that any introspective access that may exist is not sufficient to produce generally correct or reliable reports. . . . [I]nstead they [people giving reports on their internal cognitive process] may base their reports on implicit *a priori* theories about the causal connection between stimulus and response. . . . Subjective reports about higher mental processes are sometimes correct, but even the instances of correct report are not due to direct introspective awareness. Instead they are due to the incidentally correct employment of *a priori* causal theories.

The Nisbett and Wilson (1977) view is still being debated. The *strong* interpretation of their review implies that people generally have little or no access to their cognitive process; the *weak* interpretation of their review is that people in limited situations are not aware of the stimuli that cause their behavior. Nevertheless, the Nisbett and Wilson view does make one wonder about this phenomenon: when Kohlberg reported interview data, the subjects sound like the moral philosopher, John Rawls (Kohlberg et al., 1990); when Gilligan reported interviews, the subjects sound like gender feminists (Gilligan, 1982); when Youniss and Yates (in press) report interviews, the subjects say that they don't reason or deliberate at all about their moral actions.

Our contention is that production interview data (asking subjects to justify their judgments) is not a direct line into the moral mind; that production data is not a straight readout of a subject's mental program for making moral judgments; that there is no such thing as "instrument-free" assessment of cognitive structure; and that the interview excerpts quoted in many research reports are highly selected for stating the theorist's interpretation of cognitive process. This is not to say that interview material is not valuable—interview productions are valuable especially in the hypothesis-generation phase of research for suggesting possibilities of cognitive structures; also, interview productions are valuable for "think-aloud" commentary on a subject's online processing of information. But verbal productions are not open windows into the mind. Experimenters who select and trim subject reports to coincide with their own theories, and place the interpretation in the mouth of their subjects (as if the matter needed no further interpretation), are misrepresenting and oversimplifying the complex workings of the mind. The apparent "face validity" of production data is insufficient: Production data, like other data, need corroborating evidence for their validity. Every measure based on any kind of data needs to build a case for validity on its own.

Lack of Postconventional Thinking in Kohlbergian Studies

Kohlberg eliminated Stage 6 from his scoring system for lack of finding empirical cases of Stage 6 thinking. Furthermore, there is little evidence for Stage 5 scoring in Kohlbergian studies from around the world (Snarey, 1985). Gibbs (1979)—a codeveloper of the scoring system—even proposed that true Piagetian stages of moral judgment stop with Stage 4. The lack of empirical data for Stages 5 and 6—postconventional thinking—is a serious problem for Kohlberg's enterprise, because he defined the stages from the perspective of the higher stages. The seriousness of this problem is underscored by the fact that virtually every critic in the book *Lawrence Kohlberg: Consensus and Controversy* (Modgil & Modgil, 1986) find the absence of Stages 5 and 6 to be a fatal flaw.

Greater Moral Capacities of Young Children

Zahn-Waxler, Radke-Yarrow, Wagner, & Chapman (1992) stated that young children have "(a) the cognitive capacity to interpret the physical and psychological states of others, (b) the emotional capacity to affectively experience others' states, and (c) the behavioral repertoire that permits the possibility of trying to alleviate discomfort in others" (Zahn-Waxler et al., 1992, p. 127). Their point was that young children are not morally limited to egocentric responses or deference to superior power (as the theories of Kohlberg and Piaget suggest). Many psychologists argue convincingly for the greater capacities of young children (e.g., Damon, 1988; Eisenberg, 1986; Hoffman, 1991; Saltzstein, Millery, Eisenberg, Dias, & O'Brien, 1997; Turiel, 1983; see the outstandingly penetrating and judicious review of the whole field of moral psychology by Lapsley, 1996, with special regard to young children). In fact, Tisak (1995) puts the threshold for Turiel-type domain distinctions as early as 26 months of age; and domain research indicates that young children say they should defy authorities when another person would be directly hurt. All this suggests that Kohlbergians have to rethink the earlier stages of moral judgment development. DIT research can not help in this reformulation, because the DIT has a testing floor of ninth grade. However, it should be noted that changes to Kohlberg's early stages to accommodate the increased empathic capacities of children do not necessarily invalidate his claims about adolescent conceptions of the morality of society.

CRITICISMS FROM THE PHILOSOPHERS

The Problem of "Foundational Principlism"

Up through the 1960s, moral theories were commonly formulated by defining a "foundational principle" (e.g., Mill's "greatest good for the greatest number," or Kant's "categorical imperative"). The foundational principle would then be used to deduce moral judgments applied to concrete cases. In many of Kohlberg's writings (e.g., "From Is to ought," [1971/1981]; "Justice as Reversibility," [1981]), Kohlberg seemed to have adopted this approach to moral philosophy, typical of his time. Since the 1960s, moral philosophy has undergone drastic changes (DeGrazia, 1992).[2] One major development has been the criticism of "principlism" (e.g., Clouser & Gert, 1990; DeGrazia, 1992; Toulmin, 1981). Because Kohlberg's theory was formulated as a principle-based theory, it too has been criticized for its "principlism."

In the interim, moral philosophers have criticized ethical theories that assume foundational principlism. One problem is that deduction from a foundational principle is not always a sufficient guide—one often needs more guidance for action than can be supplied by foundational principles (see DeGrazia, 1992). This criticism is similar to that raised by Strike's criticism regarding the insufficiency of Kohlberg's abstract principles and the need for intermediate concepts. Kohlberg seems to have thought that Stage 6 principles contain sufficient moral directives for deducing a moral judgment for any moral dilemma (Kohlberg, 1984). For instance, Kohlberg (1984) thought that justice principles defined at Stage 6 would deductively lead to a unique moral solution to the Heinz dilemma, and would lead to a unique moral solution to the question of capital punishment. In contrast, Pritchard (1991) argued that adopting Kohlberg's Stage 6 can lead to different lines of action; Heinz could logically do different things in accord with Stage 6. In other words, Kohlberg's principles are not sufficient guides for clear direction for choosing a course of action. Although Kohlberg's principles eliminate some possible actions, more than one course of action is logically consistent with Stage 6 principles (see Pritchard, 1991).

---

[2]Our philosopher friends point out that our summary of recent moral philosophy is not comprehensive. Our objective, however, is only to cite criticisms especially germane to Kohlberg's theory.

Paradigm Cases: "Bottom-Up" Morality

A criticism related to the insufficiency of abstract principles is that principles are not the *only* source for reliable moral guidance. Specific cases can also lead to moral reflection, which in turn can supply moral guidance. Moral guidance from the analysis of specific cases is sometimes more certain and produces more agreement than difficult-to-fathom principles (Toulmin, 1981). For example, Toulmin described his experience serving with the National Commission for the Protection of Human Subjects: The 11 commissioners—a very diverse group—had the job of fashioning guidelines and policy statements for the use of human subjects in research. Interestingly, the 11 commissioners found that they could reach agreement on moral judgments about specific cases, although they could not agree on which abstract principles undergirded their judgments. In light of experiences like Toulmin's, some philosophers challenge the notion that moral thinking operates most reliably in terms of principles; they decry "principlism" (e.g., Clouser & Gert, 1990) and "the tyranny of principles" (Toulmin, 1981). Just as laws can be too rigid, absolute, and insensitive to special circumstances, so too can moral principles be abused.

Another example of a bottom-up formulation of moral guidelines comes from Beauchamp and Childress (1994):

> Consider an example from the explosion of interest since 1976 in surrogate decision making. A series of cases beginning with the aforementioned Quinlan case[3] challenged medical ethics and the courts to develop virtually an entire new framework of substantive rules for responsible surrogate decision making about life-sustaining treatments, as well as authority rules regarding who should make those decisions. This framework was created by working through cases analogically, and testing hypotheses against preexisting norms. In both ethics and law, a string of cases with some similar (and some dissimilar) features set the terms of the ethics of surrogate decision making. Even when a principle or rule was not entirely novel in a proposed framework, its content was shaped by problems needing resolution in the cases. Gradually a loose consensus emerged in the courts and in ethics about a framework for such decision making. It would falsify history to say that this framework was already available and was simply applied to new cases. (p. 18)

Notice how the process of arriving at moral guidelines in the Quinlan case is different from foundational principlism. Over time, there developed a consensus among medical practitioners and ethicists about this specific case, and it became paradigmatic. The community reflects on specific cases and reaches agreement on at least some of the cases. The logical interconnections (the framework) interpreting the cases become the "common morality" for that community; new cases are then considered in terms of their similarities and differences with the established cases,

---

[3]*In re Quinlan*, 70 N.J. 10, 355 A.d 647 (1976), at 663–64.

and new reflections refine the moral guidelines. The process for building this kind of common morality is similar to the process used to build common law. Moral case precedents are established. Instead of attempting to build a moral consensus by obtaining agreement over abstract principles, the bottom-up approach first starts with actual community agreements about specific cases and inductively works up to other cases. Beauchamp and Childress (1994) stated:

> Inductivism [the bottom-up approach] maintains that we must use existing social agreements and practices as a starting point from which to generalize to norms such as principles and rules, and inductivists emphasize the role of particular and contextual judgments as a part of our evolving moral life. A society's moral views are not justified by an ahistorical examination of the logic of moral discourse or by some theory of rationality [Kantian, Rawlsian, Kohlbergian], but rather by an embedded moral tradition and a set of procedures that permit new developments. . . . New experiences and innovations in the pattern of collective life lead to modifications in beliefs, and the institution of morality cannot be separated from a cultural matrix of beliefs that has grown up and been tested over time. (p. 18; inserted remarks in brackets are not in original)

Reed (1997) stated that there are two contradictory themes in Kohlberg's theorizing. One theme is his depiction of the isolated individual decision maker, who constructs a moral point of view from his or her own intuitive imagination. Proponents of this type of moral theory regard such a construction as the universal standard for all individuals, without consideration of their particular history and community affiliations (Kohlberg's Kantian/Rawlsian approach). The second theme in Kohlberg's work is the development of the just community, which involves group decision making negotiated through democratic process; it is intended as the affirmation of group solidarity and shared values, very much in the context of their particular history and mutual concern for each other as persons. Reed thought the more valuable contribution of Kohlberg is the second theme (as assumed in the just community). In contrast, Kohlberg's first notion was extended in Turiel's notion of a formalistic, universalistic morality, which the individual knows from his or her own inner cognitive processes, and which Turiel said is separate from the conventional domain (i.e., separate from community agreements and social-institutional patterns of communal living) (1983).

Both Bottom-Up and Top-Down in Reflective Equilibrium

A new type of philosophical approach combines both a bottom-up approach (inductive) with a top-down (deductive) approach. Beauchamp and Childress (1994—note: 4th ed.)[4] were at first criticized for their old-fashioned principlism (especially for earlier editions of their book), but with the 1994 edition they articulated a combination approach. Their book is impressive for giving guidance to hundreds of specific moral dilemmas in biomedical ethics. Beauchamp and Childress start from common morality for which there is moral consensus (common sense and tradition growing out of the reflections of a community in dealing with specific cases), and then examine the moral justifications for the specific cases. Note that, in their theory, a single principle does not function as a foundational principle. Instead, principles function as tools for analyzing the justificatory basis of social norms and action choices in specific cases. Justifications (often in the form of "stipulated" principles—see DeGrazia, 1992) provide the connective tissue for systematization and the theoretical rationale for moral consensus in building the common morality. Principles, norms, and analyses of cases are examined for their logical coherence and fit with moral experience. Beauchamp and Childress view theory building as a dialectical process of maintaining both top-down and bottom-up moral judgments in a coherent "reflective equilibrium." Principles are checked against the more settled specific moral cases, working from both ends to put them all into logical coherence, making adjustments at all levels to put them in mutual agreement (discussed by Rawls, 1971). Although we cite Beauchamp and Childress (1994) as an example of the new type of combination theory, one would hesitate to claim that nowadays moral philosophers (practical or theoretical) generally endorse any one type of ethical theory.

Common Morality and Relativism

Kohlberg might have objected to bottom-up processes by arguing that different communities might have different histories, different paradigmatic cases, different moral understandings, and therefore might develop different common moralities (just as differences in common law arise between communities). Kohlberg might have objected that a moral system based on common morality and paradigmatic cases is not universal but instead is relativistic and endlessly in flux. Kohlberg caricatured relativism as maintaining that cannibalism is right for cannibalistic societies, that human sacrifice was right for the Aztecs, and so on (1984). In contrast,

---

[4]Beauchamp and Childress have published several editions of their book, *Principles of Bioethics*. Their first editions were special targets of the critics of principlism. The fourth edition, published in 1994, explicitly dealt with these problems.

Kohlberg sought moral consensus by assuming that developmental advance leads all people ultimately to the same Stage 6 judgments, a priori, independent of a community's actual experience and settled agreements (Kohlberg & Candee, 1984).

However, contemporary moral philosophers say that a consensus based on purely a priori considerations doesn't exist now (thoughtful people do not agree on what the foundational principles ought to be, as exemplified in Toulmin's experience with the Commission on Human Subjects) and is unlikely to ever occur (e.g., DeGrazia, 1992; Toulmin, 1981). These philosophers admit that one particular community's moral system may not be identical to another community's moral system and, therefore, they have given up on the quest for a *universal* moral system. They argue that actual consensus on at least some paradigmatic cases by a particular community is a better starting place than the fruitless alternative of seeking consensus about some a priori abstract principles. These philosophers accept the untidy idea that a moral system might be forever in flux (just as science, medicine, etc., are constantly in reformulation as new data and theories are developed).

The concept of a common morality entails that a community in some specific time and place engages in moral reflection around particular cases to arrive at specific agreements about how to define moral guidelines for that community in dealing with those and similar cases. Because different cases might arise in different communities, and the community might reach consensus in a variety of ways, form alternative agreements, and build different histories of successive agreements, the common morality for each community can vary. Whereas morality is relative to a specific community at a specific time, this does not entail the endorsement of moral skepticism (the belief that all moral discourse is merely the endorsement of personal preference), nor the mindless and unquestioning conformity to established group practices and tradition, nor the abandonment of moral ideals. Kohlberg believed that relativism intrinsically embodied these vices. Reed (1997) reminded us that Kohlberg was concerned that social science have a more robust notion of ethics than wimpy relativism. Kohlberg was always concerned with providing the argument against the Nazi officers who argued that what they did during the Holocaust could not be condemned because they were conforming to group norms by following orders. However, the concept of common morality in reflective equilibrium with sharable moral ideals, arrived at through moral discussion and open debate, is a different sort of moral relativism than the one Kohlberg feared.

Guttmann and Thompson (1997) stated that morality in democratic societies inevitably involves open discussion, debate, and disagreement: "Actual deliberation has an important advantage over hypothetical agreement: it encourages citizens to face up to their actual problems by listening to one another's moral claims rather than concluding (on the basis of only a thought experiment) that their fellow citizens would agree with them on all matters of justice if they were all living in an ideal society" (p. 16).

Walzer (1983) provided many examples in which actual communities have debated specific moral issues and arrived at different solutions, yet still strive to fulfill sharable moral ideals as best suit the circumstances. For instance, Walzer (1983) addressed the ways that Athens in the fifth and fourth centuries B.C. provided for the welfare and security of its citizens, and how this differed from medieval Jewish communities in Europe. Walzer described how each community provided different services for different clienteles, had different organizational apparatuses to deal with problems, raised money in different ways, and encoded the practices differently in their moral ideologies:

> The Jews and Greeks suggest not only the range of communal activity but also, and more important, the way in which this activity is structured by collective values and political choices. In any political community where the members have something to say about their government, some such pattern will be worked out: a set of general and particular provisions designed to sustain and enhance a common culture. (p. 74)

The point here is that morality and justice may take many forms in response to different histories, circumstances, and social/political organizations of the community. Morality conceived as a social construction often incorporates the peculiarities of social history and circumstance. Once one begins to consider the specifics of distributive justice, what is considered moral is relative to group agreement and the particulars of social organization. Morality is not a separate matter from social organization and group consensus. However, this does not mean that this relativism of common morality is uncritical or mindless, because it is driven by the moral ideals in the particular histories and context of the community. Socially constructed morality that represents a reflective equilibrium of cases and moral ideals is not mindless conformity to the status quo.

KOHLBERG'S COUNTERARGUMENTS

Do the criticisms of principlism devastate Kohlberg's theory? Certainly, some people have dismissed his whole approach because its philosophy is principlism (e.g., Munsey, 1980). Kohlberg made several counter-arguments to the criticisms of principlism.[5] Kohlberg was criticized for being an absolutist in his Stage 6, failing to take context into account. However, Kohlberg distinguished between rule principlism and constructivistic principlism (Kohlberg, 1984). In the first type, rule principlism (which Gilligan, 1982; Munsey, 1980; and Murphy & Gilligan, 1980, mostly seem to have in mind), a rule is raised to an absolute status so that all other rules are lower in priority: For instance, one might say, "Preservation of human life is the absolute principle" (implying that all other moral claims have less status). In this case, the criticism of absolutism is made for not appreciating the contextualism of real-life moral dilemmas or special circumstances.

However, Kohlberg claimed that his form of principle was to prescribe a procedure for constructing a moral point of view specific to each moral situation—type two. "Moral musical chairs" and "ideal reversibility" described a way of analyzing specific situations, taking context into account—each participant simultaneously role taking the positions of all participants in a dilemma with all the contextual peculiarities of the participants included. (For a clear exposition of this idea, see Kohlberg et al., 1990). Thus, Kohlberg argued that his principlism is not rule principlism—or absolutism that neglects context—but rather a way of constructing a moral perspective that takes context into account. Although Kohlberg might be called a formalist, and he did describe Stage 6 in terms that suggest foundational principlism, it is incorrect to assert that he did not take context into account. The principle of Stage 6 is not a rule raised to an absolute, but rather a procedure for constructing a moral point of view in any situation by imaginatively taking the roles of all the participants in the situation with all the contextual information that each person has. In our view, Kohlberg successfully rebuts the charge of absolutism.

However, it is unclear to us how Kohlberg's rebuttal of this charge answers other problems of principlism (like deductivism). Kohlberg was aware of the problems of deductivism, and denied outright that his theory was subject to the problems of deductivism.[6] But we are not clear whether he succeeded on this point.

Second, in exchanges with Habermas, Kohlberg claimed that Stage 6 presumes having an actual dialogue among participants in a moral dilemma under conditions of ideal discourse (as discussed by Guttmann & Thompson, 1997, and by Habermas, 1990). Kohlberg claimed that

---

[5]We are indebted to Donald R. C. Reed and Dwight Boyd for pointing out to us these complexities in Kohlberg's theory.

[6]Kohlberg states, "We do not see our principles as *a priori* axioms from which moral judgments are deduced as geometric propositions were deduced from prior Euclidean axioms" (Kohlberg, 1984, p. 301). Kohlberg also states, Our principles "also help free the reasoner from the strictly deductive "top down" strategy of applying a principle to a case" (Kohlberg et al., 1990, 164–165).

"monologic" role taking (i.e., trying to construct a moral point of view solely within one's own head, by oneself) is merely a fall-back position in Stage 6, only invoked when the conditions of ideal discourse among several actual individuals is not possible (Kohlberg, 1984). Kohlberg's incorporation of Habermas' "dialogic" communication among other participants moves Kohlberg's position closer to Guttmann and Thompson's "deliberative democracy." However, we do not understand how Kohlberg's 1984 view would work out in detail, nor how he could maintain the notion of the universality of Stage 6, because different groups with different histories might arrive at different dialogic agreements.

Third, Kohlberg talked about Stage 6 as involving Rawls's concept of "reflective equilibrium" (1984):

> With regard to moral principles, we follow Rawls' account of the formulation of principles as a "bootstrapping" or spiral process of "attaining reflective equilibrium." According to this account, principles or methods for judging are tentatively applied to cases or dilemmas. Where there is a discrepancy between the principle and our intuitions about the right action in the dilemma, we can either reformulate the principle or decide our moral intuition was in error. (p. 301)

Again, this use of reflective equilibrium would move Kohlberg's position closer to contemporary moral philosophers, but we do not understand how Kohlberg would work out this position in detail. For instance, would Kohlberg really have agreed to modify the principles at Stage 6 if reflective equilibrium seemed to require it? Furthermore, how would he have argued for the universality of Stage 6 if different people decided to make different adjustments to the principles?

In any case, philosophers have raised criticisms with regard to Kohlberg's normative theory. We don't presume to have a solution to these problems, or even to understand them fully. Moral philosophy itself is in a period of uncertainty. The point in raising these objections by philosophers and in discussing new theories of moral philosophy (like Beauchamp & Childress, 1994) is to understand the disenchantment of moral philosophers to the Kohlbergian approach—in particular, the claims for Stage 6. Our solution is not to substitute some more recent moral philosopher for Rawls as the new embodiment of Stage 6, nor do we propose new adult stages of morality beyond Stage 6 (e.g., Gilligan & Murphy, 1979; Murphy & Gilligan, 1980). Rather, it seemed to us that the better option was to back away from the current controversies of moral philosophers and to attempt a looser definition of development that did not claim to solve the problems of moral philosophy. We don't think it is necessary to endorse any particular philosophical position as a basis for a psychological theory of development. By not attempting to argue for any specific philosopher's theory—by not attempting to argue specifically for any particular normative theory among those being currently advanced—we believe it is still possible to describe in more general terms a psychological theory of development.

Our coarse-grained depiction of development in terms of only three schemas leaves out many refinements of current debates of moral philosophers. Despite the coarseness of our proposal, we were buttressed into focusing on these broad distinctions by the vast, wide-reaching project by Martin Marty and R. Scott Appleby (e.g., 1993). Six edited volumes describe major ideological clashes in the world after 4 decades of the Cold War and the collapse of the Soviet Union. Article after article in their edited volumes describe the ideological conflicts causing factionalism, violent ethnic particularisms, civil wars, and skirmishes spilling over into border disputes, and frustrating the search for consensus (1993). The crux of the ideological disputes (in the United States and around the world) does not concern the refinements of modern philosophy (e.g., the disputes over postmodernism vs. modernism, over deontological theories vs. communitarian theories, or over virtue-based theories vs. rights-based theories). Rather, the ideological division is over fundamentalism versus secularism, orthodoxy versus progressivism, and conventional versus postconventional ideology. A case can be made that the broad-gauged distinction we draw between conventional and postconventional moral thinking is more urgent to understand than the many finer points of modern moral philosophy.

UNWARRANTED CRITICISMS

Although we have acknowledged problems with Kohlberg's theory, several criticisms have been made that we believe are unwarranted:

- Many researchers (see Modgil & Modgil, 1986) have faulted Kohlberg for the lack of evidence for a developmental sequence from conventionality to postconventionality. Frequently, they point to the lack of postconventional thinking in Kohlberg's studies. But the evidence produced by the DIT should be considered. The next chapters of this book are devoted to exploration of that point. In light of DIT research, we don't think that Kohlbergians need to change the claim that postconventionality follows conventionality.
- Kohlberg is criticized for embracing a highly formalistic account of higher development and thus disregarding the context of moral judgments (as, e.g., by Munsey, 1980; Murphy & Gilligan,1980). This criticism is discussed earlier as failing to distinguish between rule principlism and constructivistic principlism.

- Lind (1995) criticized Kohlberg for not attending to structure but instead to stage preference, and therefore by his method of assessment (relying on preference measures for a stage) he mixed affect and structural competence. This criticism was countered in Rest, Thoma, and Edwards (1997).
- Turiel (e.g., Turiel, 1983; Turiel & Davidson, 1986) faulted Kohlberg for not keeping the morality domain separate from the domain of conventionality (see chap. 7). According to Turiel, mixing up the two domains prevents precise findings in either. Yet Turiel failed to demonstrate that there are domains (in the sense that hard domains are used in cognitive science—see chap. 7). In support of a soft notion of domains, there is evidence that people do make distinctions between acts of directly hurting or helping someone via acts of etiquette and social convention. However, finding that people make distinctions is not evidence for the stronger case, that is, for hard domains, only evidence for hard domains—not soft domains—is a basis for asserting that Kohlberg was wrong that postconventional thinking follows conventional thinking.
- Shweder (e.g., Shweder, Mahapatra, & Miller, 1987, 1990; Shweder & Much, 1991) faulted Kohlberg for claiming that development accounts for the fundamental differences in moral thinking. Shweder maintained that the fundamental differences in moral thinking are better accounted for by cultural differences (see chap. 8), namely a difference between rights-based morality and duty-based morality. But inconsistent with Shweder's position, the difference attributed to cultural differences is the basic difference between Kohlberg's conventional morality and postconventional morality. Shweder did not seem to recognize that Kohlbergian theory has within it a duty-based morality and a rights-based morality; a developmental difference, not a cultural difference.

This analysis of criticisms over the past 25 years identifies elements to consider in a reconstruction of the Kohlbergian approach. In chapter 3 we present our reformulation in a neo-Kohlbergian approach using the DIT, and in chapter 4 we review the empirical evidence on validity and reliability.

SUMMARY OF CRITICISMS
OF KOHLBERG'S APPROACH

We have considered criticisms from psychologists and philosophers, and group the criticisms under four headings:

1. Limitations not requiring change in basic tenets but requiring an acknowledgement of the limits in scope and applicability of the theory:
   (a) A focus on only one component process in the larger psychology of morality to the neglect of moral motivation, moral sensitivity, and follow through in behavior.
   (b) A focus on abstract, coarse-grained markers of life-span development to the neglect of intermediate-level concepts.
   (c) A focus on justice issues to the neglect of personal/intimate relationships and the role of religion in the formation of moral thinking.
   (d) The limited scope of dilemmas.
2. Psychological problems requiring change:
   (a) The staircase-stage concept.
   (b) An interview method that is overreliant on verbal articulation.
   (c) The rarity of postconventional thinking.
   (d) The underestimation of young children's capacities.
3. Philosophical problems requiring change:
   (a) Foundational principlism and deductivism.
   (b) The failure to recognize bottom-up morality and Common morality.
   (c) The assumption that a foundational principle can produce consensus.
   (d) New conceptions of moral relativity and embeddedness in society.
4. Unwarranted criticisms (not requiring change):
   (a) Postconventional thinking does not come after conventional thinking.
   (b) Kohlberg's formalism neglects context.
   (c) Kohlberg's focus on stage preference neglects the study of structure/competence.
   (d) The need to separate the moral domain from the social-conventional domain.
   (e) Cultural differences overwhelm developmental differences.

3

꙰ ♦ ꙮ

A Neo-Kohlbergian Approach
Based on the DIT

In this chapter, we propose our solutions to the problems with Kohlberg's theory discussed in the previous chapter. First, we cite Kohlberg's own distinction between conventional and postconventional moral thinking, on which we base our neo-Kohlbergian approach.

KOHLBERG'S DEFINITION OF THE SHIFT FROM CONVENTIONAL TO POSTCONVENTIONAL MORAL THINKING

We quote Colby et al. for their definition of conventional and postconventional moral thinking (1987, Vol. 1, pp. 28–29):

> At Stage 4 the individual takes the perspective of a generalized member of society. This perspective is based on a conception of the social system as a consistent set of codes and procedures that apply impartially to all members. The pursuit of individual interests is considered legitimate only when it is consistent with maintenance of the sociomoral system as a whole. The informally shared norms of Stage 3 are systematized at Stage 4 in order to maintain impartiality and consistency. A social structure that includes formal institutions and social roles serves to mediate conflicting claims and promote the common good. That is, there is an awareness that there can be conflicts even between good role occupants. This makes it necessary to maintain a system of rules for resolving such conflicts. The perspective taken is generally that of a societal, legal, or religious system that has been codified into institutionalized laws and practices. . . .

> The Stage 5 prior-to-society perspective is that of a rational moral agent aware of universalizable values and rights that anyone would choose to build into a moral society. The validity of actual laws and social systems can be evaluated in terms of the degree to which they preserve and protect these fundamental human rights and values. The social system is seen ideally as a contract freely entered into by each individual in order to preserve the rights and promote the welfare of

all members. This is a "society-creating" rather than a "society-maintaining" perspective. Society is conceived as based on social cooperation and agreement.

Our definitions of the schemas of development (personal interest, maintaining norms, postconventional) are somewhat different from Kohlberg's stages, but we believe our revision still captures the core of Kohlberg's major ideas. Admittedly, DIT research does not address all of Kohlberg's six stages. However the distinction between conventional and postconventional thinking is one that DIT research can address and is the critical one in this book.

Other theorists have also proposed reformulations, including Weinreich-Haste (1983), Thornton and Thornton (1983), Gibbs (1991), and Lind (1995). We refer to our reformulations as "our neo-Kohlbergian view" to distinguish it from other neo-Kohlbergian formulations.

THE MAINTAINING NORMS
AND THE POSTCONVENTIONAL SCHEMA

Given the criticisms raised by philosophers and psychologists, we postulate developmental schemas instead of stages with distinct justice operations. (Note: the significance of using the term *schema* instead of *stage* is discussed in chap. 6.) Our discussion of maintaining norms and postconventional schemas will sound very much like Colby et al. (1987) to people only mildly familiar with Kohlberg's analysis, but it may sound flagrantly heretical for those who are very familiar. The core ideas are Kohlberg's, but we do take some liberties. To distinguish our notions from Kohlberg's, we use different labels (e.g., "maintaining norms" schema instead of Kohlberg's "law and order"). Our discussion of the schemas of development is more like Kohlberg's description of development in terms of sociomoral perspective (1981) than Kohlberg's description of stages in terms of justice operations (1984). It is also similar to Thornton and Thornton's (1983) scheme "the collective interest hypothesis," and to Weinreich-Haste's (1983) account of development in understanding the social order.

Maintaining Norms Schema

A "rational reconstruction" of a schema entails that the various parts of a schema be described in a manner that explicates how the parts fit together logically. It is not supposed that actual participants in a study will recite everything in this description, but the detail is given to indicate how the various notions cohere. We presume that this description represents tacit understanding, and does not require explicit verbalization. Furthermore, an actual participant may miss some of the elements, but we give here the full-blown prototype.

The schema "maintaining norms" (derived from Kohlberg's Stage 4) contains the following elements:

- *Need for norms.* If a societywide system of cooperation is to be established, then some normative rules and role systems are necessary (whatever they may be—the schema itself does not specify which particular rules or role systems to have). Some standards and stable norms are needed so that everyone need not debate every act every time somebody is to act. Coordination is necessary (e.g., if a water irrigation system is to be built, some central plan is necessary). By having some set of norms and rules, people avoid continuous conflict, disagreement, and working at cross purposes. Norms provide stability, predictability, safety, and coordination.
- *Societywide scope.* A person realizes that he or she not only has to get along with kin and friends and well-known acquaintances; people also have to get along with strangers, with competitors, and with lesser-known acquaintances. Therefore, a societywide system of cooperation needs to be established involving large numbers of people who do not know each other in a personal, face-to-face way. Formal law is particularly useful for stabilizing expectations among people who are not familiar intimates.
- *Uniform, categorical application.* Furthermore, laws are social norms that are publicly set, are knowable to everyone, and apply to everyone. "Law" is usually understood in the sense of civil, municipal law (in the sense described by Hart, 1961). This includes "secondary rules," which are rules to set up a legal system that makes, interprets, and enforces rules. But law can also be understood in terms of religious codes (see especially the discussion of orthodoxy/progressivism later in the book). Regardless of whether the law is civil or religious law, everyone is "under the law" (the law applies equally to all citizens), and everyone is protected by the law (all citizens can invoke the protection of the law).
- *Partial reciprocity.* Laws establish a reciprocity (or reversibility) among participants in society. A person obeys the law and does his or her duty, expecting that other people are doing their duties. Society in general benefits from this division of labor and mutual exchange. The maintaining norms orientation emphasizes the importance of doing one's duty according to one's station and role position in society. (We call this "partial" reciprocity, not "full" reciprocity, because under the maintaining norms schema obeying the law might not benefit all the participants in an equitable way, as is required in the postconventional schema.)

- *Duty orientation.* Maintaining norms is duty oriented and authoritarian (in the sense of affording unchallenged powers to authorities and in deferring to authorities). In an organized society, there are chains of command; that is, there are hierarchical role structures (teacher–pupil, parent–child, general–soldier, doctor–patient, etc.). One must obey authorities, not necessarily out of respect for the personal qualities of the authority, but out of respect for the social system.

For this schema, maintaining the established social order defines morality. In the maintaining norms schema, law is connected to order in a moral sense. The schema leads to the expectation that without law (and duty to one's roles), there would be no order. People would instead act on own their special interests, leading to anarchy—a situation that responsible people want to prevent. For this schema, no further rationale for defining morality is necessary beyond simply asserting that an act is prescribed by the law or is the established way of doing things. The schema commits what moral philosophers call the "naturalistic fallacy" in inferring that what "is" (the de facto norms) also "ought" to be (is ethically required). The schema, maintaining norms, is consonant with "legal positivism" (Hart, 1961) in the sense that neither appeals to moral criteria beyond the law itself. Acquisition of this schema is what gives conventional thinkers their sense of moral necessity for the maintenance of social order. In other words, the schema provides a sense of moral certainty ("I know I'm right for the sake of our entire society"), and therefore fuels the special zeal and ferocity of conventional thinkers.

In the history of human civilization, law is one of the great human inventions, along with the cultivation of plants for food, writing, and the formation of cities. Because cities were established in the earliest civilizations that we know about (e.g., the Mesopotamian, beginning approximately 5,000 years ago), informal, face-to-face relationships could no longer be counted on to establish reliable expectations about interpersonal behavior. As a result, laws began to be formalized (Kramer, 1967). The Ur-Nammu cuneiform clay tablets date from about 2100 **B.C.** and constitute the prototype for subsequent written codes of laws. Such codes include the better-known Code of Hammurabi, which is primarily a collection of case laws describing crimes and misdemeanors and the corresponding punishments (Kramer, 1967). With the demise of the Sumer civilization (about 2000 **B.C.**), poets lamented the loss of law and order (Kramer, 1967).

Laws made possible a new kind of social order: For example, laws for land use made it reasonable for people to invest in the labor of tilling and cultivating fields until the time of harvesting—a long period of investment, but one that produced much greater yields of food than did the hunting and gathering methods of nomadic life. Laws governing the building and maintenance of waterways made possible irrigation systems that took years and years to build, but put larger acreage of land into agricultural use. Laws offered protection against marauders, pirates, and plunderers. The law broke the endless cycle of killing that was mandated by the vendetta (whereby killing one's kin needed to be avenged by killing the other's kin, ad infinitum). Likewise, the establishment of law and order in the American West meant that disputes would not be settled by the fastest gun. Law established social order, an order that was morally preferable to a society without law. Law—and the social/moral order it establishes—is a natural discovery of people in developing ways to organize cooperation in a large collective. This is the sense that the maintaining norms schema—our rendition of conventionality—is better than society without law, in a normative, moral, philosophical sense.

Using a very different approach from our neo-Kohlbergian approach, Youniss and Yates (1997) reported a widening conceptualization and concern among adolescents in viewing human welfare. Change is in the form of moving from a personal perspective to a sociocentric perspective. Youniss and Yates described the small-group discussions and essays of adolescents regarding their experiences of serving in a soup kitchen for unfortunates in Washington, D.C. They noted the shift in these adolescents from viewing their experiences in face-to-face personal terms toward viewing their experiences in terms of defects in the social system. In other words, these adolescents started to think about a societywide system of cooperation (macromorality), rather than only face-to-face relationships (micromorality).

So far, we have emphasized the positive aspects of the maintaining norms schema, and the sense in which it is a developmental accomplishment. But the maintaining norms schema can become exaggerated and harmful as well: for instance, in 1950s with McCarthyism, or with George Wallace's law and order orientation. McClosky and Brill (1983)—from a very different database than the DIT—commented on what they call the "conventionally minded," and thus characterized the negative side of this orientation:

> Because the established standards tend to be accepted as correct standards, those who flout them are often seen as thoughtless, ignorant, or wicked. To choose to be different in one's attitude towards venerated objects and symbols—religion, the nation, the flag, the family, the Deity—is seen as a sign of depravity. Why should one permit, much less safeguard or encourage, recalcitrance, error, malicious scorn for objects and values that right-minded people know to be correct or even sacred? . . .

Those who believe they know the "truth" on a particular issue, and in addition, enjoy the right to expound it, may find it difficult to understand why they have an obligation to permit someone with a contrary (and hence obviously false) view to enjoy an equal opportunity for freedom of expression. If one knows that the Nazis preach doctrines that are both hateful and wrong, by what moral obligation is one bound to permit them to publish their views or to assemble and proselytize in an effort to persuade others? (pp. 14–16)

McClosky and Brill viewed the particular danger of exaggerated "conventional mindedness" in terms of being so protective of the social order that basic human rights and civil liberties are curtailed. In other words, the social order that the maintaining norms orientation endorses can be overly authoritarian and oppressive. One haunting implication of the view that conventionality is part of natural development is that the threat of fascism and authoritarian regimes is present in every generation. At a certain stage in a person's normal development, fascism cannot only be tolerated but can seem right and good as well.

Note that in defining the maintaining norms schema in this way, we are not asserting that for the maintaining norms schema, all social thinking is a moral matter. Kohlbergian approaches are sometimes criticized for putting too much in the moral domain, particularly regarding conventional morality (Turiel, 1983). But even a person thinking only in terms of the maintaining norms schema can distinguish moral matters from purely economic, aesthetic, sociological, or political matters. For instance, defining conventionality in the way that we do does not put in the moral domain statements like the following: "The Dow Jones index went over 9,000 today," "*Titanic* is an artistic movie," "There are more women than men in the United States," and "Jones won the election." (Someone making these statements or their opposites would not be regarded as immoral by a person preferring the maintaining norms schema.)

The Postconventional Schema

We do not define postconventional schema by reference to Kantian or Rawlsian moral philosophies; our definition of postconventionality is not defined in terms of any single moral philosophy. Although the philosophy of John Rawls would certainly be classified as postconventional, so would most other modern moral philosophers. We do not propose a new normative philosophical theory by our highest levels of development (attempting to resolve philosophic disputes), and we are mindful of the unsettled state of moral philosophy at the present time. Our notion of schema is a broader, less partisan definition than Kohlberg's—and one could also say it is more timid and less exact.

Philosophers over the centuries have proposed many visions for a society based on moral ideals. Different ideals have been proposed (e.g., utilitarian, social contract, virtue based, feminist, casuist, religious ideals), and they have many different starting points, elements, and assumptions. The defining characteristic of postconventional thinking is that rights and duties are based on sharable ideals for organizing cooperation in society, and are open to debate and tests of logical consistency, experience of the community, and coherence with accepted practice. Moral theories that do not fit our criteria of postconventional schema include emotivist theories of morality (who say morality is nothing but the personal expression of approval or disapproval, e.g., Stevenson, 1937); Nietzsche (e.g., 1886/1968, in regarding cooperation as a bad idea and a ploy of the weak to hold down the strong); and ethical approaches based on fundamentalist/orthodox religious views (discussed later). In attempting a rational reconstruction of the postconventional schema, we propose four elements: primacy of moral criteria, appeal to an ideal, sharable ideals, and full reciprocity.

Primacy of Moral Criteria.   The person realizes that laws, roles, codes, and contracts are all social arrangements that can be set up in a variety of ways. Tradition, law, religious codes, or existing social practice prescribe certain behaviors. But the sole fact that these are de facto directives does not entail that a person *ought* to behave in those ways. (In other words, postconventional morality does not commit the naturalistic fallacy.)

Note that this realization of the alterability and relativity of social norms at the postconventional level is similar to Turiel's conception of the separate domain of social convention. In our view, Turiel's distinction of the domain of social convention from morality is essentially one part of the postconventional schema. Conventions at the maintaining norms level are viewed quite differently than are conventions at the postconventional level. At the maintaining norms level, conventions are inviolate and the last stand against anarchy; upholding convention defines the moral for conventional morality. In contrast, at the postconventional level, the person views conventions as alterable and nonuniversal insofar as they are instruments of *moral* purposes—agreements can be renegotiated. At the postconventional level, duties and rights follow from the moral purpose behind the conventions; not, as at the conventional level, from de facto norms.

Appealing to An Ideal.   Postconventional thinking is not merely a negative attitude toward the "establishment" or the "system." The Hippie rejection of society (or far-left ideology) does not, in the rejection, propose a constructive ideal by which to transform society. The positive and constructive aspect of postconventional thinking is to provide some idealized way that humans can interrelate, some ideals for organizing society. Examples of ideals for society that have been proposed include creating the greatest good for all, guaranteeing minimal rights and protection for everyone, engendering caring and intimacy among people, mandating fair treatment, providing for the needy, furthering the common good, actualizing personhood, and so on.

Sharable ideals. To be postconventional, the ideal must be *sharable*, not an idiosyncratic or ethnocentric preference or personal intuition. Sharability is tested by the ability to justify an act or practice to those whose participation is expected. When one justifies an act, one gives more than an appeal to one's private intuition ("My conscience told me it was right"). By a justification, one is arguing that an act is not self-serving at the expense of others, that the act respects others, serves group goals, furthers cooperation and the common good, or is consistent with acceptable policy and previously agreed-on principles and ideals.

Furthermore, one's justifications are open to rational critique, and can be challenged by new experience, by logical analysis, and by evidence. Postconventional thinking is not shielded by a privileged source of authority. Transcendental commands that are not subject to scrutiny or that are in principle beyond human comprehension are not postconventional. (This does not mean that insights from religion are categorically defined out of postconventionality, but instead entails that all insights—whatever their source—are subject to scrutiny by the participants who are affected, to tests of logical consistency, and to verification by human experience.)

Full Reciprocity. Whereas *partial* reciprocity was envisioned by the maintaining norms schema (i.e., that everyone alike is under the law and protected by the law), at the postconventional level one realizes that the law itself may be biased; lawful acts may nevertheless favor some over others (e.g., such was the point of Martin Luther King's civil disobedience). "Full" reciprocity entails not only uniform application of social norms, but also that the social norms themselves not be biased in favor of some at the expense of others.

There has been—and still is—much dispute among moral philosophers about what ideals should govern society, how to optimize all the participants' welfare, who is a participant, what *fair-minded* and *impartiality* mean, what *rational* and *equal* mean, what constitutes logical coherence, and the relative importance of principles and paradigm cases. Nevertheless, we believe that the schema of postconventional morality (as defined by these features) is presupposed in most modern moral philosophies. A major difference between the maintaining norms schema and the postconventional schema is how each attempts to establish consensus: The strategy of the maintaining norms schema is to gain consensus by appealing to established practice and existing authority; in contrast, the strategy of the postconventional schema is to gain consensus by appealing to ideals and logical coherence.

In the course of human history, the ideal of establishing a moral society has been a driving force in major revolutionary movements: in the American Revolution ("Liberty"); in the French Revolution of 1789 ("Liberty, Equality, Fraternity"), and in the Russian Revolution ("From each according to ability, to each according to need"). The utopian idealism of establishing a moral society accounts in part for the deprivations and sacrifices that supporters were willing to endure for the sake of a better future for all. Of course, other goals often motivated the revolutionaries, too, such as nationalism, opportunism, and the adventure of exercising raw power. Additionally, the ideal of establishing an ideally moral society is important in explaining nonrevolutionary and incremental movements, movements in the United States such as the child welfare movement in the nineteenth century, the movement to abolish slavery in the nineteenth century, the Women's movements of the nineteenth and twentieth centuries, the Civil Rights movement, and the prohibition of alcohol in the twentieth century. (The last example, the prohibition of alcohol, is cited to remind us that not every idealistic movement turns out well.)

We adopt this looser, more tepid notion of postconventionality in order to avoid the justified philosophical criticisms of Kohlberg regarding foundational principlism, lack of a notion of common morality, the assumption that a foundational principle can produce clear directives for action and consensus among informed, fair-minded, rational participants, and so on. Given the unsettled state of moral philosophy today, we await philosophical solutions; we do not propose to have settled them by aligning with one school or another. Our notion of postconventional schema accomplishes the goal of defining a developmental sequence in psychological terms without simultaneously claiming to advance a philosophical theory of normative ethics.

Parallels of Our Schema to Adelson's "Growth of Political Ideas"

Joseph Adelson's work, undertaken 3 decades ago (e.g., Adelson, 1971; Adelson & Beall, 1970; Adelson, Green, & O'Neil, 1969; Adelson &

O'Neil, 1966; Gallatin & Adelson, 1970), addressed the same phenomena as our work: how adolescents develop concepts on the morality of society. He used a different method than the DIT, and did not base his research on Kohlberg's work. Instead, he interviewed adolescents posing this problem: "Imagine that a thousand people venture to an island in the Pacific to form a new society; once there they must compose a political order, devise a legal system, and in general confront the myriad problems of government" (Adelson, 1971, p. 1014). The interview centered on questions like: What form of government should they have? What is the purpose of laws? Should people be required to be vaccinated? Should smoking be outlawed? What if the country wants to build a road and one person whose land is in the way doesn't want to sell that land? What is the purpose of education, and who should pay for it? How should crime be dealt with?

Adelson interviewed about 450 adolescents, starting at an earlier age (11-year-olds) than we use with the DIT (we usually do not go younger than 13-year-olds). Also, Adelson ended with high school seniors (18-year-olds), whereas we go into adulthood. However, Adelson reported findings in striking parallel to our three-schema theory of development.

The youngest of Adelson's subjects (the 11-year-olds) were characterized this way: "The early adolescent's political thought is constrained by personalized, concrete, present-oriented modes of approach" (Adelson & O'Neil, 1966, p. 305). This is reminiscent of our "personal interest schema," our counterpart to Kohlberg's preconventional level. (We don't say much about the personal interest schema because this schema is already on the wane in the samples engaged with the DIT.)

Adelson goes on to make comments about what we call the "maintaining norms schema." He said, "Younger subjects [particularly the 13-year-olds] are more likely to approve of coercion in public affairs. . . . [T]hey more readily accept the fact of hierarchy. They find it hard to imagine that authority may be irrational, presumptuous, or whimsical; thus they bend easily to the collective will" (Adelson & O'Neil, 1966, p. 304).

In 1971, Adelson wrote:

> Unless and until one has spoken at some length to young adolescents, one is not likely to appreciate just how bloodthirsty they can be. . . . Though they have a rough sense that the punishment should fit the crime, their view of that arithmetic leads them to propose Draconian measures even for innocuous misdeeds. . . . The young adolescent's views on crime and punishment reflect a more general, indeed a pervasive authoritarian bias. There is in fact no topic we explored which is free of that bias; wherever the child's mind turns—government, law, politics, social policy—we find it. . . . It [authoritarianism] is, in short, a ubiquitous feature of early adolescent political thought. . . . [T]he child's authoritarianism can be seen to stem from a certain conservatism of mind, which

leads him to view values and institutions as fixed and immutable. . . . Moral judgments at this age are marked by a blessed simplicity. Good and evil do not vary over time or between situations, and we see little of the moral relativism which will later complicate clear conviction. . . . The decline and fall of the authoritarian spirit is, along with the rapid growth in abstractness (to which it is related), the most dramatic developmental event in adolescent political thought. (pp.1022–1026)

Adelson noted the upsurge in authoritarianism in adolescents (as do we in the maintaining norms schema) as they become aware of the necessity for the societywide organization of moral order, and then its decline with the advent of postconventional thinking.

Third, Adelson commented on a later development in adolescence that is reminiscent of the postconventional schema:

> With advancing age there is an increasing grasp of the nature and needs of the community. As the youngster begins to understand the structure and functioning of the social order as a whole, he begins to understand too the specific social institutions within it and their relations to the whole. . . . Thus the demands of the social order and its constituent institutions, as well as the needs of the public, become matters to be appraised in formulating political choices. (Adelson & O'Neil, 1966, p. 304)

> The steady advance of the sense of principle is one of the most impressive phenomena of adolescent political thought. Once acquired, it spells an end to the sentimentality which so often governs the young adolescent's approach to political issues; it allows the child to resist the appeal of the obvious and the attractive, particularly where individual or communal rights are concerned. Our youngest subjects are so often capricious about individual rights not merely because they idealize authority, but also because they have so little sense of those principles which should limit the sway of government. (Adelson, 1971, pp. 1028–1029).

> It should come as no surprise that few adolescents show signs of having given serious thought to the radical revision of society. That there is little interest in the construction of utopia among the youngest adolescents is hardly unexpected. As we have seen, they have such a rudimentary sense of the concept of society that it would be implausible to find them indulging in social critique, let alone proposing schemes of social betterment whether modest or exalted. (Adelson, 1971, pp. 1036–1037)

Adelson's work is a richly nuanced interpretation of adolescent political/moral thinking. Reading Adelson (e.g., 1971) is a treat. His interpretations contain many leads for future research, even after almost 3 decades.

The Structure–Content Distinction

Our difference with the Kohlberg definition of postconventional thinking has implications for the structure–content distinction. Distinguishing structure from content is basic to a constructivist, cognitive approach. The distinction is crucial for diverse purposes: distinguishing between under-lying structure and surface content; defending a structural approach to moral education in public schools that is constitutional; making cross-cul-tural comparisons when it is obvious that cultures differ in terms of specific values, customs, and practices.

It is an open question, however, as to how to make the distinction. One can draw the distinction in different ways (e.g., Kohlberg's distinction in his 1958 dissertation is a different distinction than that in the 1987 scoring system). Kohlberg spent the last decade of his life working to purge content from structure in the 1987 scoring system (Colby et al., 1987). Kohlberg wanted to have a definition of structure that would support a strong version of the stage concept and his claim to having found, in longitudinal studies, "hard" Piagetian stages in moral judgment. Kohlberg's scoring system employs a four-tier process of unraveling content from structure, each layer holding some aspect of content constant, then preceding to the next layer of distinction. By time the scorer gets to the fourth tier, there are very abstract descriptions of stage structure, indeed. For instance, the idea of law and order is viewed in the Colby-Kohlberg system as a mix of "norm" content, "value element," and stage structure. The DIT does not make these distinctions, and Kohlberg thought that DIT research hopelessly mixed up content and structure (Kohlberg, 1984). Clearly, the 1987 Colby-Kohlberg system defines stage features at a more abstract level than in the DIT.

How does one decide which level of abstraction is better? We don't believe that the important question is how abstractly one can define structure (or how pure and rarified one can operationally make structure). The question should be what definition of structure can be operationalized (can assessment be done that produces the theoretically expected range of scores?) and validated (do the scores produce information that illuminates phenomena of interest?). We argue that the content–structure distinction embodied in a measure of moral judgment ought to maximize multiple validity criteria, not just stepwise progression in longitudinal studies. In DIT research we have attended to multiple validity criteria:

- Upward movement in longitudinal study.
- Differentiation of "experts"—Ph.Ds in moral philosophy and politi-cal science—from nonexperts.
- Sensitivity to moral education interventions.
- Correlations with moral comprehension.
- Predictability to positions on controversial public policy issues.
- Predictability to various measures of "moral behavior," and so on. (see Rest, Thoma, & Edwards, 1997, for discussion of our validation strategy).

Furthermore, once one gives up the notion of justice operations as defining "hard" Piagetian stages, then it is not important to purge all content from structure. For example, in DIT research our definitions of schemas include notions of social institutions; we do not try to purge them out. (In turn, this may limit the applicability of our descriptions of schemas to societies that have certain types of social institutions, e.g., eliminating hunting-and-gathering peoples.) We define our notion of the schema of maintaining norms to include law as a social institution—we do not try to separate law from the concept of social institution. In short, we draw the distinction between content and structure at a different place than Kohlberg did. The next chapters in this book give the reader some sense of the success of this alternative in terms of the multiple criteria of validity.

THE DEFINING ISSUES TEST
AS THE METHOD OF ASSESSMENT

Our neo-Kohlbergian approach uses the Defining Issues Test (DIT). This paper-and-pencil, multiple-choice test began as a "quick and dirty" method of stage assessment (at least, "quick and dirty" was how the DIT was understood at Kohlberg's Center at Harvard in the 1970s). Kohlberg had begun to revise his scoring system then, and was mindful of the arduous task of analyzing interview material. He joked that the DIT was like alchemy—the attempt to turn lead into gold. Using simple ratings and rankings to assess development instead of the labor-intensive analysis of interview material seemed too good to be true.

Obviously, the DIT was quick (enabling mass testing and scoring by computer). As results from DIT studies came in, we began to question whether it really was "dirty" as well—at least it seemed to be no dirtier than alternatives. But its quickness has remained a liability in the minds of many Kohlbergians. In chapter 7 we discuss a reconceptualization of how the DIT works.

Recognition Versus Production Tasks

The most noticeable difference between Kohlberg's research and DIT research is in the method of data collection. Kohlberg used an interview in which participants were presented with several moral dilemmas, asked to solve the dilemmas, then asked for the reasoning behind their choices. The interviews were transcribed and scored for stage according to a detailed, 800+-page scoring guide (Colby et al., 1987).

In contrast, the DIT is a paper-and-pencil task that presents participants with six moral dilemmas; each dilemma is followed by 12 items presenting an issue for consideration in solving the dilemma. Importantly (and, it turns out fortunately for our later theoretical interpretations), the items of the DIT were based on what subjects had actually said in Kohlbergian interviews. Therefore, the items were not simply armchair arguments deduced from the six-stage theory as understood in the early 1970s, but instead represented the diverse ideas of hundreds of actual subjects. The "fortunate" part of writing items this way is that the DIT items actually contain subtleties in moral thinking that we were not aware of in the 1970s. Items representing postconventional thinking do not only reflect a Rawlsian view, but there are also some items representing a utilitarian view, a libertarian view, and other forms of postconventionality—but they all have in common an appeal to a sharable ideal that is open to scrutiny.

In the DIT, the participant's task is to rate and rank the items in terms of their importance in making a decision about the dilemma. (See Table 3.1 for examples.) The participant's task is to rate each statement according to its importance in making moral decisions (importance rating as "great," "much," "some," "little," or "no"). After rating the 12 items, the participant is asked to consider all 12 items simultaneously and to rank the most important of the 12 considerations in making a decision ("most important," "second most important," "third most important," or "fourth most important").

Ratings and rankings of the items are used to derive a participant's score. The most used index of the DIT has been the "P" score (which is the weighted sum of ranks for the "postconventional items," derived from Kohlberg's Stages 5 and 6). For instance, if a participant ranked a postconventional item as "most important," then the P score would be increased by four points; ranking it as "second most important" increases the P score by three points; ranking it in third place increases the P score by two points; and ranking in fourth place increases it by one point. The total produced in this way ranges in the six-story version from 0 to 57. (The total does not equal 60, because there are not four P items in every story.) This is referred to as the "raw" P score. Raw P scores are converted to percentages (having a base of 100 rather than 60), and therefore the P percentage scores range from 0 to 95. The P score is interpreted as the degree to which the participant thinks postconventional considerations are important. Recently, we discovered a better way to index the DIT (Rest, Thoma, Narvaez, & Bebeau, 1997). The new index is called N2 but we do not go into details of that here.

There are potential advantages of a *recognition* task over a *production* task:

TABLE 3.1

Examples of DIT Items to Dilemmas

"Heinz" Dilemma

(Should Heinz steal a drug for his dying wife if he can get the drug no other way?)

Personal interest items (derived from Kohlberg's Stages 2 and 3):

1. Is Heinz willing to risk getting shot as a burglar or going to jail for the chance that stealing the drug might help?

2. Isn't it only natural for a loving husband to care so much for his wife that he'd steal?

Maintaining order items (derived from Kohlberg's Stage 4):

1. Whether a community's laws are going to be upheld.

2. Whether the druggist's rights to his invention have to be respected.

Postconventional items (derived from Kohlberg's Stages 5 and 6):

1. What values are going to be the basis for governing how people act toward each other.

2. Whether the law in this case is getting in the way of the most basic claim of any member of society.

"Prisoner" Dilemma

(Should Mrs. Jones report to the authorities someone—Mr. Thompson—whom she recognizes as an escaped prisoner, but who has led a good life since escaping?)

Personal interest items (derived from Kohlberg's Stages 2 and 3):

1. Was Mrs. Jones a good friend of Mr. Thompson?

2. How could anyone be so cruel and heartless as to send Mr. Thompson to prison?

Maintaining norms items (derived from Kohlberg's Stage 4):

1. Every time someone escapes punishment for a crime, doesn't that just encourage more crime?

2. Wouldn't it be a citizen's duty to report an escaped criminal, regardless of the circumstances?

Postconventional items (derived from Kohlberg's Stages 5 and 6):

1. How would the will of the people and the public good best be served?

2. Would going to prison do any good for Mr. Thompson, or protect anybody?

Table 3.1 continued on next page

Table 3.1 continued

"Newspaper" Dilemma

(Should a principal of a high school stop a student, Fred, from publishing a controversial student newspaper?)

Personal interest items (derived from Kohlberg's Stages 2 and 3):

1. Would the students start protesting even more if the principal stopped the newspaper?

2. Whether the principal's order would make Fred lose faith in the principal?

Maintaining norms items (derived from Kohlberg's Stage 4):

1. When the welfare of the school is threatened, does the principal have the right to give orders to students?

2. Whether the principal should be influenced by some angry parents when it is the principal who knows best what is going on in the school.

Postconventional items (derived from Kohlberg's Stages 5 and 6):

1. If the principal stopped the newspaper, would he be preventing full discussion of important problems?

2. What effect would stopping the paper have on the students' education in critical thinking and judgment?

"Doctor" Dilemma

(Should a doctor give a suffering woman an overdose of medicine that would kill her, which the woman is requesting?)

Personal interest items (derived from Kohlberg's Stages 2 and 3):

1. Whether the doctor could make it appear like an accident.

2. Whether the doctor has sympathy for the woman's suffering, or care more about what society might think.

Maintaining norms items (derived from Kohlberg's Stage 4):

1. Is the doctor obliged by the same laws as everybody else if giving an overdose would be the same as killing her.

2. Can society afford to let everybody end their lives when they want to.

Postconventional items (derived from Kohlberg's Stages 5 and 6):

1. Is helping to end another's life ever a responsible act of cooperation.

2. Can society allow suicides or mercy killing and still protect the lives of individuals who want to live.

1. In a production task (like Kohlberg's, asking a participant to produce justifications), a participant is credited for having only *explicitly expressed* ideas—*tacit understandings* are not counted. Hence, a production task tends to underestimate what a person understands. (We think this helps to explain why Stages 5 and 6 are so scarce in Kohlberg's data.) By contrast, in a recognition task (like the DIT), there is less of a burden on verbal expression, because examples of ideas are provided to elicit a response. All that a subject must do is to rate and rank the item, thus taxing the subject's articulation abilities less.

2. In a recognition task, there is only the subject's response that varies; not, as in clinical interviews, a mixture of interpretations from three sources. First, there is variability in the respondent's interpretations—the variable of interest. Second, there is also variability due to the interviewer's interpretations (not every interviewer conducts the interview in the same way). Third, there is variability due to scorer interpretations (because the subject's responses can be variously interpreted). On the other hand, advocates of clinical interviewing claim that they standardize the test administration by accommodating to the peculiarities of the subject, and therefore achieve superior standardization by clinical adaptation. Nevertheless, the superiority of clinical standardization over standardization of stimulus materials has not been demonstrated.

3. In production tasks, if the participant does not understand what the interviewer is asking, the utterances of the participant may not be scorable. Moreover, if the participant is repetitious, makes incomplete points, or haphazardly wanders from point to point, the unit of analysis is in doubt and comparability of scores from one testing to another (or one person to another) is in doubt. In contrast, recognition tasks offer more control of the testing situation. The use of discrete items—to which the participant gives a rating or a ranking—clarifies the task for the participant and the unit of analysis for each item, and establishes comparability (Rest, 1979; Rest, Thoma, & Edwards, 1997).

4. Related to the control that a recognition task affords is that the dilemma-and-item combination can help define the task for the subject. For instance, the presence of P items signal that it is permissible for the subject to consider issues relating to the fundamental structuring of society; that to comply with the task presented by the DIT, it is not necessary to limit consideration to how only the protagonist would live out his or her own life concretely. In fact, subjects who only identify what is at stake for the individuals involved in the dilemma—and do not move to the more general level of grappling with how society ought to be set up to deal with such dilemmas (shifting to macro issues)—will not get high P scores.

5. Convenience: Instead of requiring a trained judge to score free-response interview data according to a scoring guide, the participants in effect classify their own reactions to provided stimuli, thereby making objective and computerized scoring possible. (As we joked with Kohlberg, the DIT enables the study of morality "untouched by human hands").[1]

Of course, there are problems with recognition tasks. Among them are (a) participants may randomly check off ratings and rankings without attending to the task at all, thus giving bogus data; (b) participants may respond to aspects of the test stimuli that are not intended by the test designer; (c) test items may be ambiguous, or reactions to items may be idiosyncratic; and (d) generally speaking, just as production tasks probably *under*estimate a person's development, a recognition task probably *over*-estimates a person's development. For a detailed analysis of these problems, a description of the features that are built into the DIT to minimize these problems, and evidence that these are not fatal flaws for the DIT, see Rest, Thoma, and Edwards (1997), and Rest, Thoma, Narvaez, and Bebeau (1997). Design features of the DIT include several checks on the subject's giving reliable data, the "fragment strategy" (i.e., use of short outlines of arguments rather than extensive arguments), deemphasis on action-choice advocacy, and items that are based on the actual wording of subjects rather than design abstractions. Rest, Thoma and Edwards (1997) argued that these design features give the DIT advantages over other recognition-task instruments of moral judgment that do not have these features.

On the other hand, many researchers prefer production tasks and interview data. Explanations given by subjects have immediate face validity; they do not require a long chain of inferences by the experimenter (such as our seven-point validity strategy). Many people accustomed to verbal explanations from a production task do not like rating and ranking data, because it does not seem like real data. We have already discussed the problems in assuming the face validity of interview verbal productions. Furthermore, production/interview data is not always more like real life.

---

[1]In the early 1980s, Larry Kohlberg came to the University of Minnesota to give a boost to an Educational Psychology Colloquium series. He came despite being very ill at the time. While he was here, we showed him the computerized DIT forms and the optical scanner, and demonstrated how moral judgment scores could come popping out of the computer at an unseemly fast rate. At the time, we joked with him about "doing morality research untouched by human hands"—that is, without the arduous task of analyzing free responses to interviews. He saw the humor in our statement and smiled at its preposterous implications, but in his eyes there was also a glint of "Oppenheimer" regret. (J. Robert Oppenheimer, father of the atomic bomb, after witnessing the success of the Manhattan Project had deep second thoughts, "What have I unleashed upon the world?").

Consider, for example, the way that citizens in a democracy indicate their political judgments: in elections, referendums, and polls—all in the form of recognition tasks, not production tasks. Referendums, elections, and polls are not less real life, nor do they have less effect on the flow of real-life events for involving recognition data.

Items, Task Instructions, and Scoring the DIT

The Fragment Strategy. From earlier research in the 1960s with recognition tasks (e.g. Rest, 1969), we concluded that the items on the DIT had to be short and brief (see Rest, Thoma, & Edwards, 1997). If items are too lengthy, participants tend to project many of their own ideas onto the test statements, making it difficult to know what the participants are rating and ranking. Accordingly, stimulus items that were brief and cryptic were written on the presumption that only subjects who were already thinking about the dilemma along the lines suggested in the item would be attracted to that item; thus, no item is an extensive oration giving a lengthy rationale. Presumably, if an item raises an issue that the subject could not understand, that item would be passed over for another item more meaningful to the subject. (We refer to this as the "fragment strategy," in that the items only use fragments of moral arguments.)

The most direct evidence for the fragment strategy comes from recent research by Narvaez (1998). She found that people who pick P items on the DIT are also the ones who show better postconventional recall and reconstruction of postconventional arguments embedded in a narrative text. In the Narvaez study, participants were asked to do two tasks: complete the DIT and—in stories separate to and independent of the DIT—to read and recall moral narratives with moral arguments embedded in them. We presume that when a person takes the DIT, if the person already has developed the postconventional schema, then, on encountering a postconventional item, the person is more likely to think that item is important. Similarly, when the person was asked to recall the stories that were read, the person tended to include a postconventional argument (or invent a postconventional argument in reconstructing the story, responding to his or her own schema elicitation). Hence, both the DIT and the reconstructed memory task evoked (or activated) the postconventional schema (if the person had already developed them). Therefore, the reconstructed recall task corroborated what we suppose is happening in taking the DIT—both function by evoking preexisting postconventional schemas, if the person has already developed them. (See chap. 7 for further discussion on schema activation.)

Using items that are brief and cryptic (as a way to get data on postconventional thinking) places limits on the degree of discrimination that can be designed into the DIT items. In DIT research, we are not able to differentiate all six of Kohlberg's stages, nor are we able to differentiate A and B substages (Kohlberg, 1984), or to build in features that would represent many other Kohlbergian distinctions. Our data therefore does not support finer discriminations than just the three schema clusters (personal interest, maintaining norms, and postconventional). On the other hand, this lack of support does not disprove the finer distinctions. The most important point, however, is that our data does give support for that most elusive type of thinking in Kohlberg's own research, postconventional thinking.

Item Categories.   Table 3.1 shows items written for four moral dilemmas on the DIT. We group DIT items under three headings: personal interest, maintaining norms, and postconventional (roughly corresponding to Kohlbergian Stages 2 and 3, Stage 4, and Stages 5 and 6, respectively.) The category of personal interest justifies a decision by appealing to the personal stake that an actor has in the consequences of an action, including prudential concerns and also concerns for those with whom one has an affectionate relationship. (The personal interest schema collapses Kohlberg's Stages 2 and 3, because they both are mostly past history—forms of thinking that have been outgrown—for most of our subjects who take the DIT, with its minimum age of at least 12 years). Maintaining norms justifies a decision by invoking laws, custom, or religious codes that are publicly knowable, represent established ways of behaving, and thus create a social order. Postconventional justifications appeal to sharable social ideals; that is, justifications for an act are made by arguing that the act would respect other people, that the act serves sharable social goals, that the act optimizes the welfare of all participants, and so on. (Kohlberg scoring would place some of the items in Table 3.1 at earlier stages than where we place them. However, item analysis of the rating and ranking data confirms our placement, for the purposes of DIT research anyway.)

Postconventional Thinking.   We say here that the DIT's P score stands for the extent to which a person prefers postconventional justifications. In previous publications, we said that the P score represents the extent to which a person prefers principled considerations. We use the label *postconventional* instead of *principled* in response to objections by recent moral philosophers to Principlism (cited in chap. 2). But how can we change our minds about what P represents after 20 years of research? Recall that the items for the DIT came from the actual wording that people gave in previous interviews. The P items represent a mix of postconventional judgments: some P items seem to reflect utilitarian principles (e.g., "Would stealing in such a case bring about more total good for the whole society or not?"); Some items are libertarian, rights-oriented (e.g., "Whether the law in this case is getting in the way of the most basic claim of any member of society"); and some P items are inspired by a Rawlsian view (e.g., "What values are going to be the basis for governing how people act towards each other"). What all these P items have in common is that they attempt to justify an act by appealing to a sharable social ideal.

Note that the ranking procedure in the DIT allows subjects to select among the items of a cluster. Thus, for instance, if a subject does not like utilitarian thinking, the subject can still rank another P item in first place—which would still indicate preference for P items over Stage 4 items or low stage items. In other words, a person can get a high P score by various philosophical routes. Note that what we have changed over the past 20 years is not the stimuli or data, but the theoretical interpretation of the P score (from principled to postconventional).

Shifting Distributions Versus the "Staircase"

In DIT research (Rest, 1979), we distinguish two issues:

1. Describing stages or structures—depicting the underlying logic that interconnects a line of moral argument—or to use Kohlberg's phrase, "the rational reconstruction of the ontogenesis of justice reasoning"
2. Assigning a developmental score to a particular person.

Issue 1 concerns the logical structure of reasoning, to specimens of thinking or to lines of argument. Issue 2 concerns the scores given to subjects. The two issues are not the same. Various situational conditions affect which stage is employed at a particular time. A person can use multiple stages of thinking at the same time and be inconsistent in stage use. Development is, in part, the more frequent and reliable use of higher stage thinking, not merely the first occurrence of the stage.

Whereas qualitative analysis is used to illuminate the logical interconnections describing the features of a schema, the assessment of the developmental progress of an individual is different from this qualitative analysis. According to our view, developmental assessment is not a matter of putting an individual into one stage, but rather a matter of assessing the degree to which the individual uses various types of thinking. Developmental sequence therefore is not a matter of a person abruptly changing from stage to stage (going up the staircase, step by step), but a matter of shifting distributions of stage use (using less of the lower stages and more of the higher stages of thinking).

INRC Operations and "Justice Operations"

Kohlberg compared his notion of "justice operations" to Piaget's INRC operations (e.g., 1984). Gibbs (1979) attempted a rigorous translation of Piaget's INRC operations into Kohlbergian moral stages, and found that he could only work out counterparts of Piaget's operations up through Kohlberg's Stage 4. Gibbs concluded that only Kohlberg's Stages 1 to 4 were true Piagetian stages, and that Stages 5 and 6 were elaborations of a different construct than moral judgment. Kohlberg nevertheless argued that postconventional stages were true Piagetian stages involving distinct justice operations, culminating at Stage 6 in the fulfillment of justice operations. Kohlberg was motivated to find a developmental distinction between George Wallace and Martin Luther King.

We favor a different resolution to this issue: We abandon the attempt to define moral stages in terms of logical operations (either Piaget's INRC operations or Kohlberg's justice operations). Many areas of psychology do not invoke the notion of operations to explain cognitive expertise (e.g., Ericsson & Smith, 1991). Rather than postulating distinct justice operations to define each stage, we more simply invoke the notion of "schema"—a general construct that implies some sort of cognitive structure or concept (see chap. 6). We still agree with Kohlberg that the aim of the developmental analysis of moral judgment is the rational reconstruction of the ontogenesis of justice reasoning. Our description of the developmental schemas is our rational reconstruction without reference to operations, focusing on the pan-human problem, of how to organize cooperation in society.

SUMMARY OF OUR NEO-KOHLBERGIAN APPROACH

What remains of Kohlberg's theory and what is changed in our neo-Kohlbergian approach?

1. The major legacy of Kohlberg is the starting point that he gave for research in morality: a cognitive constructivist approach that is developmental, in which one starts with the person's internal construction of the social world, emphasizing the individual's cognition and moral judgment. Piaget and Kohlberg viewed the problem of morality primarily in terms of establishing a cooperative social system (that works beyond the expression of empathy in face-to-face situations), assuming sequential development in the conceptualization of the possibilities for organizing social systems.

2. We explicitly recognize the limitations in Kohlberg's six-stage theory:
   (a) That moral judgment is only one psychological component of general moral development.
   (b) That Kohlberg's analysis of stages is of global, course-grained markers of life-span development, and that intermediate-level concepts are needed for a full decision-making model.
   (c) That Kohlberg's emphasis on justice is not a comprehensive moral theory, but predominantly deals with the morality of nonintimate relationships within society (the political side of morality rather than the personal side).
   (d) That Kohlberg's dilemmas do not cover the whole domain of morality.
       Acknowledging these limitations, we still see the usefulness of Kohlberg's starting points, but understand that these may not be the final endpoints of a comprehensive theory.

3. Kohlberg advanced both a psychological theory of moral development and a philosophical theory of normative ethics. Kohlberg's normative theory is partisan to deontological theories of a Kantian/Rawlsian type. In contrast, our definition of postconventional thinking is intended to be nonpartisan to any particular moral philosopher; the key is that postconventional thinking proposes a sharable ideal for society open to scrutiny and debate.

4. Rejected is the idea that the only way to build a moral theory is from foundational principles—a common view of moral theory in Kohlberg's day. The postconventional schema includes principled theories as well as others.

5. Kohlberg described development in terms of "hard" Piagetian stages, each having distinctive "justice operations." We describe development in terms of shifting distributions of schemas, the higher stages gaining in use whereas the lower stages diminish. We do not use the concept of justice operations to characterize development.

6. Kohlberg distinguished content from structure too starkly; we propose to include concepts of social institutions in our definition of schemas.

7. The core ideas for our schemas are essentially Kohlberg's. Our definition of maintaining norms is derived from Kohlberg's law and order; our definition of the postconventional schema is derived from Kohlberg's general discussions of Stages 5 and 6.

8. The major methodological differences between Kohlberg's approach and the DIT is that one uses a production task, and the other a recognition task. Kohlberg's method has stringent verbal requirements, whereas the DIT can measure tacit understanding and enables us to find evidence for postconventional thinking.

9. DIT research does not disprove, but neither does it support, many of the finer distinctions of Kohlberg's theory (e.g., six or seven distinct stages, A and B substages, justice operations). Perhaps someone will figure out a way to build more discriminations into items for a recognition task than we were able to do with the DIT using the fragment strategy.

THE SHORT CONCLUSION

The main problems of Kohlberg's 1987 theory are: Kohlberg overextended Piaget in his model of psychological development; he overextended Rawls in his philosophical theory of normative ethics; and his research provided too little evidence for postconventional thinking. Our neo-Kohlbergian approach follows Piaget in being a developmental approach, but we adopt a more complex model of stage development and do not attempt to define stages in terms of justice operations or the staircase metaphor. Our neo-Kohlbergian approach recognizes the Rawlsian approach to normative ethics as but one important kind of postconventional theory that appeals to a sharable ideal for organizing society, but we recognize other ways of proposing sharable ideals as well. We define postconventional thinking more broadly (or more loosely) than Kohlberg did. Finally, our method of assessment is not as dependent on verbal expressiveness as Kohlberg's production task, and allows us to credit people with more tacit understanding of postconventional thinking, the main index of the DIT.

4

വ◦ ♦ ◦ന

Validity and Reliability Studies
of the DIT

CRITICISMS OF DIT RESEARCH

The DIT has not been without its critics. Criticisms of DIT research not only include the problems with Kohlberg's approach that we discussed in chapter 2, but also the following:

1. The field of moral development is contentious, because of the difficulty in establishing the validity and generality of any measure.
2. DIT research is based on 10- to 20-year-old data.
3. Much of DIT research is unpublished and inaccessible, and the claims cannot be evaluated.
4. DIT findings are a hodgepodge.
5. Because the DIT has not been changed for 30 years, DIT research cannot address the many issues that have become part of the discussion of moral development in recent years. Being an old instrument, it does not address the criticisms leveled at Kohlberg's approach.
6. DIT research is not the start of a new field, but puts an end to an old one.
7. The DIT provides limited insights about moral development, because it uses recognition data rather than verbal production data. Recognition data cannot provide insights into moral development.

We didn't think that an adequate response to these criticisms would be, "Read the literature." Although the criticisms can be quickly made, it takes lengthy discussion and documentation to address them. One could regard this whole book as a response to these criticisms. In chapter 2, we laid out the major criticisms of Kohlberg's approach. In chapter 3, we argued our position regarding what reformulations are necessary and how DIT research attempts to meet the justified criticisms. Also in the previous chapter, we took our shot at the debate over production/interview data versus recognition/DIT data, and we concluded that any data-collection method needs to be validated on its own merits. In this chapter, we address mainly the first four of the criticisms listed at the start of this chapter, documenting the extensive research (in fact, much of it is published and accessible) that bears on the validity and reliability of the DIT. In the next chapters, 5 through 8, we elaborate on new data that have emerged—and are still emerging—from DIT research, mainly addressing the fifth and sixth criticisms.

What Is Construct Validity for a Test of Moral Judgment?

How does a person tell whether or not a test of moral judgment is valid? What is the DIT good for? What special information does one get from the DIT that cannot be obtained from existing tests? What phenomena are illuminated by the construct and its measurement? How can one tell whether one test of moral judgment is better or worse than another?

There is no standard answer to these questions. Answers involve proposing an operational definition of the construct validity for a test of moral judgment. This is an interpretative act, so different people may have different operational definitions with alternative studies in mind. We have proposed criteria for validity since the 1970s, with minor alterations. (Recently, we have shown how seriously we take these criteria by basing programmatic research decisions on them; e.g., Rest, Thoma, & Edwards, 1997; Rest, Thoma, Narvaez, & Bebeau, 1997). Our list of validity criteria has been explained in many publications over the years (Rest, 1974a, 1974b, 1975b, 1976a, 1976b, 1976c, 1976d, 1979, 1980d, 1980e, 1980f, 1981, 1982, 1985a, 1985b, 1986a, 1986b, 1988a, 1993, 1994), and our approach to validity should not be too surprising to anyone reading some of this literature. The list of validity criteria and the studies that investigate them provide a connecting thread for the diverse studies on the DIT. Keeping in mind the list of validity criteria serves to frame our response to critics about DIT studies being a hodgepodge.

Here is our proposal for defining construct validity for the DIT: A test of moral judgment should:

1. Differentiate groups assumed to be of greater or lesser expertise in moral reasoning (e.g., moral philosophers are expected to show higher scores than junior high school students).
2. Show significant upward change in longitudinal study.
3. Be sensitive to interventions designed to improve moral reasoning (e.g., show pre-/posttest gains on moral education programs).
4. Show evidence of a developmental hierarchy (i.e., that higher is better or more advanced).
5. Significantly predict to real-life moral behavior.
6. Significantly predict to political attitudes, political choices, and the way in which a person participates in the larger society.
7. Have adequate reliability. There are additional DIT studies besides the research addressing these validity criteria, but in this chapter we focus on validity research.

The organization of our presentation on validity has three parts for each of the seven criteria. First, we discuss briefly each validity criterion (how certain kinds of findings are relevant to the concept of validity).

Second, we illustrate DIT studies with an example from the early years (from the 1970s) and an example from the later years (from the 1990s). The early studies were originally used to argue the validity of the DIT, and are called classic studies. They are classic in the sense that these studies provided the first support for the DIT that was used to persuade researchers to use the DIT. Furthermore, because we at Minnesota performed many of these early studies, the raw data are available to us for secondary analysis. In discussing the validity research of the DIT (e.g., Rest, Narvaez, Thoma, & Bebeau, 1997; Rest, Thoma, & Edwards, 1997) we make frequent use of the classic studies. Research, however, did not end in the 1970s. We cite later findings to show that the results of the 1970s are still being replicated. The consistency of DIT findings between the 1970s and 1990s shows that we are not engaging in a bait-and-switch maneuver (i.e., hooking researchers on an early version of the DIT that worked in the 1970s, and then changing the DIT so that it will work now but maintaining the impression that the early studies are cumulative for the later version). Rather, the DIT has remained unchanged so that a record of validity and generality could be established over the years during a full cycle of research. It was apparent to us that we could not both establish the generality and validity of a measure and also be changing it whenever the winds shifted direction. Although we have been tempted to fiddle with the DIT (to update it in various ways), we thought that it was more important to establish a stable record. Only recently have we begun to embark on a new cycle of studies with a new updated version of the DIT (Rest, Narvaez, Thoma, & Bebeau, 1998).

Third, we will list published studies in a table of citations that accompanies each criteria or heading. There may be other published studies that escaped our notice; certainly, there are many additional unpublished studies. By our count, there are well over 400 published articles and books on the DIT—the literature is vast. For each validity criteria the tables are divided into reviews and studies. The reviews include both published and unpublished studies, but the studies sections of the table list only *published* empirical data. We understand the concern of the first four criticisms at the start of the chapter essentially to be about the accessibility and recentness of DIT studies. It is true that the Rest's, 1979 and 1986b books cite mainly unpublished references—doctoral dissertations, conference presentations, and unpublished manuscripts as the bulk of support. In responding to this criticism, we now emphasize published references. (By "published" references, we mean those articles in journals and books that have been mass reproduced, and copies sent to libraries.) In the citation tables, we refer to each published study by author and data; in the reference section we provide the full citation of the study and precede the author with an asterisk (*) if the reference is a published DIT study. Fig. 4.1 is a graph of the number of published references of DIT research (across the various topics of chaps. 4 and 5). The figure simply tallies the references by year of publication and presents the cumulative total (over 400). The

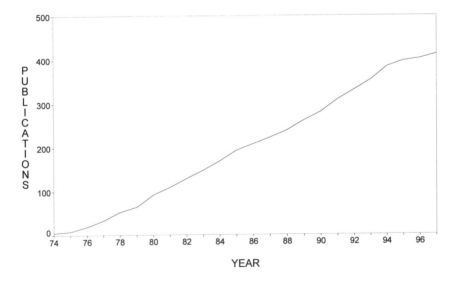

FIG. 4.1. Cumulative Frequency of DIT publications by year.

simple point we wish to make here is that the published literature on the DIT is plentiful, and has accumulated steadily since the 1970s.

Note that the published/unpublished dichotomy is not a judgment of quality. We do not mean to imply that the published studies are better than the unpublished studies. Indeed, we could cite many instances of splendid unpublished dissertations, in contrast to seriously flawed articles in journals with high rejection rates (some of which are critiqued in this book). The *reviews* cited under each heading contain both published and unpublished articles. As Gene Glass (1977) argued in meta-analytic research, when one aggregates many studies from many sources, it is best to include both published and unpublished data sets. In moral judgment research, we too have found that published and unpublished studies—both those that strike us as well crafted and those that strike us as not-so-well crafted—give essentially the same conclusions when aggregated in meta-analysis (Schlaefli, Rest, & Thoma, 1985). Nevertheless, we cite only published studies in response to critics. A more complete bibliography including unpublished data is available from the Center at Minnesota, discussed in Appendix B.

The lists of citations in the tables serve several purposes: (a) to document the fact that the study of the DIT did not take place only 20 to 30 years ago, but has continued throughout the years; (b) to document that there is *published* research on DIT findings—they are not all buried in inaccessible, unpublished sources; and (c) to provide interested researchers with an entry point into the literature (which admittedly is very scattered). In this chapter, we do not comment on every study—that is the burden of the reviews on each particular topic. As previously mentioned, the reviews reach conclusions by taking account of both published and unpublished studies.

THE STUDIES

Does Postconventional Thinking Exist?

Before moving to the validity criteria and discussion of the empirical evidence on whether conventionality comes before postconventionality, there is the prior question of whether or not there is evidence that something we call "postconventional thinking" even exists to any appreciable extent. Here, we are not concerned with the details of sample characteristics (e.g., respondents' place of origin, age, socioeconomic status, religion, etc.); we simply ask whether or not DIT research, like Kohlberg's research, fails to show postconventional thinking.

A succinct demonstration of this preliminary point involves looking at a large collection of DITs from many researchers (over 800 studies) who have used the Scoring Service of Minnesota's Center for the Study of Ethical Development. The sample is comprised of 45,856 DITs scored during the years 1989 through 1993. It is called the "Mega" sample, and was compiled by Evens (1995). The data come from the entire age range of people who can take the DIT (12 years and up), from all walks of life, from virtually every state in the United States. (See Evens, 1995, for more details on the Mega sample.)

In Fig. 4.2, a histogram of P scores for the Mega sample is presented. The P score is calculated in the way indicated earlier in this book (see Rest, 1979, for details; Rest, Thoma, & Edwards, 1997) and is converted from raw scores to percentages. The mean of this distribution is 39.1, and the standard deviation is 14.84. P scores are approximately normally distributed, ranging from 0 to 91. In short, unlike the large body of Kohlbergian research, something we call postconventional thinking is plentiful in DIT research. Thus, we can go on to ask the more interesting questions: What is the nature of postconventional thinking on the DIT? Who has it, and to what extent? Why is it useful to know someone's P score? What is the evidence that postconventional thinking is a developmental advance over conventional thinking?

Validity Criterion 1: Differentiation of Groups Differing in Expertise

One of the first kinds of studies we did in the 1970s was to compare the scores of junior high school students with senior high school students,

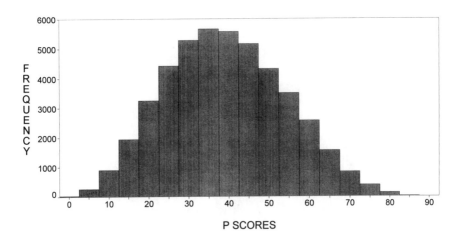

FIG. 4.2. Histogram of P scores for the "Mega" Sample.

college students, and graduate students (e.g., Rest, Cooper, Coder, Masanz, & Anderson, 1974). This is the familiar cross-sectional age/education trend study, usually one of the first kinds of studies to be done with a developmental measure. On a commonsense basis, one expects that age and education are rough indexes of development, and that as age/education increases in groups, so also should developmental scores.

One of the problems with the cross-sectional design (comparisons of different age/education groups and inferring developmental sequence from group differences) is that the groups may differ in respects other than only on development. For instance, in comparing junior high school students from poor, inner-city neighborhoods with more affluent senior high students, the differences may reflect socioeconomic status (SES) or ethnic differences as well as developmental differences. If the circumstances were reversed—say, the junior high students came from affluent neighborhoods, and the senior high students were from poor, inner city neighborhoods—the differences on developmental tests might be reversed from the usual age/education expectation. One of the ways to build more confidence in the cross-sectional design is to use large composite samples. By using many different subsamples for each of the age/educational groupings, there is less probability that some other factor (e.g., SES, region, ethnic subgroup) is systematically causing differences between the age/education groupings.

The use of composite samples came easily. As other researchers began to use the DIT, it was possible to use their samples and form large composites of subjects at different age/educational levels. Davison (1979) reported on a composite sample of 1,080 subjects made up of about 250 junior high students, 250 senior high students, 250 college students and 250 graduate students. The age range was 15 to 82 years, 424 males and 452 females (gender unknown on the remainder). The sample was a composite of 23 smaller studies from various parts of the United States, each reporting age/education as well as P score. An ANOVA produced a main effect for educational level (four levels), $F = 203.3$ ($df = 3, 1008$; $p < .001$), indicating very strong differentiation of age/education groups on the DIT. In a later composite sample of 4,565 subjects (Rest, 1979), from 136 different samples, grouping subjects by four educational levels produced an $F = 604.9$, highly statistically significant, accounting for 38% to 49% of the DIT variance (depending on whether four levels of education were used or whether the classroom was used as the grouping variable).

In 1986, Thoma compiled 56 studies into a composite sample of 6,863 subjects. Grouping by the four education levels (junior high, senior high, college, and graduate school), he found that education accounted for 52.5% of the variance, whereas sex (gender) of subject accounted for only 0.2% of the variance (data given in more detail in chap. 5).

The differentiation of age/educational groups by DIT P score is well replicated in the literature. Table 4.1 lists over 30 published studies that show many independent replications of the differentiation of age/education groups on the DIT.

We composed a composite sample (the "1995 composite sample") with the aim of providing more comparison points that just four levels of education—this composite sample was designed to have 10 levels, therefore affording a more detailed picture of the shifting distributions of the schema with development. The 1995 composite sample consists of about 1,000 subjects; again, of about 250 subjects at each of the four levels of education. However, this sample is broken down further into 10 subgroups, ranging from participants from an academically poor,

TABLE 4.1

Citation of Published Cross-Sectional Studies

Reviews:

Gielen, & Markoulis, (1994) [age/educational trends among cross-cultural studies]

McNeel (1994b); Nucci & Pascarella (1987); Pascarella & Terenzini (1991) [focus on the college years]

Ponemon & Gabhart (1994) [review of groups of accountants]

Rest (1979, 1986b); Rest, Davison, & Robbins (1978); Rest & Thoma (1985b) [general discussion of formal education]

Self & Baldwin (1994)[review of groups of medical doctors]

Self, Olivarez, & Baldwin (1994) [review of groups of veterinarians]

Studies:

Bakken & Ellsworth (1990); Baxter & Rarick (1987); Bertin, Ferrant, Whiteley, & Yokata (1985); Biggs & Barnett (1981); Boom & Molenaar (1989); Bouhmama (1987); Cohen (1982); Daniels & Baker (1979); de Casterle, Jansses, & Grypdonck (1996); Felton & Parsons (1987); Finger, Borduin, & Baumstark (1992); Ketefian (1981b); Lawrence (1987); Martin, Shafto, & Vandeinse (1977); Murk & Addleman (1992); Perez-Delgado, Garcia-Ros, & Clemente-Carrion (1992); Ponemon & Glazer (1990); Rest, Cooper, Coder, Masanz, & Anderson (1974); Self (1993); Shaub (1994); Swanson (1990); Thoma (1986); Thoma & Davison (1983); Thoma & Rest (in press); Wilson (1995) underprivileged, highly delinquent junior high school student population; through senior high school students and college students; to graduate students in moral philosophy and political science.[1] We speculated that, at the lower end, the junior high school students from the poor, inner-city neighborhoods would have lower DIT scores than would other junior high school students from privileged, upper classes. Also, we speculated that, at the upper end, graduate students in moral philosophy and political science would have higher DIT scores than would students in a medical school—not because the medical students were less bright or less academically motivated (quite the contrary), but because the academic specialization of the philosophy/political science students was expected to give them some advantage on a moral judgment test. In short, the 1995 composite sample is a speculative attempt to spread out the points of development into 10 groupings rather than just 4. The 1995 sample was analyzed in two ways: more conservatively, on the basis of the four education/age levels; and more speculatively, on the basis of the 10 subsamples.

Fig. 4.3 shows how the average *ratings* of DIT scores (grouped into the three schemas—designated Stages 2 + 3 = personal interest, Stage 4 = maintaining norms, and Stages 5 + 6 = postconventional) shift around on the 10 subgroups of the 1995 composite sample. First, note that ratings for postconventional morality (Stages 5 + 6) systematically increase as we move from the less expert groups to the more expert groups. Whereas the junior high school groups start out with higher ratings for Stage 4 than for postconventional morality, there is a crossover sometime in high school, and the college groups and graduate school groups show increasingly higher ratings of Stages 5 + 6. Whereas Stage 2 + 3 is higher than Stages 5 + 6 in junior high, it continues to decline, being lower than

---

[1]Subsample 1 was comprised of 116 junior high students from an impoverished, academically poor, inner-city school with serious delinquency problems (Rest, Ahlgren, & Mackey, 1973). Subsample 2 was comprised of 59 junior high students from an average suburban school (from Narvaez, 1993a). Subsample 3 was comprised of 71 junior high students from a private, college-prep school with exceptionally high academic standards and privileged SES family background (from Narvaez, 1993a). Subsample 4 was comprised of 72 senior high students from a working-class school (Center files). Subsample 5 was comprised of 174 senior high students from an academically average school (Center files). Subsample 6 was comprised of 87 college students, mostly lower division (Narvaez, 1993b). Subsample 7 was comprised of 155 college students, mostly higher division (Center files). Subsample 8 was comprised of 166 students at the end of their first year of medical school (Self & Baldwin, 1994). Subsample 9 was comprised of 60 seminarians from a liberal theological seminary who were in an advanced ethics course (Schomberg & Nelson, 1976). Subsample 10 was comprised of 32 doctoral students in moral philosophy or political science (Narvaez, 1996). "Center files" refers to data that are not reported in any published article but are part of the archived records of DITs scored at the Minnesota Center.

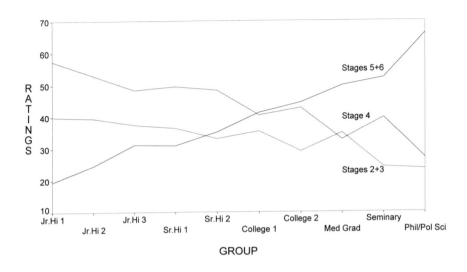

FIG. 4.3. Average ratings for clusters by age/education subgroup.

Stage 4 and Stages 5 + 6 in high school and thereafter.[2] Fig. 4.4 shows that these trends of the *rating* data are also true for *ranking* data; however, the rating data show more differentiation of the schema at the early levels than do the ranking data.

Note that the single index, the P score, based on Stages 5 + 6 (ratings or rankings), is a good indicator of development in moral judgment by itself. Stages 5 + 6 (P score) increase monotonically across the 10

---

[2]The rating data in Fig. 4.3 eliminate the three items that decrease the Cronbach alpha of their respective groupings (hence W7 is omitted from Stages 5 + 6, P4 is omitted from Stage 4 items, and N12 is omitted from Stages 2 + 3). This leaves 20 P items, 18 Stage 4 items, and 21 Stages 2 + 3 items. Also, because the 10 subgroups of the 1995 composite sample have different overall average ratings (for all 57 items), each subject's ratings are divided by the subject's overall average rating in order to standardize for use of the rating scale (i.e., individual item ratings are divided by the individual's average rating of the 57 items).

Fig. 4.4 shows the age/education trends for Stages 5 + 6, Stage 4, and Stages 2 + 3 based on *ranking* data instead of *rating* data. Comparison of Figs. 4.3 and 4.4 shows that both rating and ranking data produce nearly identical trends. For instance, Stages 5 + 6 are based on rating data correlates .85 (*n* = 992), with the P score based on ranking data. In our presentation, the switch between rates and ranks occurs for this reason: When doing factor analysis on the Mega sample, *rates* are used because of the special problems with ranking data. (In ranking data, two thirds of the items are "0" because only the top four items are ranked for each dilemma.) Note that all subsequent analyses report results using ranks (the P score), because that index is the one usually reported in the literature for the past 25 years. (Recently, we discovered that there is a better index than the P score, but here we stay with the P index and defer discussion of a new index; Rest, Thoma, Narvaez, & Bebeau, 1997).

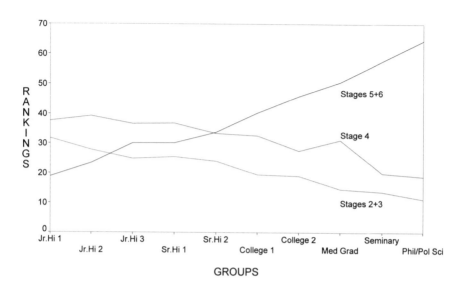

FIG. 4.4. Average rankings for "clusters" by age/education subgroup.

subgroups—the P score serves as a good single-number index of development. The correlation of P score (*ranks*) with the 10 subgroups is .69. (The corresponding correlation with Stages 5 + 6 from *rating* data is .63.) ANOVA on P scores for *rates* by the 10 subgroups produces $F = 75.992$, d.f. $= 9, 979, p < .001$. ANOVA on P score for *ranks* by the 10 subgroups produces an F of 101.331, d.f. $= 9, 979; p < .001$. For purposes of testing the sequentiality of the stages, Stage 5 + 6 (both for rates and ranks) is presented here along with that for Stage 4 and Stages 2 + 3. We see that the higher scores increase as the lower stage scores decrease. Therefore, for most research purposes, simply having a single number (i.e., P score) by itself for subjects is sufficient—it is redundant to report Stage 4 and Stages 2 + 3. If the P scores increase, we can expect the lower stages to decrease. (In *ranking* data, a rise in higher stages mathematically must be complemented by a drop in lower stages because of the ipsative nature of ranks. Although this is not mathematically necessary for *rating* data, empirically it turns out that way.)

There may be some misgiving about using the 10 subgroups in the 1995 composite sample to represent a linear scale of development. Admittedly, in reporting correlations between the P score and subgroup, it is assumed that the 10 subgroups form a linear scale of moral expertise with equal intervals between them. Therefore, more conservatively, we can represent these data simply in terms of four levels of education (junior high, senior high, college, and graduate or professional school)—4 levels instead of 10 subgroups. An ANOVA with educational level as main effect (four levels) produces an F of 256.6, $p < .001$, $n = 992$.

A discussion of the effects attributable to specific demographic variables (formal education, age, SES, region of country, gender, religion, and profession) was reported in Rest (1979). That discussion concludes that formal education is by far the most powerful demographic correlate of DIT P scores, typically accounting for 30% to 50% of the variance in large, heterogenous samples, whereas age per se in children is confounded with formal education (older children have more education). However, in adult samples, when it is possible to have very old subjects with little formal education, the two variables can be separated. We find that formal education is much more predictive of DIT P score than age (i.e., young adults with much formal education have higher P scores than do old adults with little education); and, in some studies of adults, age is actually *negatively* correlated with DIT P scores, whereas education is positively correlated (Coder, 1975; Rest, 1979). The general picture that we have of the relations of age, education, and P score is that DIT P scores tend to increase while the person is in the formal education setting, and then reaches a plateau as the person exits formal education. Thus, adults (perhaps as old as in their 60s and 70s) who ended their education, say, with junior high school, tend to have low P scores like those of current junior high school pupils; whereas adults with advanced graduate degrees have P scores like current students in that advanced degree program (Rest, 1979).

The logic of cross-sectional comparisons of groups does not depend on separating out the unique contributions of each demographic variable, but instead depends on the commonsense expectation that some naturally occurring groups are more or less expert than other groups. Nevertheless, a discussion of the separate effects of demographic variables like age, education, socioeconomic status, and region of the country is contained in Bakken and Ellsworth (1990), Murk and Addleman (1992), Rest (1979), and Wilson (1995). In addition, the demographic variables of gender, religion, and political affiliation are discussed later, as topics under their own headings. Professional/occupational group has been a very popular topic for exploration, as Table 4.2 shows with over 100 published citations. Nevertheless, the short conclusion regarding all these demographic variables is that the level of formal education is the strongest predictor of DIT scores.

Validity Criterion 2:
Longitudinal Upward Trends

Different people may show different use of postconventional thinking, but how do we know that differences in DIT scores represent a develop-

TABLE 4.2

Citation of Published Articles of Professional/Occupational Groups

Accountants, Auditors

Armstrong (1987, 1993); Arnold & Ponemon (1987, 1991); Bernardi & Arnold (1994); Icerman, Karcher, & Kennelley (1991); Lampe & Finn (1992); Loeb (1991); Ponemon (1990, 1992a, 1992b, 1993a, 1993b); Ponemon & Gabhart (1990); Ponemon & Glazer (1990); Shaub (1994); St. Pierre, Nelson, & Gabbin (1990)

Business, Managers

Baxter & Rarick (1987); Castleberry, French, & Carlin (1993); Conry & Nelson (1989); DeConinck & Good (1989); Ford, Latour, Vitrell, & French (1997); Goolsby & Hunt (1992); Jeffrey (1993); Wood, Longenecker, McKinney, & Moore (1988)

Counselors

Bernier (1980); Richmond (1989)

Dentistry, dental hygiene

Baab & Bebeau (1990); Bebeau (1983a, 1983b, 1985, 1988, 1991, 1993a, 1993b, 1993c, 1994a, 1994b); Bebeau, Rest, & Yamoor (1985); Bebeau & Thoma (1994); McCullough (1985); Newell, Young, & Yamoor (1985); Ozar & Hockenberry (1985)

Doctors

Adamson, Baldwin, Sheehan, & Oppenberg (1997); Baldwin, Adamson, Self, Sheehan, & Oppenberg (1996); Baldwin, Daugherty, & Self (1991); Benor, Notzer, Sheehan, & Norman (1984); Candee, Sheehan, Cook, & Husted (1979); Candee, Sheehan, Cook, Husted, & Bargen (1982); Cook (1978); Daniels & Baker (1979); Givner & Hynes (1983); Glazer-Waldman, Hedl, & Chan (1990); Hustead (1978); Jessee, Cecil, & Jessee (1991); Self (1993); Self & Baldwin (1993, 1994); Self, Baldwin, & Olivarez (1993); Self, Baldwin, & Wolinsky (1992); Self & Olivarez (1996); Self, Wolinsky, & Baldwin (1989); Sheehan, Husted, Candee, Cook, & Bargen (1980)

Lawyers

Hartwell (1990, 1995); Willging & Dunn (1982)

Nurses

Cassells & Redman (1989); de Casterle, Jansses, & Grypdonck (1996); Duckett et al., (1992); Duckett & Ryden (1994); Felton & Parsons (1987); Frish (1987); Hilbert (1988); Ketefian (1981a, 1981b, 1989); Krawczyk (1997); Nokes (1989); Shuman et al. (1992); Swanson (1990)

Public administrators

Stewart & Sprinthall (1991, 1994); Stewart, Sprinthall, & Siemienska (1997)

Social workers

Dobrin (1989)

Table 4.2 continued on next page

Table 4.2 continued

Sport, athletes

Bredemeier & Shields (1984a, 1984b, 1994); Shields & Bredemeier (1994)

Teachers

Bergem (1986); Bloom (1976); Cartwright & Simpson (1990); Griffore (1978); Henkel & Earls (1985); Hurt (1977); Johnston (1985, 1989); Johnston & Lubomudrov (1987); Johnston, Lubomudrov, & Parsons (1982); Maccallum (1993); McNergney & Satterstrom (1984); Reiman & Thies-Sprinthall (1993); Sprinthall & Bernier (1979); Tan-Willman (1978); Taylor, Waters, Surbeck, & Kelly (1985); Wheaton (1984); Wilkins (1980a, 1980b); Yeazell & Johnson (1988)

Veterinarians

Self (1991, 1996); Self, Olivarez, & Baldwin (1994); Self, Pierce & Shadduck (1995); Self, Safford, & Shelton (1988)

---

mental difference? Developmental theories are primarily interested in directional changes within the individual. That is, developmental theory is primarily interested in how, say, John, Andrew, and Mary at age 4 are different from John, Andrew, and Mary at ages 14 and 40; not in how John as an individual is different from Andrew and Mary as individuals. Longitudinal data is suited to address the issue of intra-individual difference in using the subject as his or her own control for between individual differences, thereby focusing on intra-individual change.

In a longitudinal study begun in the 1970s and continuing into the 1980s, a sample of subjects was followed over 10 years. Approximately half of the sample was female and half was male; half from a large urban area and half from a small town; about half going to college and half not going to college (Rest, 1986b). Three testings over 10 years for a sample of 49 Minnesotans reports P score averages at Time 1 = 33.1 (SD = 13.6), Time 2 (2 years later) = 39.6 (SD = 13.6), and Time 3 (10 years later) = 47.0, (SD = 14.2). Repeated measures MANOVA produced an F = 23.07, p < .001. Therefore, with this 10-year longitudinal study of college and noncollege adults, there is longitudinal evidence of general upward movement.

In a recent review of nine longitudinal studies, McNeel (1994b) reported changes from freshman to senior status of college students with a combined sample size of n = 755. The average effect size[3] for liberal arts colleges and universities is .80. McNeel said that this effect size is "among

---

[3]Effect size is calculated following Pascarella and Terenzini (1991) as the senior minus freshman mean difference divided by the freshman standard deviation.

the largest average effect sizes for the many college impact variables that have been studied" (1994b, p. 32). Pascarella and Terenzini (1991) reviewed the effect sizes of other variables, and finding lower effect sizes is typical: general verbal (effect size = .56), oral skills (.60), independence (.36), various value and attitudes (effect sizes ranging from .10 to .50). In short, the college experience seems to be very effective in fostering moral judgment development—college seems to prod students to reexamine their thoughts about the moral basis of society and to value postconventional reasoning more and more. McNeel's review is especially interesting in that the majority of colleges on which he reported are conservative colleges (religiously and politically), not at all bastions of liberalism, as some commentators have assumed (Emler, Palmer-Canton, & St. James, in press). The critical characteristic of a college for promoting moral judgment seems to be a commitment to critical reflection. Being in a setting that is politically or religiously liberal is not the critical characteristic for DIT gains (McNeel, 1994b).

Table 4.3 cites over 30 published longitudinal studies. Although the majority of these studies are of college students, there are also longitudinal studies of high school students, noncollege subjects, and postcollege subjects. The longitudinal data are in agreement with the cross-sectional data: Each higher level of education is accompanied by an increase of about 10 points in DIT P score. Later we discuss why it is that formal education has such a large role in DIT increases.

TABLE 4.3

Citation of Published Articles on Longitudinal Change

Reviews:

Loxley & Whiteley (1986); McNeel (1994b); Nucci & Pascarella (1987); Pascarella & Terenzini (1991); Rest & Deemer (1986); Self & Baldwin (1994); Whiteley (1986)

Studies:

Baldwin, Daugherty, & Self (1991); Bertin, Ferrant, Whiteley, & Yokata (1985); Bridges & Priest (1983); Buier, Butman, Burwell, & Van Wicklin (1989); Deemer (1989); Kaseman (1980); Kilgannon & Erwin (1992); King & Kitchener (1994); King, Kitchener, Wood, & Davison (1989); Kitchener, King, Davison, Parker, & Wood (1984); Kitchener, King, Wood, & Davison (1989); McNeel (1991, 1994a); Mentkowski & Doherty (1983); Mentkowski & Straight (1983); Rest (1975a); Rest, Davison, & Robbins (1978); Schiller (1997); Self (1991); Self & Olivarez (1996); Shaver (1985, 1987); Whiteley et al. (1982); Whiteley & Loxley (1980); Wilson & Deemer (1989); Wilson, Rest, Boldizar, & Deemer (1992)

Validity Criterion 3:
Sensitivity to Moral Educational Interventions

A different kind of study of intra-individual change is the intervention study. Moral education programs have used the DIT as a pre- and posttest instrument to assess the effectiveness of a program in stimulating development in moral judgment. Intervention studies are relevant to the issue of validity in that these studies address the question, "Can enrichment programs produce significant upward change on the DIT?" Intervention studies are like longitudinal studies in testing and retesting the same subjects who act as their own controls. Intervention studies are usually shorter in duration than longitudinal studies (e.g., typically less than 1 year, in contrast for instance up to 4 years in the freshman to senior longitudinal studies reviewed by McNeel), and they also have more control over what experiences the subjects have between testings.

A meta-analysis of 55 intervention studies was reported in Schlaefli et al., (1985), of DIT intervention studies mostly conducted in the 1970s and early 1980s. The meta-analysis reported the following major trends:

- The type of intervention having consistently the greatest pre/posteffect is the "dilemma discussion" intervention, having an effect size of .41, a significant but "modest" effect size by meta-analytic standards. (In comparison, control/nonexperimental groups show an effect size increase of only .09.)
- The kind of intervention that showed the lowest gains in DIT scores was the traditional academic course (e.g., history, social studies, literature).
- Older groups (e.g., college and adult groups) showed greater change in DIT scores than did younger groups (e.g., junior high or high school students). So, as one article put it, you can "teach old dogs new tricks" (Oja & Sprinthall, 1978). It is not the case that morals are fixed by adolescence.
- Interventions shorter than 3 weeks do not produce significant gains on the DIT.

More recent reviews of intervention studies in higher education are contained in Rest and Narvaez (1994a). Another recent treatment of intervention studies is in Rest, Thoma, and Edwards (1997). Four data sets are examined here, having a combined sample size of 516. Each of the four studies separately had a statistically significant effect in shifting the P scores of the participants upward, with matched t-tests on the individual studies ranging from 3.62 to 9.16 (all significant at $p < .001$). The

t-test for the combined sample (pre to post) was 11.2 ($n = 516, p < .001$), effect size .54.

Table 4.4 cites over 60 publications on intervention studies and the DIT. In addition to providing replications on the sensitivity of the DIT to interventions, the articles present a wealth of ideas for designing educational programs. The articles represent programs for many different populations and professional groups. For instance, there is advice to aim not solely for gains in moral judgment; advice not to isolate ethics in one concentrated course but to distribute ethics among many components of an educational program; advice to use projects along with lecture, employ active problem-solving techniques, screen films, and incorporate community service components; and to incorporate teaching of basic philosophical concepts. (More is said about moral education programs later.)

Validity Criterion 4:
Developmental Hierarchy (Higher Is "Better")

Even if we grant that there is a developmental sequence to moral judgment (that postconventional thinking increases with development), who is to say that postconventional thinking is better than conventional thinking?

TABLE 4.4

Citation of Published Articles on Moral Education Interventions

Reviews:

Bebeau & Thoma (1994); Lawrence (1980); Rest & Narvaez (1994a, 1994b); Rest & Thoma (1986); Schlaefli, Rest, & Thoma (1985); Self & Baldwin (1994); Self, Olivarez, & Baldwin (1994); Sprinthall (1994); Thoma (1984)

Studies:

Baldwin, Daugherty, & Self (1991); Bebeau (1983a, 1983b, 1985, 1988, 1991, 1993a, 1993b, 1993c, 1994a, 1994b); Bebeau & Brabeck (1987); Bebeau, Rest, & Yamoor (1985); Bernier (1980); Boss (1994); Cognetta (1977); Cook (1985); Copeland & Parish (1979); Duckett et al. (1990); Duckett & Ryden (1994); Enright, Lapsley, Harris, & Shawver (1983); Erickson, Colby, Libbey, & Lohman (1976); Eyler & Halteman (1981); Fleetwood & Parish (1976); Frish (1987); Glazer-Waldman, Hedl, & Chan (1990); Hartwell (1990, 1995); Hurt (1977); Keen (1991); Ketefian (1981a); Krawczyk (1997); Maul (1978); Mentkowski (1980); Mentkowski & Doherty (1983); Mentkowski & Strait (1983); Mustapha & Seybert (1990); Nevin & McNeel (1992); Nichols, Isham, & Austad (1977); Nucci & Weber (1991); Oja (1977); Oja & Sprinthall (1978); Page & Bode (1982); Penn (1990); Powell, Locke, & Sprinthall (1991); Reiman & Thies-Sprinthall (1993); Ryden, Duckett, Crisham, Caplan, & Schmitz (1989); Self & Baldwin (1993); Self, Baldwin, & Olivarez (1993); Self, Baldwin, & Wolinsky (1992); Self, Pierce, & Shadduck (1995); Sprinthall & Bernier (1979); Sprinthall, Hall, & Gerler (1992); Sprinthall & Scott (1989); Straub & Rodgers (1986); Thies-Sprinthall (1984); Tucker (1977); Wong (1977)

Certainly, there are sequences over the life span in which a later stage is not better, like losing one's hair. Thus, the later condition is not necessarily better. Philosophers have been particularly concerned with how this argument is made, especially claims for a normative ethical theory (e.g., Modgil & Modgil, 1986).

In DIT research, four kinds of studies have attempted to address the question, "Is a higher score on the DIT really better?" These studies:

1. Associate DIT scores with a measure of moral comprehension, showing that higher P scores are associated with higher comprehension of moral concepts.
2. Correlate the DIT with other developmental measures (e.g., ego development, reflective judgment, Kohlberg's measure of moral judgment, and Piaget's formal operations), showing that higher development on the DIT is associated with higher developmental scores on other developmental instruments.
3. Link higher stages with more desired behavior (e.g., more "prosocial behavior," more highly valued job performance)
4. Show that higher scores on the DIT are associated with better recall and reconstruction of moral argument in narratives (thus showing greater cognitive capacity for high P scorers).

In this section we consider points 1, 2, and 4, and postpone discussion of the behavior studies (point 3) for a later section.

1. The Moral Comprehension Studies. In the early studies (Rest, 1969; 1973; Rest, Turiel, & Kohlberg, 1969), moral comprehension was assessed in terms of the participant's ability to paraphrase a moral argument written to reflect one of the stages. Participants were asked to restate in their own words somebody else's moral argument. For instance, a subject might be given a Stage 4 statement and asked to paraphrase it; if the paraphrase was judged to get the gist of the prototypic statement, then the subject would be credited with comprehending that stage argument. Note that this measure of comprehension is different from measures of moral judgment, in that the comprehension measure is an inventory of concepts that the subject *understands*, not assessing whether or not the concepts are *used* to justify an action in a dilemma. We found that the moral comprehension of participants was cumulative: That is, if a participant was credited with understanding Stage 4 items, the participant would also have high comprehension for Stages 3, 2, and 1. It was not the case that higher-stage thinking obliterated or displaced lower-stage thinking. Subjects with higher-stage comprehension could easily understand the lower stages.

In addition, participants were asked to rate the statement on how much they found the argument convincing and persuasive. The finding of interest here was that of the statements that were comprehended, participants preferred the ones that represented the highest stage comprehended. Even though concepts at the less advanced stages were usually highly comprehended, the lower-stage statements were not preferred. Although the lower stages were accessible, they were not preferred. And so, for instance, a participant showing high moral comprehension up to Stage 4 would not prefer statements at Stages 3, 2, or 1, but would prefer Stage 4 statements. Some participants, when evaluating statements at low stages (lower than their own spontaneously produced stage), made remarks like, "This sounds like a kid," and "This is simple minded," and "I used to think that way but I don't anymore" (Rest, 1969). So, given the question we started out with, who says higher stages are better? One answer: *Subjects do themselves.*

These psychological findings complement the normative theoretical description of the schemas offered earlier in the book. That is, the reasons given in chapter 3 for the greater adequacy of postconventional reasoning over the earlier schema are paralleled by the psychological fact of the preference choices of the subjects themselves. The parallel between philosophical and psychological accounts for Kohlbergian stages was discussed by Boyd in terms of the "complementary hypothesis" (1984). Essentially, this is to approach the parallelism between the facts of developmental psychology and the philosophical claims (that higher levels of moral judgment are more philosophically adequate than the lower) by not reducing one side of the parallelism to the other, but maintaining the difference between *is* and *ought* while noting the two both support the hierarchy claim. The parallelism is mutually reinforcing.

The moral comprehension studies suggest the following explanation for stage usage in spontaneous production tasks: As moral comprehension increases, new ways of thinking become possible; because subjects prefer the highest stage comprehended, the newest, highest stages are used. As participants outgrow simplistic ways of thinking—as they perceive the old stages to be inadequate—they still understand the lower-level arguments but prefer not to use them.

The early studies linked moral comprehension to Kohlberg's stages as assessed by Kohlberg's interview measure. The link between moral comprehension and Kohlberg's later stage system (beyond his 1958 stage scoring system), was replicated by Walker, deVries, and Bichard, 1984. The link between Moral Comprehension and the DIT's P score uses another measure of moral comprehension. The new comprehension measure is comprised of a paragraph-length moral argument, followed by a set of four short statement alternatives. The participant's task is to indicate which of the four alternatives best represents the gist of meaning of the matching paragraph. (This is a common strategy for measuring comprehension in *reading*, except in this case the paragraphs are keyed to *moral* concepts.) Eleven such paragraphs and alternatives comprise the new moral comprehension test. Scores are the number of correct matches (0–11; Rest, 1979, 1986b). The point of these later studies was to show a significant correlation between moral comprehension and the DIT's P score.

A data set that comes from the 1970s is a study by Rest, Cooper et al., (1974) of 160 participants: 40 junior high students, 40 senior high students, 40 college students, and 40 graduate students. The correlation of P with moral comprehension was .67 ($p < .001$).

A replication of P's correlation with this measure of moral comprehension comes from a longitudinal sample reported in Rest (1986b), consisting of 101 young adults aged 24 through 29. (Because this sample is more homogeneous than the cross-sectional sample, one would expect some attenuation of the correlations due to the restricted range of the variables.) In this replication, as in the previous study, the P index was also significantly correlated with moral comprehension ($r = .38, p < .001$).

It is possible that DIT P scores might be correlated with moral comprehension due to both variables having shared variance with education. That is, it might really be *education* that explains why moral comprehension varies, and the P score is piggybacking on education. In order to test this interpretation, multiple regressions were performed, predicting to comprehension as the dependent variable, and using education and P score as the independent variables. Examining the beta-weights of each independent variable allows us to estimate the unique contributions of each independent variable in predicting to the dependent variable, moral comprehension. If it was true that the P score was really piggybacking on education for its correlation with comprehension, then we would expect a nonsignificant beta weight of P in the multiple regression (because all of its predictability in the simple correlation would be due to its shared variance with education). Table 4.5 indicates the results of this analysis. Contrary to the hypothesis that P is piggybacking on education, the P score in fact shows much larger standardized beta-weights than those for education, and the standardized beta-weights for P score are statistically significant, whereas for education they are not. This suggests that the relationship of P score with moral comprehension cannot be explained as due to education.

TABLE 4.5

Regression Analyses With Comprehension as Dependent Variable,
and Education and P Score as Independent Variables

Independent Variable	b	SE b	Beta-weight[+]
(From Rest et. al., 1974, n = 140)			
Education	.54	.18	.25**
P score	.07	.01	.50***
(From Rest 1986b, n = 99)			
Education	.24	.15	.18
P score	.07	.03	.26*

Note: *p < .02. ** p < .003. *** p < .0001. [+]Beta-weight is the standardized regression coefficient.

2. Correlations With Other Developmental Measures. A second line of evidence that "higher is better" comes from correlating DIT scores with other developmental measures. The assumption is that if higher DIT scores represent thinking that is more developed and advanced, then the DIT should be correlated with other developmental measures. For instance, significant correlations are reported for such measures as reflective judgment (r = .46 and .58; King & Kitchener, 1994), Loevinger ego development (generally r = .40; see Rest, 1979, for references), Kohlberg's test (r = .78 to .34; see Rest, 1979), ethical reasoning inventory (r = .57; Page & Bode, 1982), dental ethical sensitivity Test (r ranging from .20 to .50; Rest, Bebeau, & Volker, 1986), various aptitude and academic achievement tests (generally r is in .20–.50 range; Rest, 1979).

3. Recall and Reconstruction. A recent line of research that argues for the greater cognitive capacity of high P scorers over low P scorers comes from recall and reconstruction studies by Narvaez (1998). Narratives about moral dilemma situations that contained moral arguments were prepared (separate assessment from the DIT). College students (higher P scorers) and eighth- grade students (lower P scorers) were contrasted on their ability to recall and reconstruct the moral arguments in the narratives. In multiple regression analysis, even after controlling for differences in general recall of nonmoral material (general reading comprehension) and age/education (college students vs. eighth graders), the higher P scorers showed greater recall and reconstruction of the high stage moral arguments than the lower P scorers ($p. < 02$).

Table 4.6 cites over 30 published studies relevant to the "hierarchical" claim. Studies are subdivided into reviews, studies of moral comprehension, and studies of other developmental variables.

Validity Criterion 5: Links to Behavior

Critics of the Kohlbergian approach note that the dilemmas used to produce moral judgment scores are very limited: The dilemmas cover a limited range of possible moral dilemmas; they are hypothetical dilemmas and therefore unlikely to be the moral dilemmas actually occurring in a person's life. Earlier, we conceded this point—Kohlbergian dilemmas are limited, both on the MJI and DIT. The question then arises, what evidence is there that the scores from Kohlbergian instruments measure anything important or pervasive? Does the instrument (e.g., the DIT or MJI) relate to anything beyond itself? Are researchers engaged in logic chopping and fussing over discriminations that only have relevance to a minute spectrum of a person's

TABLE 4.6

Citation of Published Articles Relevant to Hierarchical Claim

Reviews:

Pascarella & Terenzini (1991); Rest (1979, 1983)

Moral comprehension studies:

Lawrence (1987); Narvaez (1994, 1998); Rest, Cooper, Coder, Masanz, & Anderson (1974); Rest, Thoma, & Edwards (1997)

Studies of developmental correlates:

Bloomberg (1974); Bode & Page (1980); Cauble (1976); Chovan & Freeman (1993); Connolly & McCarrey (1978); Cook (1985); Froming & McColgan (1979); Green (1980); Hendel (1991); Henderson, Gold, & Clarke (1984); Howard-Hamilton (1994); Iozzi & Paradise-Maul (1980); Keating (1978); King & Kitchener (1994); Kitchener, King, Davison, Parker, & Wood (1984); Kitchener, King, Wood, & Davison (1989); Loxley & Whiteley (1986); Lutwak & Hennessy (1985); McColgan, Rest, & Pruitt (1983); Meyer (1977); Narvaez (1993a); Oja (1977); Page & Bode (1980, 1982); Powell, Locke, & Sprinthall (1991); Rowe & Marcia (1980); Tan-Willman & Gutteridge (1980); Wilmoth & McFarland (1977) life and don't tell us anything important about the person's behavior in real life?

A serious challenge to a researcher's interpretations of participant cognitions is to demonstrate that the interpretations have something to do with some other significant variables. It is possible that the interpretations and fine distinctions of a researcher about a subject's cognitions are nothing more than the subject's fleeting jumble of verbalizations uttered in the confusion of trying to comply with a pesky researcher. Therefore, it is comforting to have the researcher's interpretations (e.g., P scores, domain distinctions, big three analysis) linked to something else (preferably important in its own right) that corroborates the significance, pervasiveness, and importance of the researcher's interpretations.[4]

Higher scores on the DIT have been linked to various "prosocial" behaviors. For instance, in the longitudinal study begun in the 1970s and continued for 10 years (Rest, 1986b), the DIT is significantly related to measures coded by Deemer from her interviews: "community involvement" ($r = .31$; which gives higher scores for activity that contributes to one's community), and "civic responsibility" ($r = .44$; which gives higher scores for stated concern about the welfare of the community). Both correlations were significant ($p < .01$). In addition, the DIT is correlated with the "Duncan scale" ($r = .38$; a sociological measure of the perceived social value of one's occupation).

Thoma, Rest, and Barnett (1986) reviewed links between the DIT P score and various behavior measures. They reported that 32 out of 47 analyses are statistically significant. Note that the measures of behavior in the studies of this review include significant links with delinquency, experimental measures of cheating, cooperative behavior in the prisoner's dilemma game, whistle blowing on misdeeds at work, mock jury trials, conscientious objection to the Vietnam War, a distributive justice experiment, nurses' decisions about medical care, coaches' ratings of aggression among athletes, and clinical performance ratings of medical interns. In short, the DIT has significant correlations with a great variety of naturalistic and experimental measures of behavior; with prosocial and antisocial measures; and with measures based on self-report, ratings by others, and laboratory measures of behavior.

---

[4]Note that we are not subscribing to the notion that moral judgment is to be validated by "predictive validity." (Predictive validity is particularly useful, e.g., in the case of having a simple, inexpensive, hand-eye coordination test that predicts well to who will make a good jet-fighter pilot. We don't intend that kind of use for the DIT by looking for its correlations with job performance.) We think the relations of moral judgment with behavior are complex and determined by many variables (see Narvaez & Rest, 1995; Rest, 1983; Thoma, 1994a, 1994b). Rather, the issue is whether or not the researcher's interpretations of another person's cognitions are valid at all when those interpretations have no relation to anything at all.

More recently, an edited book on moral development in the professions (Rest & Narvaez, 1994a) contained several dozen additional links of the DIT to professional decision making and job performance of professionals (e.g., the DIT is significantly linked to nurses' clinical performance ratings, schoolteachers' perceptions of classroom discipline, auditors' detection of fraudulent financial reports, and accountants' perceptions of management's competence and integrity). Table 4.7 cites over 60 published studies relating DIT scores to various measures of behavior and decision making.

In sum, there is much evidence that the limited, hypothetical dilemmas of the DIT do tap something important in human functioning because of the many links to other measures outside the test. It remains for other measures of moral thinking (e.g., those based on real, experienced moral dilemmas in the subjects' own lives) to show that they predict to an array of measures outside the test. If these new measures based on other dilemmas (and scoring features) show their superiority in actual empirical

TABLE 4.7

Citation of Published Articles on Behavior and Decision Making

Reviews:

Chang (1994) [teachers]; Ponemor. & Gabhart (1994) [accountants & auditors]; Shields & Bredemeier (1994) [sport]; Thoma & Rest (1986) [behavior, decision making, and attitudes]

Studies:

Adamson, Baldwin, Sheehan, & Oppenberg (1997); Bagarozzi (1982); Baldwin, Adamson, Self, Sheehan, & Oppenberg (1996); Berg, Watson, Nugent, Gearhart, et al. (1994); Bernardi & Arnold (1994); Bloom (1978); Brabeck (1984); Bredemeier & Shields (1984a, 1984b, 1994); Bruggeman & Hart (1996); Candee, Sheehan, Cook, & Husted (1979); Candee, Sheehan, Cook, Husted, & Bargen (1982); Cartwright & Simpson (1990); Cassells & Redman (1989); Cook (1978); Cook & Margolis (1974); Fincham & Barling (1979); Forsyth & Berger (1982); Foster & Sprinthall (1992); Gaertner (1991); Givner & Hynes (1983); Glover (1994); Graham, Turnbull, & La Rocque (1979); Gunzburger, Wegner, & Anooshian (1977); Hay (1983); Hernandez & DiClemente (1991); Heyns, VanNiekerk, & Le Roux (1981); Hilbert (1988); Holt, Kauchak, & Person (1980); Houston (1983); Johnston (1985, 1989); Johnston & Lubomudrov (1987); Ketefian (1981b); Leming (1978); Lupfer, Cohen, & Bernard (1987); Maccallum (1993); Mason & Collison (1995); Mayton, Diessner, & Granby (1993); McColgan, Rest, & Pruitt (1983); McNergney & Satterstrom (1984); Miceli, Dozier, & Near (1991); Parish, Rosenblatt, & Kappes (1980); Parsons, Holt, Kauchak, & Peterson (1983); Ponemon (1992a, 1992b, 1993b); Priest, Kordinak, & Wynkoop (1991); Renwick & Emler (1984); Richmond (1989); Roffey & Porter (1992); Rotenberg, Hewlitt, & Siegwart (1998); Sheehan, Husted, Candee, Cook, & Bargen (1980); Shuman et al. (1992); Taylor, Waters, Surbeck, & Kelly (1985); Thoma (1994a); Thoma, Rest, & Davison (1991); Wheaton (1984) demonstrations, then it is time for replacing or adding to the Kohlbergian dilemmas.

In saying there is a link between DIT scores and behavioral measures, we are not saying that high P scores will bring happiness, occupational success, public acclaim, and a cure for toe fungus. In short, we are not claiming that everything good follows from a high P score. In fact, there is evidence that happiness is largely independent of P score (Schiller, 1997, in press; Thoma, MaloneBeach, & Ladewig, 1997); that in some occupations, high Stage 4 (not P) is related to career success (Lawrence, 1987; Ponemon, 1992b); that sophistication in moral judgment can put a strain on friendship relations (Thoma, MaloneBeach, & Ladewig, 1997), and even that exceptionally high postconventional thinking can get one killed (Kohlberg, 1981). (Kohlberg's favorite exemplars of moral development were Socrates, Martin Luther King, Jr., and Janusz Korczak. Yet all three were killed for their moral beliefs. Advancement to the highest levels of moral development seems to be hazardous to one's health.) Rather, our main point is that these linkages of DIT scores with behavioral measures argue against the view that Kohlbergian dilemmas and methods of data collection are meaningless, and not tapping anything significant about real life.

Validity Criterion 6:
Links to Political Attitudes and Political Choice

Criterion 6 (political attitudes) is similar to Criterion 5 (behavior) in relating the DIT to external, outside-the-test variables. Whereas in the previous section we looked for a statistically significant link of the DIT to behavioral measures, in the political realm we expect a stronger association than just beating chance. On Criterion 5, the strength of association between moral judgment and behavior might typically account for 5% to 20% of the variance of the behavioral measure. On Criterion 6, the variance accounted for should be higher (it is over 40% in some studies).

The political realm is concerned distinctively with how people relate to each other in society (macromorality). In personal moral issues (micromorality), we are concerned with the web of personal relationships; in the political realm we are concerned with a wider web of relationships. In the democratic state, individuals have the opportunity to participate in forming the policy and practices of the state that determine their mutual destiny. When the individual participates in state policy decisions, the individual is morally related to other individuals in a different way than in direct face-to-face relationships. In the political realm, individuals are related to others through laws, institutions, and establishing general practices. Political choices (e.g., an election or referendum) involve choosing to establish a law or policy direction that affects the whole body politic; it is a decision about how the society is supposed to work generally. The individual is not making a decision about only his or her own affairs and personal behavior (as is often the case in Criterion 5), or responding empathically to another specific person. A political decision concerns the structure of society; it concerns a wider web than the web of personal relationships.

The concept of *society* is a cognitive construction—just as are concepts of the universe, tectonic plates of the earth's crust, biological evolution, and subatomic particles. A person does not directly see society, the universe, or subatomic particles, but evidence is assembled in imagination to constitute the concepts. How the construction of society is cognitively assembled is the heart of the Kohlbergian theory of development. Other theorists using different methods have also commented on the "discovery" of society in adolescents. Youniss and Yates (1997) described how adolescents show growing awareness of "The System," and question the morality of society. Adelson (1971) described adolescence as "a watershed era in the emergence of political thought . . . struggling to formulate a morally coherent view of how society is and might and should be arranged" (p. 1013). We argue that DIT scores are especially illuminating of political decision making and behavior. How people respond to the old Kohlberg chestnuts (like "Heinz and the drug") yields very useful information in understanding "red meat" political controversies of the day (e.g., abortion, prayer in the schools, legalities in arresting and convicting the accused, rights of homosexuals, free speech, and women's roles).

In DIT studies, political attitudes have emphasized issues of political toleration (attitudes toward the rights of outgroups; see Marcus, Sullivan, Theiss-Morse, & Wood, 1995) and civil libertarianism (see McClosky & Brill, 1983). Table 4.8 gives a sampling of the items used in various measures. Appendix A gives the entire political attitude instrument devised by Getz (1985), the "Attitudes Towards Human Rights Inventory" (ATHRI), asking for people's positions on abortion, free speech, and the like. Note that although we refer to these measures as assessing public policy issues, we do not mean to suggest that these issues cover the gamut of such issues. Our emphasis on political toleration and civil libertarianism (concerns central to the U.S. Constitution's Bill of Rights) does not address many issues studied in political psychology, such as unemployment, urban unrest, defense spending, the budget deficit, foreign policy toward Russia and Central America, and so on. Rather, our use of the blanket term "public policy issues" is meant to signal the distinction between matters of personal morality (how I should act in my own life) and matters of public morality (what policies I think should govern how our state should

TABLE 4.8

Examples of Items Measuring Political Attitudes Used in DIT Research

Law and Order Attitudes (Rest, 1979)

1. Under what conditions do you think people should be prevented from speaking their opinions? (Check one under each heading.)

    a. Those criticizing the president

    ___ Prevented from speaking or punished for speaking

    ___ Prevented in some cases

    ___ Not prevented

    b. Those teaching communism in schools or colleges

    ___ Prevented from speaking or punished for speaking

    ___ Prevented in some cases

    ___ Not prevented

    c. Those speaking of overthrowing our government by force or violence

    ___ Prevented from speaking or punished for speaking

    ___ Prevented in some cases

    ___ Not prevented

2. Under present laws it is possible for someone to escape punishment on the grounds of legal technicalities, even though the person may have confessed to performing the crime. Are you in favor of a tougher policy for treating criminals?

    ___ Strongly agree with tougher policy

    ___ Mildly agree

    ___ Mixed agreement and disagreement

    ___ Mildly disagree

    ___ Strongly disagree

Political Tolerance Attitudes

1. If a person wanted to make a speech in this city favoring communism, he should be allowed to speak. (agree/disagree)

2. People should not be allowed to march on public streets in support of political ideas or causes. (agree/disagree)

3. Books written against churches and religion should be kept out of our public libraries. (agree/disagree)

Table 4.8 continued on next page

Table 4.8 continued

Attitudes Toward Human Rights Inventory ("ATHRI," Getz, 1985)

[strongly agree to strongly disagree on a 5-point scale]

1. Abortion is any woman's right

2. If we let atheists teach in our schools, they will try to indoctrinate our children.

3. Homosexuals shouldn't be hired for jobs requiring considerable contact with the public.

4. We should not waste time having costly trials for people we are 100% sure are guilty.

5. A terminally ill and suffering patient should be able to have the doctor "pull the plug".

6. Laws should be passed to regulate the activities of religious cults that have come here from Asia.

act). Three measures used in DIT studies ("law and order attitudes," "political tolerance," and "attitudes towards human rights") examined the tension between human rights (e.g., freedom of speech) and the need to protect society in general and to honor authorities.

Table 4.9 is a review of the association of the DIT's P score with political attitudes in studies that span the 1970s through the 1990s of samples with some heterogeneity. We see that the DIT's P score is strongly and consistently associated with measures of political attitude and choice over the years.

The consistency of this relation is notable especially because America's political views have been changing from liberalism to conservatism.[5] In the 1960s and 1970s liberal political attitudes were prominent, and one might have explained the correlation between a cognitive-developmental measure and political attitudes as being due to learning the dominant ideology of one's culture (i.e., the cognitively advanced learn faster). However now, when liberal political attitudes are out of favor, the correlation of a cognitive-developmental variable with political attitudes is not so easily explained as learning the dominant ideology (Thoma, 1993).

McClosky and Brill (1983) found that education was highly predictive to political attitudes. They stated that people who are better educated and better informed are more prone to endorse the civil libertarian position

---

[5]The correlation between P and law and order at Time 1 was $-.39$, and the correlation between P and law and order at Time 2 was $-.58$, both statistically significant $p = .001$, $n = 64$.

On a different matter, the change in the overall political climate of the United States between the 1970s and 1990s is manifest in presidential politics: Contrast the 1976 campaign of Carter/Mondale, who assumed it was good to be liberal, with the 1992 and 1996 campaigns of Clinton, who denied he was a liberal; it is also manifest in the resurgence of the Republican party on conservative issues, taking over the U.S. House and Senate in the 1990's for the first time in decades.

TABLE 4.9

Correlations of DIT P score with political attitudes and political choice

Study	Sample	Measure	Correlation
Rest, Cooper, Coder, Masanz, & Anderson (1974)	140 Ss,[a] jr. high to grad school	Law and order	-.58**
		Political toleration	.59**
Coder (1975)	87 adults (mixed education)	Law and order	-.49**
Rest (1975a)	88 Ss, sr. high and college	Law and order	-.52**
Lapsley, Sison, & Enright (1976)	65 college females	Attitude to authority	-.29*
Thornlindsson (1978; translated DIT)	46 Icelandic Ss (mixed education)	Law and order	-.45**
Rest, Davison, & Robbins (1978)	55 young adults (mixed education)	Law and order	-.47**
Nardi & Tsujimoto (1978)	179 college Ss	Survey of ethical attitudes	-.32**
Gutkin & Suls (1979)	284 college Ss	Survey of ethical attitudes	-.27**
G. Rest (1979)	47 college Ss	Issues in 1976 presidential election	-.47**[c]
	64 adults	[Chi-square	-.39***[c]
Eyler (1980)	135 college Ss	For majority rule	27.8**
		For minority rights	3.8*
		For partisan conflict	4.7*]
Letchworth & McGee (1981)	24 college Ss	Equal Rights Amendment	.55**

87

Table 4.9 continued

Study	Sample	Measure	Correlation
Lonky, Reihman, & Serlin (1981) (short form DIT)	287 Ss from eighth grade to college	Majority rule	.45**
		Minority rights	.52**
		Equality	.37**
		Civil liberties	.42**
		Freedoms	.47**
		Social welfare	.20**
		Military policy	.31**
		Foreign policy	.29**
		Respect	.37**
Emler, Resnick, & Malone (1983)	73 college Ss	*New Left Scales:*	
		Traditional morality	-.49**
		Machiavellean tactics	-.42**
		New left philosophy	.39**
		Machiavellean cynicism	.04[b]
		Revolutionary tactics	.09[b]
DeWolfe & Jackson (1984)	113 college Ss	Attitude toward capital punishment	-.41**
Getz (1985)	172 Ss (adults and college)	ATHRI	.66**
Rest (1986b)	102 adult Ss (mixed education)	Law and order	-.60**

Table 4.9 continued

Study	Sample	Measure	Correlation
Curtis, Billingslea, & Wilson (1988)	105 undergrads	Impersonal authority	-.60**
		Personal authority	-.37**
Thoma (1993)	128 college Ss (juniors and seniors)	1988 election issues	[curvilinear]
		Candidate preference	*
		Voting intention	*
Emler, Palmer-Canton, & St. James (in press)	23 college Ss	New Left Scales:	*
		Traditional moral.	-.61**
		Machiavellean tactics	-.65**
		New left philosophy	.11[b]
		Machiavellean cynicism	.08[b]
		Radical tactics	.05[b]
Narvaez, Getz, Thoma, & Rest (in press)	96 adults	ATHRI	.65**
	62 college Ss	ATHRI	.55**
Rest, Narvaez, Bebeau, & Thoma (1998)	194 high school through professional school	ATHRI (x DIT2)	.52**[d]

Note: Studies listed in order of date.

[a]Ss = subjects, followed by education levels in sample. [b]Expected to be nonsignificant. [c]Used D index rather than P for DIT. [d]Used DIT2-N2 rather than original DIT with P score.

on rights than are people who are less educated and less informed: "The more one knows and understands about public affairs (as measured by our scales of political information and sophistication), the higher the probability that one will respond favorably to the various libertarian rights included in the omnibus civil liberties scales we developed for each study" (p. 371). They also wrote: "Essentially similar results turn up when we assess the level of cognitive awareness by measures of 'intellectuality'" (p. 373). These authors thought that political attitude would be related to education for the following reasons:

> It is especially difficult for people with little knowledge or interest in public affairs [to be advocates of human rights]. Having little exposure to information and discussions about the meaning of civil liberties, they have had less occasion to ponder such matters as the implications of freedom, the scope of the rights set forth in the Constitution, or the subtle and recondite arguments fashioned by judges and other commentators on human rights about the nature and limits of free speech, press, assembly, religion, privacy, or due process. (p. 375)

McClosky and Brill used the phrase "conventionally minded" and came very close to Kohlberg's notions of conventional morality. Their discussion of the role of education comes very close to Kohlberg's theory of cognitive development in moral thinking. (Of course, there is more to civil libertarian attitudes than more or less cognitive development/education, but the 1995 review by Marcus et al. indicates that this is a major factor.) The question arises of whether the association of P with civil libertarianism is due to its shared variance with education. (In other words, is the P score of the DIT actually piggybacking on education to get its predictive power to civil libertarianism?)

In order to check out this possibility, two samples were used: Rest et al. (1974) and Rest (1986b). Multiple regressions were run, predicting to the civil libertarian measure ("law and order attitudes")—the dependent variable—and entering both education and P score as independent variables. Examining the standardized beta-weights of education and of the P score in predicting to civil libertarianism allows us to estimate the unique variance due to each independent variable in predicting to the dependent variable. If it were true that the P score was really piggybacking on education for its correlation with law and order, then we would expect a nonsignificant beta-weight of P in the multiple regression (because all of its predictability would be due to its shared variance with education). The results are presented in Table 4.10. The standardized beta-weights in Rest et al. (1974) are -.29 for education and -.38 for the P score. Both education and P score have significant unique predictability to the dependent variable, but P is more powerful. A similar picture emerges from the data collected in Rest (1986b): The beta-weight for education is -.20 and for

TABLE 4.10

Regression Analyses, Predicting to Law and Order as Dependent
Variable, From the Independent Variables of Education, and P Score

Independent Variable	b	SE b	Beta-Weight[+]
(from Rest et al., 1974; n = 140)			
Education	-.73	.23	-.29**
DIT P score	-.06	.01	-.38***
(from Rest, 1986b; n = 99)			
Education	-.32	.14	-.21*
DIT P score	-.01	.00	-.50***

Note: Beta-weights are all negative because the dependent variable law & order is negatively
keyed—that is, higher scores represent lower civil libertarianism.
*p < .05. **p < .002. [+]Standardized regression coefficient. ***p < .0001.

P score is -.50. (Note that beta-weights are negative because the law and
order scale is negatively keyed—i.e., the higher score in law and order
represents less civil libertarianism). Therefore, the predictability of P
score to civil libertarianism cannot be accounted for by education—and, furthermore, of the two predictors, P is more powerful than
education.

Furthermore, we can ask, in addition to accounting for inter-individual
differences, can the P score be used to account for intra-individual
developmental differences? That is, what evidence is there that, as individuals change over time in P score, this change is related to change in
political attitude? To address this question, we use the 10-year longitudinal
study, reported in Rest (1986b). One way to represent these data is to
calculate a change score for the law and order attitude test (at Time 1 and
10 years later), and also a change score for the P score (at Time 1 and 10
years later), and then to correlate the change scores. Because the law and
order scale is negatively keyed (i.e., higher scores indicate less civil
libertarianism), we would expect a negative correlation (gains in P score
should be related to losses in the law and order score). Therefore, we
expect a negative correlation between the two change measures. This is
indeed what we find: Law and order change is correlated -.39 with P
change (n = 64, p < .001). Inspecting a scatterplot of change scores for
the DIT and also for law and order over two times, the distribution of
points shows a downward slope, consistent with the negative correlation
of -.39. In short, this is longitudinal evidence that intra-individual pro-

gressive shifts in postconventional thinking are associated with progressive shifts in civil libertarianism.

In general, we contend that at least some of the differences that exist in public policy controversies regarding human rights are due to intra-individual *development*. That is, as people develop from a conventional to a postconventional moral orientation, they change in their political orientation. Put in terms of Shweder's categories, as people develop, they shift from a duty orientation to a rights orientation. People are not simply born into a culture that makes them duty oriented or rights oriented throughout their entire lives. We do not claim that *only* development affects moral orientation and political attitudes. We do not deny other sources of variance, such as the impact of group ideologies that vary from cultural differences, family or subgroup allegiances, prevailing ideologies, and so on. In fact, the political socialization literature suggests that social learning plays an important role in the acquisition of political attitudes (e.g., Hess & Torney, 1967). However, we argue that at least part of the variance is developmental.

Internal Structure and Reliability

The last heading of this chapter is on the internal structure of the DIT. The narrower topic of reliability (i.e., Cronbach alpha) is not strictly a *validity* criterion. That is, we do not consider that small differences in Cronbach alpha for two measures constitute grounds for saying one test is more valid than the other. Essentially, reliability is a threshold condition: any valid test requires an adequate level of reliability, but increasing the reliability of a test does not necessarily increase its validity.

The quick answer to Cronbach alpha on the DIT is given in Table 4.11—estimates for 20 years of Cronbach alpha for the DIT has been in

TABLE 4.11

Cronbach Alphas of P and N2 Indexes

	Cronbach alpha	
Sample	P index	N2 Index
1979 composite sample, n = 994	.76	.80
1995 composite sample, n = 932	.78	.83

Note: Only participants who gave complete data on every story are included in this analysis.

the high .70s and low .80s, depending on the index and sample. We consider this level of internal consistency to be adequate.

However, the internal consistency of a test (like that expressed in Cronbach alpha) is only one aspect of the internal structure of a test. In the early days of DIT research, we were more concerned about another aspect of reliability: the possibility that some subjects might not be taking the DIT seriously, and were turning in ratings and rankings that were randomly chosen. The possibility of "garbage" data is a worrisome possibility with group-administered, multiple-choice tests (especially when participants are guaranteed anonymity). To deal with this problem, we designed several reliability checks into the DIT so that we could detect subject unreliability. If subjects do not meet certain reliability checks, their protocols are invalidated and discarded from analysis. Our checks seem to have worked satisfactorily, as discussed in Rest, Thoma, and Edwards (1997).

Also in the early years, Davison (1979) addressed several other issues concerning reliability and internal structure. He reported on test–retest reliability (from several studies, in the range of $r = .7$ to .8); the Gutman simplex of correlations of stages, and the multidimensional scaling of items. He reported results generally supporting the theoretical view of stages of moral judgment.

A recent study of the internal structure of the DIT was performed on the Mega sample, $N = 45,856$. A factor analysis was performed on the ratings of the 72 items from the DIT (12 items from each of six dilemmas). The most interpretable solution was a three-factor solution (using VARIMAX, listwise deletions for missing data, eight iterations). The three factors that emerged were a postconventional factor (loading mostly on our Stages 5 and 6 items), a maintaining norms factor (loading on Stage 4 items), and a personal interest factor (loading on Stages 2 and 3). The merging of Stages 5 and 6 into one factor will come as no surprise, because (a) the theoretical distinctions between Stages 5 and 6 are still being argued, and (b) the short, brief items of the DIT limit how finely these distinctions can be made. The merging of Stages 2 and 3 will come as more of a surprise, because Kohlberg defined three levels (Preconventional, Conventional, and Postconventional) and two stages within each level (1 and 2, 3 and 4, 5 and 6). However our view of the matter is that the merging of Stages 2 and 3 is likely to be an instrument artifact and a sample-specific phenomenon. Recall that the DIT is used only for older participants, 12 years or older in reading level. In DIT research, using an older population, much development in moral judgment will have already taken place; and Stage 2 and 3 are likely to be "past history" for most subjects (i.e., stages that subjects have already gone through and discarded). Both Stages 2 and 3 are regarded generally as primitive by our subjects and therefore the two stages are fused as "Personal Interest" items.[6]

The internal structure of the DIT in the Mega sample is shown in Table 4.12 in several ways. Let us explain Table 4.12:

1. The heading "Item Type" is the intended theoretical stage that the item was originally designed to represent (see Rest, 1979, for description of specific features used to formulate DIT items).

2. The *first row* in Table 4.12 presents the number of items in each of the three stage groups (postconventional = Stages 5 + 6, maintaining norms = Stage 4, and personal interests = Stages 2 + 3). The issue of having unequal sets of items is discussed at length in Rest, Thoma, and Edwards (1997).

3. The *second row* in Table 4.12 represents the median factor loading for the items written at that particular stage. For instance, take the first P item on the DIT, H-8 (Heinz dilemma, item 8); it has a factor loading of .5076 on the factor we identify as the "postconventional" factor. (Note that it is methodologically possible for any item to have high loadings on any of the three factors or none at all, or to have high loadings on several factors.) Row 2 reports the median factor loadings for items as theoretically grouped (e.g., all items written to represent Stage 4). The next row (*row 3*) gives the range of such factor loadings. From row 2 we see that median loadings on the appropriate factors are about .4, but row 3 shows some items are significantly below this.

4. *Row 4* presents the proportion of items in the three groupings (postconventional, maintaining norms, and personal interest) that have loadings at an "adequate" level on the appropriate factor. Our criteria for an adequate item is that the item load on the appropriate factor at least .3 or greater; that the item have its highest loading on the theoretically appropriate factor; and that the item not have a loading of .3 or more on any other factor. From this definition of adequate items, we see that over 90% of the postconventional and lower-stage items and 74% of the Stage 4 items are adequate. All together, about 85% of the DIT items are "adequate" items by these criteria.

---

[6]The fusion of Stages 2 and 3 in the factor analysis is thought to be due to most subjects regarding both of these as primitive, *not* to there being no theoretical difference between Stages 2 and 3. If we look only at the least developed subjects taking the DIT, we find that Stages 2 and 3 do separate into different factors. Thoma and Rest (in press) showed that the factor loadings for Stages 2 and 3 are significantly different for the bottom 10% of the Mega sample (i.e., Stage 2 separates from Stage 3 for the subjects with least development); however, Stages 2 + 3 fuse for the entire mega sample of 45,000+ subjects. Our explanation for the fusing is that the generally older subjects consider both Stages 2 and 3 to be primitive considerations.

TABLE 4.12

Internal Structure of Mega Sample

	Item Type[a]		
	Postconventional (Stages 5+6)	Maintaining Norms (Stage 4)	Personal Preference (Stages 2+3)
Number of items	21	19	22
Median factor loading[b]	.41	.39	.42
Range of factor loadings[c]	.10–.53	.09–.63	.10–.56
Proportion of adequate items that meet criteria[d]	.91	.74	.91
Cronbach alpha	.77	.74	.80

[a] Item type in terms of a priori stage keying.

[b] Median factor loading on the appropriate factor extracted from Mega sample.

[c] Range of factor loadings for item type on the appropriate factor.

[d] The criteria are that an item have at least a loading of .3 on the appropriate factor, have the highest loading on that factor, and have no loadings of .3 or greater on any other factor.

5. *Row 5* presents the Cronbach alpha index of internal consistency for the three groups of *ratings* (not *rankings*) on the Mega sample. In each of the three groups, there are "inadequate" items (i.e., items that, if left out of the calculation of Cronbach's Alpha, would have improved the level of internal consistency). In conclusion, this level of internal consistency for ratings is comparable to the internal consistency for rankings (Table 4.11) and is adequate but not outstanding.

Some confidence that the Mega sample and the 1995 composite sample are not quirky samples comes from the fact that there is good agreement on average item ratings between the Mega sample (having the virtue of large numbers—over 45,000) and the 1995 composite sample (having the virtue of the full distribution of education possible for the DIT—junior high school students to Ph.D.s in moral philosophy). The correlation on average item ratings for the 72 items between the Mega and 1995 composite samples is .95. The correlation on average item ratings between the highest subgroups of the 1995 composite sample (seminary students and Ph.D.s in moral philosophy/political science) and the high P group in the Mega sample (subjects with higher P scores than 60) is .94. The corroboration between samples gives us some confidence in both composite samples as generally representative.

A last issue with regard to internal structure concerns devising an index for the DIT. An index concerns how the various ratings and rankings are put together into an overall score representing a subject's development in moral judgment. We treat this issue very briefly, because two articles were recently published on the matter: Rest, Thoma, and Edwards (1997), and Rest, Thoma, Narvaez, and Bebeau (1997).

The general premise of the indexing studies is that an index reflects what the test constructor believes to be the internal structure of the test items. As mentioned previously, the P score has served as the main index for the DIT for the past 25 years. A great deal of work has gone into investigating various ways of indexing the DIT—dozens of indexes have been devised and tested. The strategy has been to reanalyze data from the validity studies and to ascertain whether the new index shows stronger trends (i.e., has a higher r, or F, or t, etc.) than other indexes. It turns out that the P score is the index to beat, and up until recently, no new index produced stronger trends. For years, we believed that a better index would come from some sort of scaling algorithm (using multidimensional scaling, as in Davison, 1979; Evens, 1995) weighing the items according to their scaling values as determined empirically.

However, recently we concluded that scaling the items was not the best approach. Instead, we formulated a hybrid index (called N2) that takes two types of information into account: (a) the extent to which the subject ranks in top place the postconventional items—virtually identical with the traditional P score; and (b) the difference in ratings of items of Stages 2 + 3 from Stages 5 + 6. The second part of the index measures how discriminating the subject is in making distinctions between the lowest items and the highest items. The idea for the second part of the hybrid index was discovered on noticing in intervention studies that people change not only in selecting more high-stage items, but also in systematically rejecting the lower-stage items. The two parts of N2 reflect the view that developmental advance is marked by acquisition of new high-stage items and also by discriminating high from low items. Both parts of the N2 index together (ranking of postconventional items, and also the degree to which ratings of Stages 5 + 6 items are discriminated from ratings of Stages 2 + 3 items) seem to act synergistically (when one part is too high, the other part is lower; when one part is too low, the other part is higher) such that the combination of both parts generally produce stronger trends than the old standard, the P index. In addition to stronger trends on the validity criteria, N2 has slightly better Cronbach alpha internal reliability, as shown in Table 4.11.

CONCLUSION

This review of six validity criteria, plus reliability, explicates what we mean by "construct validity" and documents the extensive support for our neo-Kohlbergian approach. Many studies are cited that were performed by many independent researchers in many different parts of the country. Many studies are published and accessible. As a whole, the validity research has been consistent and mutually reinforcing.

5

∎   ◆   ∏

New Issues, New Theory, New Findings

Successful research is never final or completed. One solid finding leads to further questions, conjecture, and theorizing, which in turn lead to further research. Sometimes—happily—the new directions lead to fruitful new theories and new findings. As active areas of research gain prominence, they invite the scrutiny of critics. Appropriately, critics have a way of coming up with challenges and new proposals that call for readjustments and redirection in the plans conceived by the original researchers. DIT research also has been redirected in this way.

The DIT was an offshoot of Kohlberg's work. In the 1970s, we borrowed heavily from his work but took some different methodological and theoretical directions. We wish we could claim to have been prescient about how many issues in psychology and philosophy would work out over the next 25 years, but dumb blind luck has been an important factor in our research.

In the 1970s, we attempted to see how useful a new task collecting recognition data would be in telling us something about moral judgment. The use of recognition data has been a fortunate choice for the DIT, in view of the problems that subsequent psychological research has demonstrated with interview data that rely on the subjects' verbal articulateness and their ability to explain the inner workings of their own minds. Using recognition data has also allowed us to find postconventional thinking—the lack of which turned out to be a major problem with Kohlberg's use of interview/production data. Furthermore, in the 1970s we didn't anticipate that, as time passed, developmental psychology would be kinder to our concept of development ("shifting distributions") than to Kohlberg's "hard" stage staircase notion. In addition, developments in moral philosophy have favored backing away from equating the highest stages of development too closely with the justice operations of a Kantian/Rawlsian normative theory, as Kohlberg himself did. Also, moral philosophers in recent decades have stressed the concepts of common morality, morality from the bottom up, and the cultural embeddedness of morality. These developments have led to a different notion from Kohlberg's of the structure-content distinction and of the relativism-universalism issue. In this book, we present our reformulation of what we believe is a more defensible definition of postconventionality, which is still mainly Kohlberg's.

Although the issues of validity and reliability of the DIT provide a coherent thread through hundreds of DIT studies throughout the years (as discussed in chap. 4), DIT research is not confined to issues of validity and reliability. As new issues and fresh challenges have been raised in the field, they have fostered new ways to explore the tried and true, and spurred invention in terms of constructs and method. The next section begins discussion of some of the new ground that has been explored using the DIT as a platform for further exploration.

MORAL JUDGMENT AND THE OTHER PARTS OF THE PSYCHOLOGY OF MORALITY

If the Kohlbergian six-stage model of moral judgment is not the whole of the psychology of morality, then what else is there and how does it all fit together? Several new lines of theory and research have come from grappling with the issue of what Kohlbergian moral judgment is *not*, and what else there is. Having a way to measure moral judgment has made it easier to study what moral judgment is not. This section concerns the other parts of morality and their relations with moral judgment.

The Four-Component Model

When one reviews the existing, multifaceted literature of articles that claimed to say something about the psychology of morality (Rest, 1983), very quickly one is struck by the multiplicity of approaches, constructs, and phenomena that constitute this vast and diverse literature. Either one has to say that all the other approaches that differ from one's own are mistaken, or one has to say that there are truly different facets to morality and that morality is a multiplicity of processes. If one chooses the latter alternative, then the question becomes one of how do all these different facets relate to one another. The *four-component model* is an attempt to come up with a synthesis. It has been elaborated over the years (e.g., Narvaez & Rest, 1995; Rest, 1983; Rest, Bebeau, & Volker, 1986; Thoma, 1994a, 1994b).

The basic idea behind the four-component model is that various (four) inner psychological processes together give rise to outwardly observable behavior. The four processes, briefly, are as follows:

1. Moral *sensitivity* (interpreting the situation, role taking how various actions would affect the parties concerned, imagining cause-effect chains of events, and being aware that there is a moral problem when it exists)
2. Moral *judgment* (judging which action would be most justifiable in a moral sense—purportedly DIT research has something to say about this component)
3. Moral *motivation* (the degree of commitment to taking the moral course of action, valuing moral values over other values, and taking personal responsibility for moral outcomes)
4. Moral *character* (persisting in a moral task, having courage, overcoming fatigue and temptations, and implementing subroutines that serve a moral goal).

Moral judgment, then, is conceived as one component (2) amid at least three other processes. The model helps explain why the DIT consistently correlates with behavioral measures but not all that powerfully (typically explaining less than 20% of the variance of the behavior measure). The reason for this loose connection is that other components co-determine behavior and, if the other components are left to vary randomly, the correlation between moral judgment and behavior is attenuated. The hopeful part of this position is that by combining information from all four components, the prediction of behavior will become more powerful and precise (there is some evidence that when more than one component is measured, the prediction to behavior is strengthened; Rest, 1983). The four-component model was originally used to classify various studies in morality that focused on different phenomena and used different theoretical starting points. Later, it was used as a heuristic tool in conceptualizing the psychology of morality as a whole.

This book focuses on Component 2, moral judgment, as measured by the DIT. Bebeau has conducted the most programmatic work to date assessing what we call Component 1, moral sensitivity (Baab & Bebeau, 1990; Bebeau, Rest, & Yamoor, 1985). Whereas tests of moral judgment like the DIT present a dilemma in which much of the process of moral sensitivity is already completed, in contrast, tests of moral sensitivity assess what the subject considers as possibilities for action, how the situation can be interpreted as presenting a moral dilemma, and how various actions are going to impact the participants in the story. Logically, Component 1 (sensitivity) precedes

Component 2 (judgment), but the components do not follow each other in a set temporal order—as there are complex feed-forward and feed-backward loops, and complex interactions (see Rest, 1983).

A quick summation of the work on Component 1 is as follows: Bebeau found that her measure of moral sensitivity produces considerable variance in students in dentistry, that moral sensitivity can be improved through educational intervention, and that moral sensitivity is distinct from moral judgment in that they are only modestly correlated. Bebeau made some forays into studying Components 3 and 4 as well (Bebeau, 1994b; Bebeau, Born, & Ozar, 1993; Thoma, Bebeau, & Born, 1997). Reviewing this research, however, is beyond the focus of this book. In sum, we believe that the overall progress in the larger enterprise of moral psychology can be viewed in terms of how well research progresses in all four inner psychological components leads to outwardly observable moral behavior.

The four-component model has been useful also in thinking about moral education programs, illustrated by Bebeau (1994b; Bebeau, Rest, & Narvaez, in press) in the education of dental students, and by Duckett and Ryden (1994) in the education of nursing students. The four-component model suggests that the advancement of moral judgment is one of the desired outcomes of a moral education program, but acknowledges the desirability of other outcomes as well. Bebeau (1994b) and Duckett and Ryden (1994) have many suggestions for building experiences and curriculum elements in professional education programs that address all four components.

In thinking about moral education at the K–12 level in public schools, the four-component model helps make sense of the shifts in goals for moral education in the United States (Bebeau et al., in press). At any one time, the type of moral education in vogue in public schools reflects the ideological emphasis of American society, largely responding to what society perceives as its greatest threat at the time. For instance, in the aftermath of Sputnik, American education was focused on producing enough engineers, scientists, and mathematicians in order to stay ahead of the Russians. At that time, the emphasis was not on the "frills" of moral education, but on learning the hard sciences that contributed the most to weapons and space technology. Later, as a result of the student protest movements and the advent of hippies, American society was concerned with curbing wayward ideologies. Accordingly, the focus in public school moral education was on developing more robust moral philosophies (Component 2). Currently, the chief concern of American society is about the destructiveness and aggression of some youth—committing felonies, using drugs, begetting children, and using drive-by shootings to resolve conflict. Accordingly, moral education is focused now on Component 4—impulse control, self-discipline, and directly teaching "moral literacy" in the hope of instilling moral character.

The response to the latest fear about youth destructiveness is a flurry of activity in the name of "character education." A large number of public schools, K–12, are reported to have instituted character education programs (*Educational Leadership*, 1993), but these efforts are largely undocumented and unresearched. Recent books (Kilpatrick, 1993; Lickona, 1991; Wynne & Ryan, 1993) begin by describing the failures in the primary socialization of many of our nation's youth. William Bennett's book, *The Book of Virtues* (1993), was on the *New York Times* bestseller list for over a year, and emphasized the need for "basic moral literacy," the premise being that reading about virtues would instill virtuous behavior. The political campaigns of many office seekers have emphasized "the moral crisis," "breakdown of family values," "America's moral decline", "moral illiteracy," and "the values crisis" (cf., *U.S. News*, August 4, 1994; *Newsweek*, June 13, 1994). We hear about the new Character Education Partnership, the character education network, the Aspen Declaration on Character Education, and the publicity campaign "Character Counts." Education journals report many new initiatives for character education in schools (e.g., *Educational Leadership*, November, 1993). There is a lot of activity going on, but it is unclear what it is and how well it is working (Leming, 1997).

The country needs more than a flurry of activity. Taking some lessons from the Head Start Movement of the 1960s (which also started as a flurry of educational activity largely unfocused and undocumented), we need to develop—what Head Start eventually did— a research tracking system to record what interventions work, with whom, and under what conditions. In the same way that the preschool movement eventually tracked what was going on and documented successes, research in moral education is the means for constructing reliable theories and profiting from past experience. But, in moral education, what variables are worth tracking? We believe that the researchable variables will not likely come from the simplistic view that morality consists of three parts: emotion, cognition, and behavior. Something more complex is needed to adequately capture the complexity of moral psychology, something like the complex picture of the four component model (Bebeau et al., in press; Rest, 1983). We suggest inaugurating a systematic tracking system for moral education programs that incorporates researchable variables such as those characterized by the four-component model.

Intermediate Concepts

As described in chapter 2, further thinking about what the Kohlbergian scheme does not account for has led to the notion of "intermediate concepts" (Bebeau & Thoma, 1997). As discussed earlier, this level of conception is used in day-to-day ethical decision making. It is at a level less abstract than the maintaining norms and the postconventional schemas. Examples of intermediate concepts are paternalism, informed consent, professionalism, patient/client autonomy, due process, and surrogate decision making. One way to study intermediate concepts is by describing cases that are likely to arise in the course of occupational/professional life, and then asking the respondent for full and specific decision making about what to do in the situation. "Better" decision making is defined in accordance with what experts in the field regard as more defensible (following a process not unlike that used for establishing a common morality). If we are successful in defining intermediate concepts as a psychological variable, then some questions that can be addressed are: Do students get better at ethical decision making (using intermediate concepts) after going through a professional ethics course? Are students who have high P scores on the DIT at admission to college better able to assimilate an ethics course than are those who do not? Are they better able to transfer learning to new cases? Do they have the "conceptual bedrock" that enables ethics instruction to be understood better? (See Bebeau & Thoma, 1997.)

The Utilizer Score

Another spinoff from DIT research coming from reflection on the relation of moral judgment to behavior was the proposal by Thoma of a moderator variable—the "utilizer" score (Thoma, 1994a; Thoma, Rest, & Davison, 1991). The utilizer score is based on the idea that there are differences among people not only in their concepts of justice (as measured by the DIT), but also in the degree to which those concepts are *utilized* in moral decision making and behavior. The hope is that taking into account a utilizer variable (used as a moderator variable between DIT scores and behavior measures) increases the predictability of moral judgment to behavior.

For instance, consider a study by Lawrence (1987). She found that radically fundamentalist seminarians could comprehend moral judgment concepts much higher than those they used to make moral decisions (the DIT's P score). This was a case in which a Kohlbergian schema was not being utilized in moral decision making. The seminarians said that making moral decisions was not up to their own mortal and fallible judgment to decide; rather, God told people what moral values to have in the Bible. In talking aloud about what they were thinking while taking the DIT, the seminarians said that they were setting aside their own intuitions about what was fair and turning instead to religious teaching to tell them what was transcendently revealed as the thing to do. Even though the seminarians had shown on a moral comprehension test that they understood concepts of justice at a level commensurate with their level of education, nevertheless on the DIT they did not use these justice concepts. We would call this an example of "low utilization."

Thoma's strategy was to devise an index of utilization (the extent to which a subject uses justice/Kohlbergian concepts in moral decision making). His approach was to examine the degree of fit between DIT item endorsement and subject's action choice on DIT dilemmas. For instance, suppose a subject responds to the "Heinz" dilemma by ranking in first place the item "Whether a community's laws ought to be upheld"—then that subject would be expected to choose "Heinz should *not steal*" as an action choice. Alternatively, a subject who ranks in first place the item "Isn't it only natural for a loving husband to care so much for his wife that he'd steal" is expected to choose the action choice "Heinz *should* steal." The U score represents the degree of match or fit between items endorsed as most important and the action choice on that story. A high U score represents good fit between item endorsement and action choice; a low U score represents poor fit. Having devised a measure of the Utilizer dimension, Thoma (1994a) then went for the payoff. He found that, in a reanalysis of five behavior and attitude studies, the relation between DIT score and the behavioral/attitude measure increased in strength of prediction when the U score was used as a moderator variable.

The DIT and Job Performance

One last point about the relation of the DIT to behavior: Duckett and Ryden (1994) reported a study in which the DIT was administered at admission into a nursing program. Later in the program, as juniors and seniors, the students were rated by supervisors on their job performance as nurses. DIT scores as freshmen predicted to these job performance ratings, $r = .58$ ($n = 48$, $p < .001$). Surprisingly, their general aptitude score (scores on the ACT) predicted only $r = .42$, and GPA (grade point average) predicted $r = .29$. This finding raises the question of why, theoretically, should the DIT outperform the standard predictors used in admission decisions.

This is not a one-time occurrence. Several previous studies have reported a significant relation of the DIT to clinical performance ratings of medical interns (Cook and Margolis, 1974; Sheehan, Husted, Candee, Cook & Bargen, 1980); and of professional behavior of doctors (Adamson, Baldwin, Sheehan, & Oppenberg, 1997; Baldwin, Adamson, Sheehan, & Oppenberg, Self, 1996). Other researchers have reported a significant predictability of the DIT to clinical performance ratings of physical therapists (Sisola, 1995) and to aspects of teacher's professional lives (Chang, 1994).

Predicting to job performance has long been a practical goal of research. But when grades in school and aptitude tests for the various professions don't predict very well to job performance, why does the DIT work? Is it because the professions have such a large moral component in their jobs (and the DIT, assesses a dimension of morality)? Or is the DIT doing its work indirectly, by tapping into the dimension of making judgments in ill-structured situations?

To pursue this latter possibility, consider what is involved in making judgments in ill-structured situations (see Simon, 1973, for discussion of ill-structured problems). An ill-structured situation is one in which there is no one unique best answer, and there is much uncertainty about the facts of the case and about cause-effect sequences. Perhaps the DIT is predicting to clinical performance because it is indirectly measuring the making of judgments in uncertain social situations (in contrast to standardized aptitude tests or school grades that are largely based on well-structured problems having uniquely correct answers). King and Kitchener (1994), with their research on a construct called "reflective judgment," were especially inventive and productive in exploring this idea of rationality in ill-structured situations by developing a test instrument and conducting impressive programmatic research.

Another possibility is that the predictability of the DIT to later job performance may be more complicated than either interpretation given earlier (that the DIT predicts because it taps into morality, or ill-structured thinking). A dissertation in progress (Schultz, in preparation) finds that the DIT taken before entry into a professional nursing program does not contribute significant predictability in multiple regressions to later clinical performance ratings. It is not clear why the DIT predicts so well in some multiple regression studies to later job performance, but not in others.

DISCRIMINANT VALIDITY

Finding that the DIT consistently produces significant trends on the validity criteria, it is reasonable to ask, "Could the trends be actually caused by some other underlying variable?" In other words, if the DIT produces cross-sectional trends, longitudinal trends, correlations with other variables, and so on, could these findings reflect the workings of some other variable that is actually causing the trends? Maybe the findings summarized under the validity criteria are true, but our interpretation of them is not. Could the DIT be piggybacking on some other construct? Three alternative interpretations of DIT findings have received extended attention: (a) The DIT is reducible to verbal intelligence, or cognitive development in general; (b) the DIT is reducible to political attitude, or political identification, or liberalism-conservatism; and (c) the DIT may be valid for males but it does not work for females, who naturally have a "care" orientation.

Verbal Ability

Recently, Sanders, Lubinski, and Benbow (1995) stated, "The DIT is simply another way of measuring verbal ability. . . . If we are to continue using the DIT in psychological research . . . it is imperative that a well-established marker of verbal ability be used" (p. 502). Sanders et al. suggested that the DIT can be reduced to verbal ability, and that they are the first to raise the issue of the discriminant validity of the DIT (e.g., "Yet [no studies] have specifically examined the uniqueness of moral reasoning . . . ," p. 409). They claim that the DIT is really measuring verbal ability based on their finding that the DIT did not correlate with their selection of personality trait variables but was modestly correlated with cognitive measures.

Actually, DIT research has attended to discriminant validity for over 20 years. In Rest (1979) there is a section entitled, "The Distinctiveness of Moral Judgment" that cites six studies that control for verbal ability and general cognitive ability—the sort of thing that Sanders et al. recommended be done. Sanders et al. cited the Rest (1979) book, but did not mention anything about the section of the book dealing with discriminant validity. Rest (1979) provided information leading to the following conclusions: Partialling out the Differential Aptitude Test ("DAT"), the semi-partial correlation of the DIT with moral comprehension is still highly significant: $r = .51$ ($n = 73, p < .01$). The semi-partial correlation of the DIT with political attitudes after controlling for the DAT is .36 ($n = 73$, $p < .01$). (One observer dubbed this as the "DIT and DAT findings.")

Furthermore, semipartial correlations of the DIT with comprehension and political attitudes after partialling out the Iowa Test of Basic Skills (rather than the Differential Abilities Test) are even higher, because the ITBS is less correlated with the variables. Therefore, the information of the DIT in predicting moral comprehension and political attitudes is uniquely statistically significant; and neither benchmark of general cognitive ability (DAT or ITBS), when partialled out, renders the DIT statistically insignificant. (We report the full aptitude test scores rather than only verbal ability scores, because the full test scores are a more formidable threat to the DIT than are the narrower measures of verbal ability.) These are the very findings that Sanders et al. (1995) suggested wouldn't occur.

In support of their claim, Sanders et al. (1995) showed that the DIT does not correlate significantly with their selection of personality trait variables. But in another place (Rest, 1979), nonsignificant correlations were cited for personality trait variables. Rest (1979) stated: "Of approximately 150 correlations between the DIT and personality measures, most are non-significant. . . . The DIT is more related to cognitive processes than to personality traits" (pp. 197–198). The Sanders et al. data are actually a confirmation, not a refutation, of findings reported nearly 20 years ago.

But more to the point of discriminant validity, Sanders et al. (1995) did not use the correct criteria for testing the discriminant validity of the DIT. They should have examined the six validity criteria discussed here in chapter 4, not correlations with personality trait variables. That is, the proper test would be to see if the trends claimed for the DIT (discrimination of expert-novice groups, longitudinal trends, correlations with comprehension, links with behavior, etc.) are wiped out after partialling out verbal ability (or general cognitive aptitude, etc.). Thoma, Narvaez, and Rest (1997a; Thoma, Narvaez, Rest, & Derryberry, in press) reviewed the literature over the past 20 years on this point. They reported that the DIT still produces significant trends, even after controlling for verbal ability (or IQ, or general cognitive ability, etc.). No variable (verbal ability, IQ, general cognitive ability, or GPA) accounts for the trends in the validity criteria better than the DIT.

As to the suggestion by Sanders et al. (1995) that no study use the DIT without also including a measure of verbal ability (so that verbal ability can be partialled out), we view this suggestion as a tremendous waste of effort, given that the discriminant validity of the DIT in reference to verbal ability has been monitored for decades, in no instance has the reduction to verbal ability interpretation been supported, and there are so many other interesting questions to pursue.

Political Attitudes

A more formidable alternative interpretation of the DIT is that moral judgment in the Kohlbergian tradition is actually measuring political attitude rather than the development of concepts for organizing societal cooperation. Whereas the verbal ability explanation attributes a role to developing cognitive capacity (Sanders et al., 1995, would have said that the cognitive capacity is not distinctively moral, but rather plain verbal ability), the political attitude explanation says that moral judgment is really liberalism-conservatism masquerading as developmental capacity. This argument goes: Because Kohlberg himself preferred liberal political views, in effect he was claiming that liberalism was more highly developed than conservatism. In reality—so the argument goes—liberalism and conservatism are really two alternative political views with equal sophistication; liberalism is not more highly developed than conservatism; conservatives are not retarded liberals. Emler, Resnick, and Malone (1983) implied that the information that one gets from the DIT is essentially no more than asking a person whether they are liberal or conservative. The DIT is a very expensive way to get information that one could get from a simple, single self-report item.

There is a long history to arguments that Kohlberg's developmental theory is really the expression of a political bias in disguise. Among early critiques, an article entitled "Moral Development Research: A Case Study of Scientific Cultural Bias" (Simpson, 1974) communicated the gist of that view. More recent criticism of Kohlberg's liberal bias and his speaking from a provincial perspective of eighteenth-century liberal enlightenment is found in Shweder's review (1982) of Kohlberg's Volume I (1981), which he characterized ironically, "Liberalism as destiny." The political context favoring liberalism in which Kohlberg developed his theory in the 1960s (and which we described in chapter 1) has been noted by these critics. What was popular in the 1960s is not so popular nowadays.

Reducing moral judgment to political attitudes has been argued not only on theoretical grounds, but also empirically on the basis of two very different kinds of studies. The first, by Georg Lind (1995), makes the claim by arguing that the DIT and MJI (Kohlberg's interview) are *preference* measures. The task asked of a subject requires the subject to make a preference about the stage of reasons given, or items selected. Lind said that preferences for liking or disliking something are essentially attitude measures. The proper way to assess a cognitive developmental construct is by assessing the *consistency* of ratings, not attending to the *preferences* of stage endorsement. Lind used individual MANOVA techniques to measure consistency that he said is a pure measure of cognitive capacity, whereas the preference measures employed by Kohlberg and the DIT are attitudinal (preference) measures. Lind carried out a systematic program of studies using his stage consistency approach (1995). Lind's claims were examined at length in Rest, Thoma, and Edwards (1997). In brief, we found that Lind-like stage consistency measures show poorer trends on all six validity criteria than the usual stage-preference indexes. The Rest, Thoma, and Edwards study provides detailed empirical evidence that scores based on preference measures (the P score) outperform scores based on a consistency algorithm.

The second kind of study that argues for an interpretation of DIT scores as political attitudes was typified by Emler and colleagues (Emler, Palmer-Canton, & St. James, in press; Emler, Resnick, & Malone, 1983). Emler's empirical support for the reduction of the DIT to attitudes was most striking in studies that manipulate test instructions of the DIT (more colloquially referred to as the "faking" study). In Emler et al., (1983) subjects were instructed to take the DIT with special test-taking instructions, such as "Fake like a radical liberal." The point of these studies is to show that instructing subjects to take the DIT like a radical liberal increases the DIT's P score (above the score obtained by usual test instructions), whereas instructing the subject to fake like a conservative lowers their P score. Therefore, asking a subject to respond as a liberal or a conservative produced a range of DIT scores. Hence, it is argued that DIT scores really indicate how much a subject wants to appear to the researcher as a liberal or a conservative, telling us little about cognitive development.

In a subsequent study, Emler et al. (in press) demonstrated that subjects can systematically rate candidates for political party who endorse certain DIT items. For instance, if a candidate gives Stage 4 considerations (from DIT Stage 4 items), that candidate is rated by subjects as more suitable for the Conservative party; however, if a candidate gives Stage 5 considerations, that candidate is rated by subjects as more suitable for the labor (i.e., liberal) party.

Emler et al. (1983; in press) showed that by directing subjects to attend to certain attributes of DIT items, that British college students associate DIT items with their perceptions of British political parties. Because subjects (when directed to by special instructions) associate certain political parties with certain DIT items (e.g., conservative party with Stage 4 items), it is claimed that this fact illuminates the process whereby subjects ordinarily take the DIT under standard instructions. In effect, Emler et al. claimed that evidence regarding social perceptions of political parties is also evidence regarding the discriminant validity of the DIT—namely, that the DIT is really measuring political attitude. Emler et al. (1983) stated:

> Moral reasoning and political attitude are by and large one and the same thing. . . . (p. 1073)

> We believe that individual differences in moral reasoning among adults—and in particular those corresponding to the conventional-principled distinction—are interpretable as variations on a dimension of political-moral ideology and not as variations on a cognitive-developmental dimension. (p. 1075)

> These findings [of the 1983 study] accord with our more general claims that moral and political attitudes are substantially overlapping domains and that Kohlberg's conventional-principled distinction as applied to the moral reasoning of adults is one of ideological content rather than structural complexity. The

difference between Stages 4 and 5 appears to correspond to the conservative-radical distinction in political attitudes. (p. 1079)

Emler et al. strengthened their case by pointing to the high correlations of the DIT with political attitudes. Actually, we agree with Emler et al. (1983, in press) that DIT scores are highly correlated with various measures of political attitudes and political identity. Reviews indicate that the joint variance is as high as 40% (Table 4.9, correlations in the .60s). But our interpretation of this correlation is different from Emler's (that despite the high correlations, the two constructs are distinct), and we argue that questions of discriminant validity are not addressed by the study of manipulating test instructions (see Barnett, Evens, & Rest, 1995; Thoma, Barnett, Rest, & Narvaez, in press, for a detailed critique of the Emler et al. studies).

Our view is that the high correlations of the DIT with political attitudes do not mean that the DIT is, by and large, the same as political attitude. In our view, moral judgment describes how a person conceptualizes different ways to organize societal cooperation. Typically, studies show that in secondary school the individual begins to conceptualize cooperation in society in terms of the maintaining norms schema. The person realizes that cooperation involves not only friends, family, and people with whom one has a face-to-face relationship, but also strangers, competitors, and little-known acquaintances. Thus, the person understands the usefulness of social norms in establishing a societal network of cooperation.

We describe development in moral judgment in terms of acquiring schemas as solutions for creating a societywide system of cooperation. The DIT's P score is especially sensitive to the shift from maintaining norms to the postconventional schema. This shift in moral schema is accompanied by a shift in attitude toward authority (shifting from unquestioning support to holding authorities accountable). Furthermore, there is also a change in attitudes about the importance of maintaining established social norms (shifting from supporting all established practices to supporting only those practices that serve the community's shared moral ideals). Therefore, development in moral judgment is accompanied by shifts in political attitude. Often, conservative positions are more supportive of authority and established practices, and, usually, postconventional thinkers find liberal political positions more congenial. However, the association between political attitude and moral judgment does not mean that they are identical.

The developmental schemas are not the same thing as the distinction in political theory between right-wing and left-wing (conservative political theory versus liberal political theory). Both right-wing and left-wing political theories have a course of development, each starting from

simplistic assumptions and evolving to more sophisticated positions. Both
orientations can be at the maintaining norms stage (e.g., George Wallace's
law and order orientation, or the political correctness of the 1980s). Both
left and right can be at the postconventional stage: for example, liberal
(as, e.g., Rawls, 1971), conservative (e.g., Sandel, 1982), communitarian
(Walzer, 1983), or libertarian (Nozick, 1974). Both right and left can be
criticized for injustices (e.g., McCarthyism in America in 1950s, and the
moral critique of left-wing political correctness by Gross & Levitt, 1994).
Moral critiques of both right-wing and left-wing views indicate that moral
judgment is not the same thing as the right-wing, left-wing distinction in
political thinking.

We also regard as important the distinctions among other political
constructs. Political attitude and ideological differences do not reduce to
the single variable of liberalism/conservatism. We distinguish among the
constructs of authoritarianism (e.g., Adorno et al., 1950), civil libertarianism (e.g., McClosky & Brill, 1983), political tolerance (e.g., Marcus et
al., 1995), self-identified political liberalism/conservatism (e.g., Emler et
al., 1983), dogmatism and closed-mindedness (e.g., Rokeach, 1960), and
orthodoxy/progressivism (e.g., Hunter, 1991). All of these variables—including moral judgment—do not completely reduce to one common
factor of liberalism-conservatism. There are many facets of political
identity, political ideology, and moral judgment, and it is a mistake to lump
them all together.

A recent study by Narvaez, Getz, Thoma, and Rest (in press) made this
point empirically. Two facets of ideology (political, religious) and moral
judgment were assessed, and these variables did not reduce to one common variable of liberalism/conservatism. The study used as a dependent
variable the Attitudes Towards Human Rights Inventory (ATHRI; Getz,
1985, see Appendix A). It measures the subject's opinions on controversial
public policy issues (abortion, prayer in state-supported schools, rights of
homosexuals, women's roles, rights of the accused, etc.). The predictor/in-
dependent variables included a measure of political ideology (i.e., self-reported political identity as conservative or liberal); a measure of religious
ideology (i.e., literal interpretation of the Bible); and moral judgment (i.e.,
the DIT's P score).

We found that whereas all of the predictor variables were highly
intercorrelated in simple bivariate correlations, in multiple regressions
they each predicted significantly and uniquely to the dependent variable
(ATHRI). (Standardized beta-weights for each independent variable significantly and uniquely predicted to ATHRI.) The three variables did not
reduce to each other nor to some common variable of liberalism/conser-
vatism. Moreover, when these three variables were combined according
to their beta-weights from the multiple regression, the combination of

these three variables was much stronger in predicting to the dependent variable than any one of them alone. Recently, this study was replicated for the third time (Rest, Narvaez, Thoma, & Bebeau, 1998). These studies support our general view: Although various political and religious ideology variables are significantly correlated with moral judgment, they each contain independent information and do not reduce to the common variable of liberalism/conservatism.

In further disagreement with Emler et al. (1983, in press), we dispute that a study that manipulates test instructions can also address questions of discriminant validity (i.e., whether or not the DIT measures moral judgment or political attitudes). These questions are different and require different kinds of studies. We acknowledge that the studies by Emler et al. are informative regarding how subjects perceive different political parties. By directing subjects to attend to certain features of DIT items (e.g., does this item sound like the conservative party or the labor party) we learn how subjects understand certain social categories. This strategy could also be used to study subjects' perceptions of other social categories as well (e.g., religion, institutional ideologies, cultural ideologies, etc.). But the manipulation of test instructions is ill suited to study discriminant validity.

To illustrate the problem of the faking study in addressing issues of discriminant validity, we describe a facetious study that no one has actually proposed but whose design makes clear the logic (and shortcomings) of Emler's manipulation of test instructions. We want a design—like Emler's—that also directs subjects to attend to certain researcher-chosen attributes of DIT items (e.g., attending to whether the DIT item sounds more like the conservative party or the labor party), and which then allows us to use ratings and rankings of the DIT items thus construed to arrive at a Stage 4 score and a P score. Imagine the following facetious study with two experimental conditions: One group of college students is instructed to fill out the DIT by always choosing the even items: 12, 10, 8 and 6 (called the "fake even" group). A second group of college students is instructed to always choose odd items: 1, 3, 5, and 7 (called the "fake odd" group). If our subjects follow these instructions (and one consistent finding in faking studies is that college students do faithfully follow instructions), then the "even" group will have a P score averaging somewhere around 47, and the "odd" group will have a P score averaging around 23. Because a typical score of college students averages around 40, the "findings" suggest that the "fake even" condition will produce an increase in scores over the usual average, and the "fake odd" condition will produce a decrease in scores. Thus, this manipulation of test instructions can produce a range of DIT scores, both higher and lower than under standard conditions.

Now the critical question: Does this kind of study produce evidence that the DIT in reality reflects the disposition to present oneself as an even-item test taker or odd-item test taker? After demonstrating test manipulation effects we can always ask, "What evidence is there that subjects under normal conditions base their ranking/rating of items on the DIT on the odd/even dimension—or even think about odd/even attributes?" This facetious example illustrates a methodological point: Directing subjects to attend to experimenter-chosen attributes of test stimuli does not tell us to what attributes they usually attend.

Classical measurement theory holds that the test items *and instructions* are an integrated whole; changing the instructions is presumed to alter the test and what it measures (e.g., Brown, 1976). Thus, manipulation of test instructions can produce variance in DIT scores, but this kind of study is insufficient to say how subjects normally produce the variance of DIT scores. The manipulation invalidates the very process we want to study.

We acknowledge that we have changed our position on the use of the faking study; formerly we used to include it as a validity criteria, now we don't. Earlier we reported test manipulation studies of McGeorge (1975), Hau (1990), and Bloom (1977), who asked subjects to "fake high" their DIT responses to show how a "moral," "fair," "just," or "principled" person would fill out the DIT. We had supposed that this instruction mirrors the process usually used by subjects anyway (thinking that they were already rating/ranking items on the basis of what they thought was fair, just, principled, morally mature, etc.). Therefore, we expected that the "fake high" condition would produce the same scores as the usual condition, if indeed the process of the usual condition was the same as that given in our special directions. The findings of these studies confirmed this expectation. Similarly Emler et al. (in press) reported "self-defined right wingers saw the Stage 4 arguments as more relevant to a morally sophisticated person . . . than did the self-defined left wingers" (p. 12) who saw the morally sophisticated person in terms of P items. In all these studies (the three mentioned, plus Emler et al., in press), directing the subject to choose items on the basis of imagining what is fair, just, and morally sophisticated is the same test-taking set that we supposed subjects have under normal conditions. We were asking subjects to indicate in response to specific dilemmas what, in effect was their conception of fairness, justice, mature moral judgment, and so forth.

In contrast, Emler et al. (1983) contended that *differences* in P score between the normal conditions and the "fake high" condition (not *similarity*) constituted evidence that reveals the true DIT process under normal conditions—a very different logic than McGeorge, Hau, and Bloom. With the "difference logic," one could with equal plausibility argue that subjects are really using the odd-even dimension, because test instructions to attend to odd or even attributes of items result in different DIT scores than those under standard conditions (and therefore argue the DIT really measures the self-presentation as an odd or even test taker).

However, we are now aware that neither type of faking study (anticipating "same" or "different" scores from manipulations) actually provides direct evidence for the process used under normal conditions. We are aware that such a tangle of inferences and interpretations of the faking study are possible that we have changed our position (bowing to unanticipated empirical findings), and have eliminated the faking study from our set of the validity criteria. In summary, the faking study does show the logical *possibility* to account for a range of DIT scores (according to the process embodied in the special test instructions), but the faking study has no way to argue that it has accounted for the *actual* processes that subjects use under usual conditions. So the issue remains of how do test instructions that ask the subject to fake one way or another illuminate the processes that subjects ordinarily employ when filling out the DIT. We would say manipulation of test instructions are not useful in addressing discriminant validity.

There is a better way to test the discriminant validity of the DIT—to test whether or not the DIT contains information above and beyond its shared variance with political attitudes. As in our discussion of discriminant validity before, the appropriate strategy for testing discriminant validity is to see if the DIT still produces significant trends on the six validity criteria, even after controlling for the supposed alternative variable (in this case, political attitude). Thoma, Narvaez, and Rest (1997b), and Thoma, Narvaez, Rest, and Derryberry (in press) reviewed studies doing this, and found that consistently the DIT does present unique information above and beyond that accounted for by political attitude measures. Because political attitude measures (when partialled out) do not reduce the trends of the DIT to nonsignificance, we contend that the DIT cannot be reduced to political attitude.

Gender Differences

Gilligan's writings on moral development (e.g., 1977, 1982) have stimulated many studies of gender differences in moral judgment (see reference list of published studies in Table 5.1). For more than a decade, a frequent question about DIT research was, "But didn't Carol Gilligan disprove all of that? Isn't the justice orientation only for men and the care orientation only for women?" For instance, Nokes (1989) stated that Kohlbergian justice-oriented theories had little place in the thinking or training of nurses, because nurses scored so low on the DIT and were oriented to

TABLE 5.1

Citation of Published Articles on Gender Differences

Reviews:

Brabeck (1983); Rest, Thoma, Moon, & Getz (1986); Thoma (1986)

Studies:

Bakken & Ellsworth (1990); Bebeau & Brabeck (1987, 1989); Dobrin (1989); Friedman, Robinson, & Friedman (1987); Galotti, Kozberg, & Farmer (1991); Garwood, Levine, & Ewing (1980); Leahy (1981); Leahy & Eiter (1980); Lonky, Roodin, & Rybash (1988); Marron & Kayson (1984); McGraw & Bloomfield (1987); Orchowsky & Jenkins (1979); Parish & Copeland (1981); Perez-Delgado, Garcia-Ros, & Clemente-Carrion (1992); Pratt, Golding & Hunter (1984); Pratt & Royer (1982); Self & Olivarez (1993); Watson (1995); Wilson (1995); Wilson & Deemer (1989)

"care" rather than "justice." However, Duckett et al. (1992) pointed out that Nokes in reporting low DIT scores for nurses was using *raw* P DIT scores compared to *percentage* P scores. When the DIT scores for nurses were compared on the same metric (percentages with percentages), nurses looked quite good on the DIT in comparison with other professional groups. The difference between raw scores and percentage scores is illustrated by the fact that a *raw* P score of 30 equals a P *percentage* score of 50. Researchers are cautioned to convert all raw scores to percentage scores.

Regarding evidence for sex differences, Rest (1979) stated that "22 studies assessing gender differences were reviewed . . . and only two had a significant difference in P score between males and females. . . . In both of these studies, females had higher scores" (p. 120). The most thorough examination of gender differences on the DIT was reported by Thoma (1986) as a meta-analysis of 56 DIT studies, involving over 6,000 subjects. In brief, Thoma found that gender differences accounted for .002 of the variance of DIT scores, whereas education was over 250 times more powerful. When there are differences between the genders, females have higher averages. Table 5.2 presents the descriptive statistics for Thoma's meta-analysis. Since 1986, we know of no evidence to challenge the conclusion that gender is a trivial variable in accounting for DIT variance. The whole realm of macromorality is dismissed when one contends that morality only concerns unswerving loyalty to friends and kin, that people are interrelated only by bonds of affection, and that moral virtue consists solely of dedication to special face-to-face personal relationships. Dismissing macromorality is to overlook the organization of people at the state level whereby strangers, competitors, and diverse ethnic and religious groups are interrelated by formal roles, laws, and institutions in which the

TABLE 5.2

Descriptive Statistics for the Meta-Analysis of Gender Differences
(Thoma, 1986)

Statistic	Junior High	Senior High	College	Graduate School	Adult
Males					
Mean	19.1	28.7	44.1	61.0	42.8
SD	(6.2)	(11.8)	(12.2)	(14.0)	(11.8)
n	528	424	449	52	90
Females					
Mean	19.8	30.4	45.9	63.0	46.0
SD	(6.3)	(10.9)	(12.2)	(10.9)	(12.9)
n	519	436	436	42	183

Note: Groups are students in junior high school or senior high school, college students, graduate students, nonstudent adults. The graduate student and adult groups were not included in the secondary analysis due to their relatively small sample sizes.

moral virtues of impartiality and nondiscrimination make possible the cooperation of larger groups of people.

RELIGION

Shweder (Shweder et al., in press) made a good point that religion is important to study for its role in determining moral thinking. (In chap. 8 we state our misgivings about the particular way that Shweder studied the role of religion.) Other researchers, too, have stated that Kohlbergian approaches to moral thinking have underplayed the role of religion (e.g., Colby & Damon, 1992; Walker, Pitts, Henning, & Matsuba, 1995). So how does one study the role of religion?

Getz (1984) reviewed 22 DIT studies concerning religion, and discussed seven ways that religion has been conceptualized as a variable. Although it is hazardous to briefly summarize a review of many studies, nevertheless we quote one statement: "The most striking finding from the literature relating religious measures to moral judgment development is the consistent relationship between DIT P scores and religious beliefs" (Rest, Thoma, Moon, & Getz, 1986, p. 131). Table 5.3 cites the published studies on religion and the DIT.

TABLE 5.3

Citation of Published Articles on Religion

Reviews:

Getz (1984); McNeel (1991, 1994a, 1994b); Rest

Studies:

Bouhmama (1984b); Brown & Annis (1978); Bruggeman & Hart (1996); Buier, Butman, Burwell, & Van Wicklin (1989); Clouse (1985, 1991); Dirks (1988); Ernsberger & Manaster (1981); Glover (1997); Holley (1991); Lawrence (1987); Richards & Davison (1992); Sapp & Gladding (1989); Shaver (1985, 1987); Smith (1990); Wahrman (1981)

Narvaez et al. (in press) presented further thinking on the role of religion and moral development. We go into some detail here in describing this study, because it serves as an entry point to our theorizing about the joint influence of individual cognitive development (as measured by the DIT) with group-based ideologies (religious, political, and cultural ideologies). As briefly described in the section on "political attitudes," the study examines the role of religious and political ideology, in conjunction with moral judgment development, in determining moral opinions on controversial public policy issues (Getz's ATHRI).

Step One.   We begin in a way similar to Jensen (1996, 1997), by first identifying two church congregations with opposite reputations for being conservative or liberal. The two congregations were matched on locale, size, age, and education of constituents, but had contrasting reputations for their religious beliefs and their political/social outlooks. To use a current construct describing these differences in ideology (Hunter, 1991), the one congregation was "orthodox" and the other congregation was "progressive." "Orthodoxy" finds moral authority in traditional, transcendent religious sources (Hunter, 1991, p. 44). "Progressivism," on the other hand, finds moral authority in "the spirit of the modern age, a spirit of rationalism and subjectivism" (Hunter, 1991, pp. 44–45). (Note that Jensen also characterized the differences between the two congregations in her study as orthodox and progressive.) The first step in the procedure was to confirm the reputations of the churches in terms of three psychological measures: self-identified political liberalism/conservatism, DIT P score, and a measure of religious fundamentalism (literal belief in the Bible—using the inventory of religious belief, from Brown & Lowe, 1951). Table 5.4 gives the mean scores on these three measures. All three measures showed significant differences between the two congregations,

TABLE 5.4

Differences (Means and Standard Deviations) Between Congregations
on Psychological Measures and Political Choice

Measures	Baptist (n = 50)	U.C.C. (n = 46)	t-Test Difference
Religious ideology (fundamentalist)	71.90	51.59	13.68**
SD	(2.62)	(9.75)	
Political identity (liberal/conservative)	3.88	3.09	4.49**
SD	(.75)	(.96)	
Moral judgment (DIT P score)	32.44	41.72	3.35*
SD	(11.29)	(15.33)	
ATHRI (Controversial public policy issues)	128.42	149.42	5.85**
SD	(15.92)	(19.70)	

*$p < .001$. **$p < .0001$.

confirming the general reputation of the churches for differences in worldview.

Step Two. This step was to develop a measure of political choice on concrete public policy issues. Getz (1985) developed the Attitudes Towards Human Rights Inventory (ATHRI), discussed in chapter 4, which surveys opinions about controversial issues such as abortion, homosexual rights, public speech, women's roles, and rights of the accused. (The full ATHRI is printed in Appendix A. Originally, in 1985, there were 40 public policy issues in the ATHRI; more recently we have added eight items. However, the analyses here report on the original 40 items.) Table 5.4 shows that in addition to the differences between the congregations on moral judgment, political identification, and religious ideology, there were also significant differences on the concrete public policy issues (i.e., the ATHRI).

Step Three. Besides finding differences between the congregations, there was variance on the psychological measures and on the measure of political choice (ATHRI) within congregations, suggesting that the differences between the subjects in each congregation cannot be explained entirely in terms of the adherence in each group to a group ideology. Hence, we moved beyond church membership by using the three psychological variables as a more direct measure of the construct, orthodoxy/progressivism, than was church affiliation. In multiple regression predicting to the dependent variable, ATHRI, we entered the three psychological measures (religious fundamentalism, political identification, and moral judgment). (Recall this procedure from the previous discussion of discriminant validity and political attitude.) The multiple R of the regression was .79, accounting for 62% of the variance of ATHRI. Thus, the combination of the three psychological measures was more powerful in predicting positions on public policy measures (62% of the variance) than church membership alone (church membership accounted for 27% of the variance of ATHRI). We interpret this as supporting the view that our combination psychological measure is a better measure of the construct, orthodoxy/progressivism, than church membership per se. Also, as mentioned earlier, by examining the beta-weights of the independent variables in the multiple regression, we note that each of the three psychological variables had a unique and significant predictability to ATHRI.

Step Four. A cross-validation was conducted on a separate student sample (Narvaez et al., in press, Study 2). The student sample differed from the church sample (consisting of the two congregations) in age, responsibilities in life (being a student rather than holding responsibilities to a job and family), and membership in a secular rather than a sectarian institution. Using the same regression weights for the three psychological measures as in the church sample (serving as the measure of orthodoxy/progressivism), the measure of orthodoxy from the first sample significantly predicted to ATHRI (59% of the variance of ATHRI) in the second sample. When the church sample was combined with the student sample ($n = 158$) in a new multiple regression, the three ideology variables produced an $R = .82$, accounting for 67% of the variance of ATHRI.

Step Five. Using our combination ideology measure (from the first church sample) as a measure of orthodoxy/progressivism to reexamine the two congregations, we found that the more conservative congregation had 80% of the group with high scores for orthodoxy and only 18% of the progressives; whereas the liberal congregation had the opposite pattern: 13% were orthodox and 46% were progressives (remaining participants were in the "mixed" category). The student sample was like the liberal church, 48% progressive and 11% orthodox. Thus, there was some heterogeneity in all groups—in other words, the official ideology of the congregational groups (orthodox or progressive) did not account for the mixture of views within the groups. The two facts (the mix of ortho-doxy/progressive in all three groups, and the greater predictability to ATHRI of the individual psychological measures over group membership) suggest that the determination of ATHRI responses is at least in part an *individual* phenomenon, not simply a phenomenon of *group* ideology.

Step Six. We noted that people who were high on religious funda-mentalism were high in Stage 4 on the DIT (the correlation between Stage 4 and fundamentalism is .52; $(n = 158, p < .001)$. Ideological measures of political thinking and religious thinking were combining in significant ways with the developmental construct, moral judgment. But what sense did this make? Why would a cognitive developmental measure (the DIT) produce such a potent combination when joined with political and relig-ious ideology measures? What does all this say about the role of religion in moral thinking?

Even though we have argued that moral judgment and fundamentalism are distinct variables, when they converge in the individual's thinking they can create the ideological complex we call orthodoxy. We speculate that the role of *cognitive development* concerns the way that the orthodox worldview is formed. We believe that the orthodox worldview is crystal-lized at the stage in development when people are acquiring the schema of maintaining norms; at that time the person is especially impressed with strong authority, clear norms, and societywide systems for transforming the collective into a moral order. If, during the time that Stage 4 thinking is especially compelling, the person is recruited into a fundamentalist religion (most typically, if the person is born into a family and subculture that is fundamentalist), the normative system that the person embraces may become rooted in a religious rather than a secular base. In other words, the maintaining norms schema provides the conceptual bedrock for fundamentalist religious ideology to be especially meaningful, and the norms that are maintained become religious norms rather than secular, civic norms.

If orthodox religious teachings emphasize that moral authority that is transcendent, supernatural, and beyond attempts at human under-standing—and that it is improper and sinful to question, critique, or scrutinize its authority—then orthodoxy may reinforce itself, making difficult move-ment out of orthodoxy. Over time, the orthodox person may become increasingly oriented to Stage 4, rejecting both developmentally lower forms and developmentally higher forms of moral thinking. The lower forms of thinking (personal interests) are rejected because they are seen as selfish; the higher forms (Postconventional) are rejected because the person is blocked from formulating newer, more critical ideas, because logical reflection and rational scrutiny are viewed as heretical and sinful. Empirical evidence for this interpretation is the significant positive correlation of maintaining norms (Stage 4) with religious fundamentalism.

Note that the DIT and the measure of religious ideology are not redundant and are not measuring the same thing. The DIT involves *civil* authorities (e.g., a high school principal, the police, a doctor, a college president, a businessperson). The DIT does not ask about *religious* authorities (e.g., priests, clergy, or religious prophets) or religious issues, but it does ask about civic matters. In orthodoxy, the unquestioned respect for authority of the *religious* doctrines generalizes to *civil and political* authority. In sum, we are not saying that orthodoxy is a simple matter of more or less development in moral judgment—we do not reduce all moral thinking to moral judgment. Rather, we see the development of concepts about the moral basis of society (in particular, the maintaining norms schema) as providing the conceptual bedrock in which fundamentalist ideologies take root. The maintaining norms schema provides orthodox ideologies with an intuitive appeal (i.e., orthodoxy makes sense). The ideologies in turn proscribe strong and clear norms. Therefore, this is an instance in which moral judgment development and cultural ideology interact to reinforce and determine each other.

The bipolar construct, orthodoxy/progressivism, is useful in understanding the clashes of opinions on many public policy issues (e.g., those measured by the ATHRI), the divisive splits in religious denominations, the paralysis of communities in cooperating for their common good, the overheated rhetoric of radio talk shows and direct mail campaigns, and the formation of many special interest groups, and so on. As irreconcilable worldviews, orthodoxy and progressivism undergird many of the passionate debates of public policy. There is doubt that the United States can harmoniously develop a "common morality" while this split persists and polarizes communal life (e.g., Hunter, 1991).

Antireligious?

We wish to comment on whether or not our characterizations of orthodoxy belie a hostility toward religion. Shweder criticized Kohlberg as being antireligious: Kohlberg's moral theory is "secularism that rejects divine authority" (Shweder et al., 1987, p. 24). Shweder said that Kohlberg assigned all religious expressions to Stage 4 rather than to the higher stages, because "Kohlberg does not believe in superior beings who have privileged access to truths about natural laws" (p. 24). Are we subject to the same criticism?

Guttmann and Thompson (1997) are very useful in what they said on this issue:

An appeal to divine authority per se is thus not what creates the problem for a deliberative perspective. The problem lies in the appeal to *any* authority whose conclusions are impervious, in principle as well as practice, to the standards of logical consistency or to reliable methods of inquiry that themselves should be mutually acceptable. . . . [We do] not exclude religious appeals per se, . . .[but] any claim fails to respect reciprocity if it imposes a requirement on other citizens to adopt one's sectarian way of life as a condition of gaining access to the moral understanding that is essential to judging the validity of one's moral claims. This requirement stands in contrast to the many moral claims in public life that can be assessed and accepted by individuals who are conscientiously committed to any of a wide range of secular and religious ways of life. (pp. 56–57)

And so, the *source* of inspiration (religious or otherwise) does not determine whether moral thinking is classified as postconventional or not. Indeed we could agree, as Shweder put it, that there are "superior beings who have privileged access to truths about natural laws" (Shweder et al., 1987, p. 24), and these superior beings may inspire individuals with their messages. But more important, at the postconventional level it is presumed that the messages need interpreting in the light of human experience. The messages may not be completely understood, and therefore may need continual exploration and dialogue in the light of the ongoing experience and reflection of the participants in the community. Many people of faith have a postconventional understanding of their religion, and its moral meaning for their lives (e.g., Niebuhr, 1943; Tillich, 1957).

We realize that our position on religion will not be pleasing to everyone. For example, Richards (1988) believed that the DIT is unfair to Mormons. (Kohlberg's theory and the DIT are biased against conservatively religious people who, instead of social justice, view moral questions in terms of "living in harmony with divine law"; Richards & Davison, 1992, p. 469). People with Orthodox worldviews will find that our position does not endorse the transcendent authority of their religious beliefs.

As the U.S. Constitution anticipated, the problem with endorsing any *one* transcendent authority on matters of public policy is that *other* transcendent authorities are not endorsed. We live in a pluralistic world and have seen the prospects of unending religious wars. The resolution of pluralism envisioned by the U.S. founding fathers—which we believe is still a good solution—is to protect the individual's freedom of religious belief. But for matters of public policy—where policies of the state affect all the participants of a community, believers and nonbelievers—the state should not endorse any one transcendent authority. This entails that questions of public morality (those matters that affect the common destiny of the participants of a community) be open to scrutiny, use acceptable methods of inquiry, and conform to logical consistency—features that eliminate the validity of appeals to one particular, unquestioned, transcendent authority. This is why our notion of postconventionality may be displeasing to orthodox believers. (For complexities of this issue, see Guttman & Thompson, 1997; Holmes, 1993; Rawls, 1993. Further discussion of religion is covered in chaps. 7 and 8.)

LIFE EXPERIENCES

Table 5.5 cites published studies on the topic of life experiences that affect moral judgment development. Much of this literature deals with zeroing in on what it is about formal education—particularly the college experience—that is key to fostering moral judgment development. From previous studies, we know that years in school promote DIT P scores. Colleges do a good job at increasing the P score. Why is this so? The more one thinks about it, the more possibilities one can imagine (Rest, 1988b). Is it a simple socializing effect, so that the more years one spends in college, the more one begins to sound like a college professor? Is it a matter of learning more stuff so that you sound more knowledgeable and can decorate your language with verbiage that gets one higher scores on the DIT? Does it have to do with the formal curriculum or with the informal curriculum—the general social milieu of academic institutions? Is it that colleges are always asking for reasons and evidence for opinions, and this generalizes to asking for reasons and evidence for moral judgments as well, which pushes one's DIT score into postconventionality?

First, we realize that there is a problem with using simple age or number of years to index development, despite the reliance in many areas of research on longitudinal studies to make a case for intraindividual devel-

TABLE 5.5

Citation of Published Articles on Life Experiences

Reviews:

Pascarella & Terenzini (1991); Rest (1988b, 1991); Rest & Deemer (1986); Rest & Narvaez (1991); Rest & Thoma (1985b)

Studies:

Bertin, Ferrant, Whiteley, & Yokata (1985); Biggs & Barnett (1981); Biggs, Schomberg, & Brown (1977); Cohen (1982); Deemer (1989); Hood (1984); Lonky, Kaus, & Roodin (1984); Marlowe & Auvenshine (1982); Marron & Kayson (1984); Mentkowski & Strait (1983); Nevin & McNeel (1992); Rest (1975a); Rholes & Bailey (1982); Whiteley (1980, 1986); Whiteley et al., (1982); Whiteley & Loxley (1980); Wilson & Deemer (1989); Wilson, Rest, Boldizar, & Deemer (1992)

---

opment. Development is more a matter of richness of experience and stimulating experiences than the mere passage of years. Chronological age is at best a rough proxy variable for development; development involves the cumulative impact of people trying to construct moral meaning in their lives in response to stimulating social experiences. Time is a condition for developmental experiences and developmental processes, but time does not directly measure these developmental experiences and developmental processes. The challenge is to devise ways to measure richness of experience or stimulating experience.

Second, a number of attempts have been made to capture stimulating experience in terms of a checklist of possible enriching experiences. Such checklists include items such as "work experience that exposed the individual to persons of more mature thinking," "experiencing brutality or suffering," and "experiencing a significant decision involving a family member." (See Rest, Deemer, Barnett, Spickelmier, & Volker, 1986, for review of nine studies). These studies yielded weak and inconsistent findings.

Third, Deemer (1986) tried another approach. Rather than specifying experiences and analyzing them separately, she used global, clinical categories that encoded both the external opportunity and also the subject's own positive or negative reaction to the stimulus. Prior to Deemer's research, we had assumed that the march of science was always toward more cleanly defined, objectively described events; in contrast, Deemer's move was toward more "squishy," clinical categories. In a longitudinal study, Deemer (1986) interviewed participants about their previous experiences over the previous 10 years. She coded the participants' life experiences in terms of variables like "continued intellectual stimulation" and "richness of social environment." The life experience codes were clinical judgments of aspects of life pattern as discerned in several hours of interview (but were explicitly set forth in a scoring manual and checked for reliability by another independent judge). In other words, Deemer's work represents a serious attempt to go beyond the convenient variable of "passage of time" to get at the more complex construct of "richness of experience," and doing so in a global, clinical manner. The pattern of results that she obtained was more powerful than anything we had seen before.

The relations of P to Deemer's more complex ways of indicating life experience are shown in Table 5.6, indicating the correlations of four codes with moral judgment, tested when participants were young adults, ages 25 through 28 ($n = 101$). The experience codes are significantly correlated with P when life experiences are characterized in terms of continued intellectual stimulation, life richness, or richness of social

TABLE 5.6

Correlations of P With Indicators of "Richness" of Life Experience

	Indicators of Life Experience			
Index	Continued Intellectual Stimulation[a]	Composite Richness Code[b]	Richness of Social Environment[c]	Educational Completion[d]
P score	.58*	.61*	.68*	.54*

Note: Numbers are correlations of the P score with various indicators of life experience.

[a]"Continued intellectual stimulation" is Deemer's (1986) code for ongoing cognitive stimulation and support of learning over the 10-year period.

[b]"Composite richness code" is a composite variable constructed (the sum) by Evens (1995) from five of Deemer's codes.

[c]"Richness of social environment" is Deemer's code for the stimulation from the social environment (spouse, friends, institutional affiliations).

[d]"Educational completion" is a more objective variable reflecting how much schooling has been completed (high school only, some college, college graduate, graduate/professional school).

*$p < .001$.

environment, and are significant even when years of formal education and initial DIT scores in high school are partialled out (Rest & Deemer, 1986).

Following Deemer's lead, Schiller (1997, in press) went back over the interviews collected by Deemer and developed her own set of clinical experience codes from the perspective of the adult development literature (rather than the more delimited interest just in moral judgment development). This has involved defining new codes, writing new coding guides, and establishing interjudge reliability. Schiller's study set out to code for the developmental tasks that adult developmentalists postulate for this age group; then to relate how well the person was performing the age-appropriate developmental tasks to three outcome variables: moral reasoning (as in Deemer's analysis), occupational attainment, and life satisfaction.

First, Schiller found that the three outcome variables do not intercorrelate very highly: moral judgment correlates only .12 with life satisfaction, and .37 with occupational attainment; life satisfaction correlates .37 with occupational attainment. (And thus having a high P score does not entail that the person is happier.) Second, Schiller found that the developmental tasks predicted differently to the three outcome variables. The developmental task variables, "relationship intimacy" and "career commitment," were most related to life satisfaction (rs in the .50s). As Deemer found, cognitive-intellectual experiences were most related to moral judgment. And a developmental task variable called "presence of the dream" (as discussed by Levinson, Darrow, Klein, Levinson, & McKee, 1978), plus career commitment and education, were most related to occupational attainment. Because the interviews were conducted with young adults aged 28, the continuation of this project as the subjects grow older will be interesting.

CROSS-CULTURAL STUDIES

Kohlberg believed that his stages of moral judgment were universal. He said, "Almost all individuals in all cultures go through the same order or sequence of gross stages of moral development, though varying in rate and terminal point of development" (Kohlberg, 1971, p. 176). According to Reed's (1997) interpretation of Kohlberg, the issue of universality was important to Kohlberg because he saw it as the bulwark against relativism; and the fight against relativism was to prevent abominations as the Nazi Holocaust.

A review of 54 cross-cultural studies using Kohlberg's interview was conducted by Snarey and Keljo (1991; Snarey, 1985). Their review is commonly summarized in this fashion: (a) Kohlbergian Stages 1 to 4 are found in virtually all cultures, with little Stage 5 or 6 found anywhere; (b) the more educated, cosmopolitan areas of the world (usually Western) show more Stage 4 than the less educated, more tribal/traditional, less Western areas of the world; and (c) there is some evidence for alternative forms of postconventional moral thinking (especially communitarian themes) that are not in the standard Kohlberg scoring guide.

In comparison to the findings with Kohlberg's interview method, Moon (1985) summarized 20 cross-cultural studies using the DIT (usually a translated and modified version of the DIT). Numerous characteristics of these studies were described and compared, but the most striking finding was the similarity in age/educational trends of DIT scores. Both Western and Eastern countries showed that postconventional thinking does exist across cultures, and support the claim that the shift from conventional moral thinking to postconventional moral thinking occurs in the diverse countries studied. The United States did not come out on top in any age/education level of the countries. If Kohlberg's intent in devising his stage scheme had been ethnocentric—to put his own brand of morality arbitrarily at the top of a developmental hierarchy—he didn't do a good job of putting the United States there.

Gielen and Markoulis (1994) reviewed cross-cultural research using the DIT and report age/education on 15 studies in 14 countries. Their view was that Kohlbergian stages are universal (or at least that the postconventional schema is universal). They considered the general schema of post-

conventional morality to be broad enough to apply even to some moral
ideals of non-Western cultures. They wrote:

> Cultural ideals in their most developed forms "fill out" universal intuitions about
> the nature of moral excellence. Whereas Western secular ideals emphasize the
> dignity and personhood of individuals, religious Tibetans emphasize the "Bud-
> dha-nature" inherent in everyone, Hindus uphold ideals of universal nonvio-
> lence (*Ahimsa*), and Confucians focus on humanistic ideals of
> human-heartedness (*jen*). These cultural ideals are based upon different meta-
> physical assumptions, but they all emphasize a concern for human dignity,
> solidarity, and justice. Moral and cultural relativists have failed to perceive the
> underlying archetype that unites the moral imaginations of men and women
> living in different places at different times. (p. 87)

Supporting Gielen and Markoulis, Roetz (1996) conducted an extensive
examination of the foundational Zhou era of Chinese culture (11th
through 3rd century **B.C.** writers who laid the basis for Confucianism),
and stated: "contrary to the view of the skeptics, Kohlberg's categories are
not simply a product of modern Western male, educated middle-class
ideology, but are well suited to describe the genetic structure of the thought
of the Chinese 'axial age'"(Roetz, 1996, p. 336).

Gielen and Markoulis cited DIT research (including translations) from
a variety of Anglo-Saxon countries (Australia, Ireland, and the United
States); two European countries (Poland, Greece); two English-speaking
countries in the Caribbean (Belize, Trinidad, and Tobago); three East Asian
countries (Hong Kong, South Korea, and Taiwan); three Arab countries
(Egypt, Kuwait, and Central Sudan), and one sub-Saharan African country
(Nigeria). They stated:

1. Studies typically report age/education in terms of junior high, senior
   high, and college students (at least three points in time). And,
   typically, the P scores show age/education trends (i.e., higher education is associated with higher P scores).
2. "The main dividing line for the data is not between Western,
   Anglo-Saxon, English-speaking countries and non-Western, non-
   English-speaking countries, but between industrialized Western or
   East Asian countries with demanding educational systems and Third
   World, less-industrialized countries with less-demanding educational systems" (p. 85).
3. "The three studies conducted in Egypt, Kuwait, and Sudan do not
   portray clear developmental trends. In addition, there are signs in
   these studies that the DIT may not be a satisfactory test of moral
   reasoning in these societies" (p. 85).

TABLE 5.7

Citation of Published Cross-Cultural Studies

Reviews:

Gielen & Markoulis (1994); Rest, Thoma, Moon, & Getz (1986)

Studies:

Bouhmama (1984a, 1984b); Chiu (1990); Cortese (1982); Deka & Broota (1988); Dickinson & Gabriel (1982); Ford, Latour, Vitrell, & French (1997); Gielen, Ahmed, & Avellani (1992); Gielen, Cruckshank, Johnston, Swanzey, & Avellani (1986); Hau (1990); Ma (1985a, 1985b, 1988a, 1988b, 1989, 1992); Ma & Chan (1987); Park & Johnson (1984); Perez-Delgado, Garcia-Ros, & Clemente-Carrion (1992); Plueddemann (1989); Zeidner (1988); Zupancic & Svetina (1993)

Table 5.7 cites published cross-cultural studies.

We hasten to admit that there are immense problems with cross-cultural research using the original DIT and the DIT in translation. Among the problems are:

- Translating the DIT produces an instrument with uncertain validity and equivalence to the usual DIT (i.e., how do we know that a P score of 40, say, means the same thing with various translations?). Translation is particularly problematic given the "fragment" strategy used in designing DIT items. How do we know that translated instruments are valid at all?
- All the samples are convenience samples, not truly random samples that are representative of a whole country's population (e.g., how do we know that the Korean sample represents *all* Koreans?).
- The samples are biased in terms of being the more educated, more Westernized people in a country.
- We don't include some researchers' favorite sample (e.g., the Moose people from Burkina Faso, or people from the temple town of Bhubaneswar, India).

There is, however, a more important shortcoming in DIT research that limits its use in testing the idea of moral universality. Being a structured test, employing a recognition task, the DIT is limited in what set of alternatives is presented to subjects. It was designed to present alternatives of justice-based thinking. (We use the term *justice-based thinking*—for wont of a better term—rather than Shweder's term *rights based*, because the DIT contains items from Stage 4 that are duty-based notions.)[1] The participant's job is to say which of these alternatives (all justice based) is preferable. If the participant has a fundamentally different alternative in mind (e.g., Shweder's "divinity" morality), there is no way to register that alternative when taking the DIT. Therefore, DIT data cannot be used to establish that Kohlbergian stages are universal to the exclusion of other conceptions of morality. The DIT findings—such as we have reported in previous sections—are grounds for claiming that justice-based thinking is important in the United States and elsewhere. Currently, we don't know to what extent justice-based thinking applies to all people, or whether it applies only to one or two billion people of the world's population, or whether it applies only to those influenced by the European Enlightenment.

What do we make of these data? Actually, we are surprised by the degree to which they support the universality claim. Vine (1986), for instance, gave strong arguments for expecting quick and uniform disconfirmations of universality claims from cross-cultural research. By analogy, if this were a sporting event—say, a 10-round boxing match, with universalism in one corner and nonuniversalism in the other—from Vine's scathing critique of Kohlbergian cross-cultural research we should have expected a knock-out of universalism in the first minute of the first round. Instead, several rounds have passed and there is still no knockout. However, the match is far from finished.

Several possibilities are still live options. One possibility is that some reformulation of Kohlberg's stages (including, e.g., the communitarian themes of Snarey & Keljo, [1991]) will be supported as universal. Another possibility is that the next round of studies will disprove the ubiquity of Kohlbergian ideas of development as too parochial (too American, too individualistic, and too rationalistic). A third possibility is that the three more general schemas employed in DIT research will be supported, but not the specific Kohlbergian concepts of Stages 5 and 6. A fourth possibility is that the DIT schemas will describe moral judgment development only in communities that have democratic institutions and formal educational systems, but not in others that are without such institutions or are governed by fundamentalistic religious norms. A fifth possibility is that whatever generality the schemas have across communities, in contrast, the intermediate-level concepts will be particular to one community. In sum, there are many permutations and possibilities; there is much work to do. (Issues regarding the diversity of moral thinking are again discussed in chaps. 7 and 8.)

---

[1]The term *justice-based* follows Kohlberg's characterization of moral thinking as studied by his six-stage theory. We realize there are problems with this characterization (cf. Blasi, 1990; Döbert, 1990; Habermas, 1990), but it is at least a more inclusive term than *rights-based*.

We take note of the cross-cultural work of Snarey and Walker. Snarey (Snarey & Keljo, 1991) and Walker (Walker et al., 1995) are researchers who have made many important contributions to the Kohlbergian literature, who have worked in cross-cultural research, but who argue for the need to take account of other ways in thinking about morality beyond Kohlberg's scheme, including religious ways and communitarian ways. (See chaps. 7 and 8 for some suggestions for study.)

MERGING MORAL JUDGMENT RESEARCH WITH DISCOURSE COMPREHENSION RESEARCH

Drawing from two research areas in psychology, moral judgment and research in discourse comprehension, Narvaez illuminated four issues: (a) how both the DIT and reading moral stories involve the elicitation of schemas (Narvaez, 1998); (b) the nature of expertise in moral judgment (Narvaez, 1997); (c) the understanding of moral messages in stories (Narvaez, Gleason, Mitchell, & Bentley, 1999); and (d) how cultural moral schemas affect moral text processing (Narvaez, in press).

The first point, the elicitation of schemas, was discussed earlier as evidence for the "fragment strategy" in designing items for the DIT. Recall that by the fragment strategy the items of the DIT do not spell out a complete oration with extended moral argument, but rather use fragments of a line of moral argument that presumably would be recognizable by someone who understood the line of thinking. Narvaez (1998) supported the claim that DIT items elicit moral schema (e.g., the maintaining norms schema, postconventional schema), finding that moral schema are elicited by reading stories that contain fragments of moral arguments. Narvaez showed that those subjects who had high P scores on the DIT were the subjects who were more likely to recall and reconstruct the postconventional arguments in stories. The tie-in between performance on the DIT and performance on the recall and reconstruction task was that both tasks evoked postconventional schema for only those subjects whose development had progressed to acquiring them.

The second issue, the nature of expertise in moral judgment, takes off from the well-established fact that some groups do score higher on the DIT than do other groups. For instance, doctoral students in moral philosophy score higher than do college undergraduates (chap. 4). What mental processes are the doctoral students doing that the college students are not doing? What does this difference between those with more and less expertise really mean in terms of psychological processes? Expertise research suggests that the following kinds of differences underlie expertise: (a) the ability to perceive larger, more complex, meaningful patterns in given information; (b) having better schema selection as well as schema availability; (c) the ability to immediately transfer information to or activate a larger long-term memory network; (d) the ability to derive a set of retrieval cues that facilitate the recall of meaningful information later; or (e) the ability to efficiently suppress inappropriate associations. So when it comes to moral judgment expertise, what are the experts doing?

Narvaez (1998) used research strategies from discourse and text comprehension research to gather this information, including how subjects recall and reconstruct material containing instances of moral argument; asking subjects to "think aloud"—that is, report what comes to mind as the subject reads a text that has embedded moral arguments; and asking subjects, after reading a text, to give "moral advice" to the protagonist in the story. Using these research strategies, Narvaez (1999) found that experts not only recall and reconstruct more higher-stage moral argument, but also, while reading, the experts are much more active in processing the text information in explaining the text, making predictions, evaluating the text, and noticing things that don't make sense. Regarding giving advice, experts are more likely than are novices to pick up and endorse the postconventional advice in moral stories.

Narvaez et al. (1999) considered a third issue: how well children at various ages understand the theme of stories with a moral message. Understanding a moral theme entails that the reader integrate various sources of information about actors, their circumstances, each of their interests, and how their interests converge. The reader must draw inferences about the actors' intentions, be able to recognize some facts as secondary or incidental to story events and therefore suppress them, and understand how the events of the story unfold so as to suggest a general way of behaving in similar social situations.

Third graders, fifth graders, and adults were given moral stories to read. Among other tasks, subjects were asked to identify the theme of the story (a one-sentence gist of the story) from among a list of themes, and to pick, from among three vignettes, the vignette with the same theme as the story just read. Highly significant differences were found among the three groups of subjects for their accuracy on both tasks, ranging from nearly all wrong for the third graders to nearly all correct for the adults. The third graders chose, as comparable themes to the stories, the vignettes that contained superficial similarities to the stories (like having characters with the same names) rather than similar moral themes. They also tended to choose, as one-sentence themes for the stories, statements with no special relevance to the story, rather than choosing matches with the theme of the stories. One educational implication from this research is that simply reading moral stories to children may not promote moral character if the children don't even understand the stories' moral messages. Another far-reaching implication of this research is that the study of story-theme comprehension may open a new window on the development of moral cognition.

The fourth issue being explored by Narvaez, Mitchell, and Linzie (1998) is how moral schemas are activated by moral texts based on cultural background. Preliminary results show that a stronger collectivistic perspective of getting along with others (in contrast to an individualistic perspective) is related to inferences about moral behavior in texts. More generally, this research illustrates using the techniques of cognitive science research (in studying reaction time to primed words in order to assess what readers are inferring about text material). Drawing on cognitive science theory is the topic of the next chapter.

6

℘ ◆ ℭ

Stages or Schemas?

In the previous chapters we used the term *schemas*, rather than *stages*, to describe what the DIT was measuring. We adopted this terminology to signal that the type of cognitive structure we envisioned was *not* like Kohlberg's stages in several important ways: (a) We do not define cognitive structures in terms of "operations" (like Kohlberg's "justice operations" inspired by Piaget's INRC operations); (b) we do not endorse Kohlberg's "hard stage" concept of development based on the staircase metaphor, nor the assumption that people are in one stage at a time; (c) we do not make the a priori claim of universality for the moral schemas (for us, the extent of cross-cultural uniformity in schemas is an empirical question); (d) we do not endorse Kohlberg's radical purging content from structure in the Colby-Kohlberg scoring system. And, therefore, to signal exception with these assumptions, we used the term *schema*. We do keep Kohlberg's notion that moral judgment structures are actively constructed by the individual, and that they follow a developmental sequence. We regard the core of Kohlberg's theory as postulating a developmental sequence from conventional to postconventional thinking. As attached to the concept of stage as Kohlberg was, he did say, "I'd be happy to stop patching up Piagetian assumptions if I could see another boat on the horizon which handled my problems and data better than the stage concept" (Kohlberg, 1984, p. 425).

Researchers in the subfield of social cognition may find our use of the term *moral schemas*, to be odd and strained. They will quickly notice differences in their research from DIT research. Thus, either we must find a new term other than *schema* or explicate how the cognitive structures assessed by the DIT are schemalike. A discussion of these matters is facilitated by a wonderfully clear and concise chapter by Taylor and Crocker (1981) on schema theory. We use their chapter to frame the points of this discussion.

SCHEMAS

Bartlett (1932) is credited with promoting the term *schema*, to refer to a general knowledge structure, residing in long-term memory, that is invoked (or "activated") by current stimulus configurations that resemble previous stimuli. The story of cognition starts out with the observation that people notice similarities and recurrences in their experiences, and encode them in memory. The similarities and recurrences are the basis for building cognitive structures such as expectations, concepts, hypotheses, categories, and stereotypes, which are further elaborated into topologies, belief systems, theories, and worldviews.

Schema theory is concerned with the application of organized generic prior knowledge to the understanding of new information. When people are processing new information, several activities are involved: selecting items to attend to, taking in information about those items, and either storing it in some form—so that it can be retrieved later for consideration— or using it as a basis for action. Hypotheses (or concepts) about how the world works provide expectations or preconceptions used for focusing attention, giving structure to experience, and subsequently providing a basis for how the information will be used.

A schema is a cognitive structure that consists of the mental representation of some stimulus phenomena, including the relationships among the elements. Schema are general cognitive structures in that they provide a skeletal conception that is exemplified (or instantiated) by particular cases or experiences. That is, a schema has "slots" that can be filled in by particular instances. (This idea is similar to Piaget's notion of assimilation.) If the slots are not filled in by stimuli, then a schema supplies default values. What schemas do is enable the perceiver to identify stimuli quickly; "chunk" an appropriate unit; fill in information missing from the stimulus configuration; and provide guidance for obtaining further information, solving a problem, or reaching a goal. Schemas need not be available to consciousness or be describable by the subject through verbal articulation, because they can be tacitly and automatically invoked, working "behind the scenes." The major tenet of schema theory is that people simplify reality by storing knowledge at a molar, inclusive level, rather than squirreling away, one by one, all the original individual facts of experience (Fiske & Taylor, 1991; Taylor & Crocker, 1981).

OPERATIONS VERSUS CONTENT

Schemas are general *content* representations of the world. They are not defined in terms of different mental operations that the cognizer uses to make them possible (operations such as the INRC operations described by Piaget). For Kohlberg, the story of development was told in terms of the later stages, using more complicated mental operations than did the earlier stages. According to Kohlberg, people develop insofar as they become able to juggle more things in their minds in more complicated ways. In contrast, the story of development according to a schema concept defines cognitive structure in terms of product or content. (People develop insofar as their concepts are more complicated and normatively adequate.) Social cognition researchers have much to say about how the social world is represented. Frequently studied are content representations such as the following: person schemas (e.g., conceptions like extravert and introvert); role schemas (e.g., fire fighter, professor, cowboy); and event schemas (e.g., attending a wedding, eating in a restaurant). Schemas represent the general structure of some content stimulus configuration.

DIFFERENCES OF MORAL SCHEMA
FROM SCHEMA IN COGNITION RESEARCH

Having sided with schema theory, it is probable however that researchers in cognition will find our discussion of moral schemas strange. Several aspects of our use of the term *schema* (in "moral" schema) are different from the typical use of the term in cognitive research. First, person, role, or event schemas—the most frequent phenomena studied in social cognition—are at a more concrete level of conception than something as abstract as conceptions of the moral basis of society. Moral schemas are perhaps *schemas of schemas* (i.e., conceptions of how roles are organized into a societywide cooperative structure). Whereas the usual schemas of cognition research are more concrete than our use of the term, there is precedence for the study of schemas at this more abstract level—for instance research on "political schemas" (e.g., Fiske & Taylor, 1991, pp. 171-172; Iyengar & Ottati, 1994, pp. 143-188).

Furthermore, Taylor and Crocker stated (1981, p. 93): "[There is] apparent consistency of processing functions across levels of abstraction. . . . [I]t may be that important processing differences dependent upon levels of abstraction will emerge with more research, but as yet these differences have not materialized." The important question to ask is whether or not there are phenomena that can be illuminated by regarding them as abstracted general knowledge structures, such as our moral schemas that explain how people understand, remember, and evaluate current experience. For instance, were the hippies, yippies, and flower children in the 1960s evaluating the morality of society in terms of some general knowledge structure? Were the differences in behavior between Alabama governor George Wallace and Martin Luther King, Jr., understandable in terms of general knowledge structures? Is there such a thing as the law and order orientation? How do we explain the excesses of anticommunist McCarthyism in America in the 1950s?

A second way in which our research is different from social cognition research is that DIT research emphasizes *development,* whereas social cognition research emphasizes *memory.* These differences are not absolute, because crossover studies exist in both subfields. Nevertheless, social cognition research typically emphasizes dependent variables like recall and reaction time, and the hypotheses of studies in social cognition are typically about memory effects and efficiency in coding. Our research emphasizes change over time, and whether or not the later-developed cognitive structures are more advanced in some sense than are the earlier structures. In moral judgment research, the emphasis in development comes at the beginning of defining the constructs—we define the elements of preconventionality, conventionality, and postconventionality to depict a logical sequence from simple to complex.

For social cognition researchers, development is studied (if studied at all) after the constructs have already been defined—the constructs do not anticipate a logical sequence from simple to complex in their definitions. For example, in moral judgment research, the maintaining norms schema is set up as a logical preliminary to postconventional schema. In contrast, social cognition research (Fiske & Kinder, 1981; Fiske, Lau, & Smith, 1990) keys on the distinction between liberal/conservative ideology, but liberalism and conservatism are not logically ordered from simple to complex; instead, they are two endpoints of equal sophistication. Hence, not finding development in many constructs of social cognition may be a result of not building probable developmental distinctions into the definition of the constructs from the beginning.

The important issue here is not whether DIT researchers can obtain permission to use the special word of other researchers, *schema.* There may be another term that is more appropriate (*world view? belief? meta-schema? developmental schema? general knowledge structure?*). The important point is that we find much of the theoretical discussion of schemas by cognition researchers illuminating for "concept-driven" (i.e., hypothesis-driven, top-down) processing of information. We find advantages in attempting to blend American cognitive psychology (e.g., emphasizing content conceptions, tacit processes) with Swiss cognitive psychology (e.g., emphasizing development, valuative judgments). Taylor and Crocker (1981) summarized major ideas of American schema theory in seven propositions (abbreviated in the section that follows as T&C). We use their points to discuss DIT research (abbreviated as DIT).

TAYLOR AND CROCKER'S
SEVEN PROPOSITIONS

1. T&C: Schemas Lend Structure to Experience (p. 94).   When   a stimulus configuration is encountered in the environment, it is matched against a schema from the long-term memory store, and the ordering and relations among the elements of the schema are imposed on the elements of the stimulus configuration. Thus, the schema is activated (or triggered or elicited) from long-term memory in the perceiver.

DIT.   It is the meaning-making, constructivistic function of schemas that are most like the Kohlbergian, cognitive-developmental notion of stage. The notion of concept-driven processing is central both to social cognition and moral judgment research. Our discussion in chapter 3 of the maintaining norms and the postconventional schema are our characterizations of the cognitive structures in moral judgment that give meaning to basic moral ideas such as justice, rights, duties, and social/moral order.

2. T&C: Schemas determine What Information Will Be Encoded or Retrieved From Memory (p. 98).   Which schema is activated makes a difference in the interpretation of stimuli events. Imposing a schema on a stimulus configuration increases overall recall, especially recall of schema-relevant material.

DIT.   The DIT is essentially a device to activate moral schemas. Which schemas are activated by the set of dilemmas and items and to what degree is measured by the subjects' patterns of ratings and rankings. In comparison to social cognition research, relatively little DIT research has been conducted to date using recall as the dependent measure (Narvaez, 1998). Schema research in social cognition suggests that future DIT research should test hypotheses about cognitive structure by making greater use of recall measures and reaction time as the dependent variables, and formulating hypotheses in terms of effects on memory.

3. T&C: Schemas Affect Processing Time, Speed of Information Flow, and Speed of Problem Solving (p. 101).   A schema is an efficient means for moving information speedily through the human processing system. For example, chess experts can "read" and solve chess board configurations more quickly than can novices (Chase & Simon, 1973).

DIT: Similar to the T&C comment: Theoretically, experts in moral judgment should respond more quickly and efficiently to familiar schemas. We are testing this proposition now.

4. T&C: Schemas Enable the Social Perceiver to Fill in Data Missing from an Input Stimulus Configuration (p. 103).   Schemas supply missing information when there is a lack of information, or ambiguous data.

DIT.   Direct confirmation of this phenomenon comes from recent DIT/text comprehension research (Narvaez, 1998). When postconventional schemas are activated while reading moral stories, subjects supply part of the postconventional argument from schemas, even when the story text does not contain those elements. Also, on a more general level, coming to a belief about the morality of society involves an inferential leap beyond the particulars of one's own experience (e.g., the hippies' rejection of society as immoral; the McCarthy alarm over communists within American government), and therefore is an instance of filling in missing data by a schema.

One interesting and frequent fill-in from the maintaining norm schema is the prediction that if an authority is challenged, or some social norm is countered, then the assumption is made that social chaos will result—as if the whole fabric of society will unravel without the vigorous maintenance of all norms and authorities.

When there is good fit between the general cognitive structures coming from long-term memory (i.e., the schemas) and experience (i.e., when many parts of experience seem to be ordered in the way that the schema is organized), the person gains a sense of moral necessity and moral certainty. Zealotry (as in McCarthyism or political correctness) may derive from well working schemas. Accordingly, convictions that are said to be deeply held are those cognition structures that assimilate experiences well and are chronically accessed or frequently rehearsed.

5. T&C: Schemas Provide Bases for Solving Problems (p. 107).   As schemas provide an interpretation of events in the world, this interpretation also suggests courses of action and lines of decision making for solving problems.

DIT.   The basic problem to solve in making moral judgments on macromoral issues (according to Kohlbergians) is how to organize societywide cooperation. The moral schemas such as those we described in chapter 3 are different strategies for organizing cooperation.

Evidence in support of the function of schemas in directing problem solving comes from Thoma and Rest (in press). In this study, a measure of consolidation/transition on the DIT was significantly correlated with the utilizer score. That is, when subjects showed high use of one of the moral schemas (high consolidation), their moral decision making had a better fit with their item endorsement on the DIT (high U scores); however, subjects in schema transition (less consistent use of any one schema), had lower U scores (less fit between DIT item endorsement and their advocacy of action choices). Both cognitive-developmental and schema theory predict this finding. Cognitive-developmental stage theory predicts the episodic consolidation and transition of a stage and the corresponding waxing and waning of decision making in accord with stage acquisition. Schema theory predicts that the problem-solving effects from schemas are more pronounced the stronger the schemas are (e.g., Fiske & Taylor, 1991).

6. T&C: Schemas Provide a Basis for Evaluating Experience. (p. 109). A corollary to this proposition is that people with highly developed schemas make more confident and extreme evaluations; that is, the stronger that different schemas are activated, the greater the polarization of evaluations.

DIT. The Narvaez, Getz, Thoma, and Rest study (in press) sought to find two church congregations who had worldviews as extreme orthodox or extreme progressive. The two groups were highly polarized on a series of public policy issues; group membership in either congregation accounted for about 30% of the variance of public policy issues. Moreover, directly measuring in individuals the strength of having or not having certain distinct schemas (going beyond the demographic information of church membership to individual measures of cognition) accounted for over 60% of the variance of opinions on the controversial public policy issues. This supports the idea that it is schema strength and only indirectly church affiliation that leads to extreme evaluations.

7. T&C: Schemas Provide a Basis for Anticipating the Future, Setting Goals, Making Plans, and Developing Behavioral Routines to Deal with Them. (p. 111). Schemas don't just describe and catalogue experience; they also suggest prescriptions for action.

DIT. DIT research (especially the research relating to validity criteria 5—links to behavior—and 6—links to political attitudes—discussed in chap. 5) supports this proposition. Namely, support comes from the many significant correlations of the DIT with various behavioral and political measures. There is much evidence that the DIT predicts to various measures of decision making, behavior, and political choice.

A RECONCEPTUALIZATION OF THE DIT

With the benefit of hindsight, schema theory provides a richer way of conceiving how the DIT works than do the notions that originally gave rise to the DIT. Assume for a moment that the DIT does work (i.e., consistently produces the trends discussed in chaps. 4 and 5). This leads to the question "How does it work?" We summarize in eight points:

1. The DIT can be viewed as a device for activating (triggering, eliciting) moral schemas from long-term memory to process what is in working memory. The dilemmas and items serve to activate moral schemas if the subject has developed them. That is, to the extent that the subject has acquired the postconventional schema through development, the DIT activates it. Otherwise, if the subject has not formulated the postconventional schema (i.e., if the subject is less developed) the maintaining norms or personal interest schema will be more evident in the subject's ratings and rankings.

2. The process of schema activation need not be conscious or reflective. The subject need not articulate how his or her mind is working, nor be able to tell why an item seems like a good idea. In other words, the process can activate tacit schemas as well as deliberate, reflective thoughts.

3. A subject gives an item a high rating/ranking in importance if two things are true: The item means something to the subject, and is perceived as more adequate than other items. DIT items are like bumper-sticker slogans on a car—they are short, cryptic stimuli that might trigger recognition and assent, or be unintelligible, or be intelligible but seem unintelligent. Presumably, if a subject does not get the point of a DIT item (or recognizes the point but rejects it), the subject passes over the item and goes on to select another item as important.

4. We do not suppose that every rating and ranking to every item is truly diagnostic of moral schemas. There may be some idiosyncratic interpretations of items and some idiosyncratic ratings and rankings. Also, perhaps there are systematic biases as well (e.g., ethnic, geographical, religious, cohort, SES, political attitude differences). But by and large, the

overall patterns of ratings and rankings to DIT items do in fact produce trends that behave largely like the moral judgment construct is supposed to behave (chap. 4). We view DIT assessment as probablistic—over several dilemmas and over large enough samples, it works well enough to be useful for diagnosing the development of moral schemas.

5. DIT items must strike a balance between too much information and too little information. There must be enough information in an item so as to suggest a definite line of thinking, but not too much information so as to discourage concept-driven (top-down) processing. The fragment strategy in writing items is that the items are not so well defined that they invite data-driven (bottom-up, stimulus-driven) processing. Because we are most interested in assessing the subject's concepts—what the subject is bringing to the information processing—the stimuli must encourage concept-driven processing.

6. The extensive research on different ways to index the DIT (e.g., P score, N2 score; Rest, Thoma, & Edwards, 1997; Rest, Thoma, Narvaez, & Bebeau, 1997) is not just dabbling in psychometrics. Rather, it is an attempt to discover which pattern of ratings and rankings best represents the activation of schemas. With the new index, N2, we find that a combination of rating and ranking data is most diagnostic: (a) using *rankings* to indicate which item group (i.e., of personal interests, maintaining norms, or postconventional schemas) is chosen in a forced-choice competition (e.g., the extent to which a postconventional item is ranked as most important across the six dilemmas); and (b) using *ratings* to indicate the extent of discrimination of the low item group (personal interest schema items, as a whole) from the advanced item group (postconventional items, as a whole). These two patterns taken together give the most diagnostic information on the DIT (Rest, Thoma, Narvaez, & Bebeau, 1997).

7. Subjects who have low N2 scores also tend to check off the "can't decide" category on a separate inventory of public policy issues (e.g., they don't have definite views on policy issues, such as "In a democratic society, the press should be free from government censureship"). This relation is not simply due to a general response set of disengagement from answering questionnaires, because on a religious ideology questionnaire the same subjects don't indicate uncertainty (they are sure that "Jesus was born of a virgin," and that "Christ will visibly and personally return to earth," but not so sure about freedom of the press). This suggests that moral schemas function to direct action choices in moral dilemmas.

8. On the other hand, strongly schematic subjects who are orthodox (a combination of religious ideology along with political conservatism and maintaining norms moral judgment) have dramatically different views on

public policy matters than do strongly schematic subjects who are progressives (also a combination of religious ideology, political ideology, and
postconventional moral judgment). This suggests that moral schemas
afford a sense of moral certainty and polarize evaluation of public policy
issues.

CONCLUSIONS

Schema theory has much to offer moral judgment research—even if it
turns out that the cognitive structures studied by moral judgment are best
not called *schemas* but use some other term connoting concept-driven
processing. Perhaps because of the differences of moral judgment research
from research on person schemas, role schemas, and event schemas, there
is ground for progress. Juxtaposing the two research traditions with an
eye on each other may stimulate a creative tension. From schema theory,
the use of memory and reaction time as dependent variables open new
doors for moral judgment research. From moral judgment research, not
only do we proposed a new type of schema (moral schema), but also offer
a way to study development and to link the construct, using an array of
real-life variables, with social cognition.

7

℘ ♦ ℭ

Integrating With the
Domain Approach

In considering fresh approaches to the psychology of moral thinking
(those that have proposed not following Kohlberg's approach), we first
attempt to present the arguments for diverging from a Kohlbergian
approach.

THE BASIC STORY OF DOMAINS
IN SOCIAL COGNITION

A main challenge to the validity of Kohlberg's six-stage theory has come
from one of Kohlberg's first supporters, Elliot Turiel (e.g., 1966).[1] As a
student at Yale, Turiel had become familiar with Kohlberg's approach
(Kohlberg was an assistant professor at Yale for 2 years.) After a period of
staunchly defending Kohlberg's ideas, Turiel learned that another student
of Kohlberg's, Richard Kramer (1968), had found reversals in a longitudinal study of Kohlberg's stages. In addition, Turiel was aware that
Kohlberg was dissatisfied with his scoring of moral judgment development
and had begun a drastic overhaul of his scoring system. Over the years,
Turiel came to the view that Kohlberg was mistaken in his stage sequence,
and began to formulate an alternative to Kohlberg's stage scheme (e.g.,
Turiel, 1975, 1978a).

Turiel proposed that conventional morality does not precede postconventional morality; rather, it has a separate developmental pathway. That

---

[1]For the sake of simplifying the presentation, we identify a research tradition in terms of its
leading proponent ("Kohlberg," "Turiel," "Shweder"). Of course, many people have made key
contributions to these research programs, and dozens of names are connected.

is, thinking about social convention is distinct from thinking about morality: They develop as domains in parallel, not in sequence. Each domain has its distinct pathway of conceptual transformations and generates its own epistemological categories. Turiel seemed to take the view that Kohlberg's theory was too global—mixing up different strands of development that need to be separated if we are really to understand the sequences of social cognitive development. At the same time of this dissatisfaction with Kohlbergian theory, there was impressive research on domains in cognitive psychology (e.g., Kim & Berry, 1993; Resnick, Levine, & Teasley, 1991; see discussion of Pinker, 1997, later in this chap.). Similarly, Turiel sought to define domains in social cognition, arguing against the "global" moral stages of Kohlberg. Instead of universal stages, Turiel proposed that separate *domains* of morality and convention is what is universal in human development.

The separation of social convention from morality is the hallmark of Turiel's domain approach. In one of Turiel's earlier articles (1978b), he stated: "It has generally been assumed that morality and convention are part of one domain and do not develop independently of each other. In contrast, I [Turiel] have proposed that social convention is part of a conceptual domain that is distinct from the moral domain. . . . [M]orality is distinct from social convention" (p. 46). Turiel went on to explain that both Piaget and Kohlberg assumed that "development progresses from a state of conformity to the conventions of the social system to a state of autonomous and principled moral reasoning. . . . I [Turiel] have proposed an alternative view of social convention. Convention is part of the individual's conceptualization of nonmoral aspects of the social interaction and develops alongside the development of justice concepts" (pp. 58–59). Turiel was proposing an alternative view to Kohlberg's.

Note that Turiel's argument was not that Kohlberg's definition of convention was too imprecise, or that Kohlberg's concept of conventionality needed to be tidied up. Rather, his argument was that Kohlberg's use of social conventional thinking to define stages of morality was misguided, because social conventional thinking is in a different domain from the moral domain.

Turiel has been ingenious in devising a method for research in social judgments, called "domain analysis" (e.g., Turiel, 1983). The method lends itself to variation in contexts and contents, and is less dependent on verbal skills than Kohlberg's method. Domain analysis can be modified for use with very young children (even as young as 2 years old). Turiel's research has uncovered moral capacities in very young children, unanticipated from the theories of Piaget and Kohlberg (Tisak, 1995).

The basic method of domain analysis consists of the following three steps. First, comprise a list of acts that involve transgressing some moral or social norm. Examples are: At a playground, one child pushes another child off a swing and then hits him, causing him to cry; a child greets a nursery school teacher one morning by using her first name rather than using her title ("Good morning, Mary" instead of "Good morning, Ms. Smith"); a student chews gum in a school classroom; a person eats lunch with fingers instead of a knife and fork; a person steals someone else's doll; and a youngster takes off his or her clothes on the playground.

Second, for each transgression the interviewer asks the participant several questions designed to distinguish the domains—these vary slightly from study to study, but the general gist is as follows):

Alterability—if there were a rule against the act, could the rule be changed?

Contingency—if an authority says it is all right to act that way, would it be all right?

Generality—if people in another country (school/culture) don't have a rule against the act, and they perform the act, is it all right for them to do it?

Seriousness of transgression, punishability—is this act good or bad? How bad is it (on a rating scale)?

Third, findings are typically reported in these terms: Moral acts are not alterable, whereas social conventional acts are; moral acts are not contingent on authority, social practice, or group agreement, but social conventional acts are; moral acts are judged as wrong in any society, but social conventional acts are judged as wrong only where there are rules against the act; acts in the moral domain are judged as more serious transgressions than are acts in the social conventional domain. There is substantial evidence that people of various ages in various countries do make domain discriminations (see Helwig, Tisak, & Turiel, 1990, for a review of 48 studies that separate the domains using alterability, contingency, generality, and seriousness of transgression as criteria.)

Turiel's method of domain analysis invites exploration with different contexts, actors, conditions, and motives. Recent years have seen an astounding number of and variability in studies using domain analysis (e.g., placing the action at home, at school, at the playground; varying acts by consequence and familiarity; varying age, gender, and culture). In contrast, Kohlberg's method of data collection does not invite much tinkering with stimulus materials or scoring procedures. In fact, formulating the 1987 scoring guide (Colby et al., 1987) for the Kohlberg dilemmas required the efforts of many dedicated people over a decade to prepare, and over 800 pages to describe. Few researchers have the resources to engage in such a process. Even with a complex scoring guide, many people believe that there is more to moral reasoning than Kohlberg's six stages (e.g., Blasi, 1990; Edelstein &Nunner-Winkler, 1990; Habermas, 1990; Strike, 1982). In contrast, Turiel's method provides a way to explore more specific moral concepts than Kohlberg's global stages. Turiel has encouraged the exploration of moral thinking in differentiated contexts and at a more refined level than Kohlberg's or Piaget's global stages (e.g., see reviews by Smetana, 1995; Tisak, 1995).

"HARD" AND "SOFT" DOMAINS

We distinguish two senses of the notion of "domain"—there is a hard (or strong) interpretation, and a soft (or weaker) version. The hard notion is exemplified in Steven Pinker's book (1997), *How the Mind Works:* "The mind, I claim, is not a single organ but a system of organs, which we can think of as psychological faculties or mental modules" (p. 27), and "The mind has to be built out of specialized parts because it has to solve specialized problems" (p. 30). An example of a specialized module is the visual machinery that works to encode retinal information from many individual sensory receptors so as to recognize objects. The visual module serves to integrate this information. A second example is the motor machinery necessary to calculate movement of our various muscles in order to throw an object. Throwing an object requires the coordination of many muscles.

If the mind were a general problem solver (having one, general-purpose method for solving problems), it would not learn quickly enough to perform the specialized functions carried out by the separate modules. The specialized modules have evolved to ensure the survival of the human species in primeval habitat (e.g., homo sapiens living hundreds of thousands of years ago on the African savanna in hunting-and-gathering bands). The modules are "hard wired" into the brain and function fairly automatically, even when their functioning is inappropriate to modern circumstance (that they once benefited our progenitors in their primeval habitat gave the modules an evolutionary advantage and ensured their genetic inheritance). A module's special preprogramming enables it to process information in ways that solve intricate problems.

In contrast to the hard domain notion is the weaker assertion (soft domains) that the architecture of social knowledge is divided and grouped into networks of associated ideas/schemas. (If there were no architecture or subdivision of social knowledge, then all social knowledge would be contained in a single list in long-term memory, the whole list being scanned every time social knowledge is needed—a very inefficient way for social cognition to be organized.) The notion of *soft* domains only entails that there are distinguishable parts of our knowledge structure, and that different parts of this structure are activated to perform some function whereas other parts of the structure are not activated. In contrast, note that the *hard* domains notion entails the stronger assumption that there are separate hard-wired mechanisms for information processing, involving different parts of the brain; that the modules are preprogrammed by evolution and genetically transmitted.

What difference does it make whether domains are hard or soft? The key lies in different senses of the term *distinct*. Both hard and soft versions affirm that domains are distinct. But in the soft notion, *distinct* means distinguishable, whereas in the hard version, *distinct* means altogether separate cognitive mechanisms. Consider the point with this homely example: Husbands and wives are distinguishable from each other, yet they are highly related in families, and their individual identities are defined in their relation to each other (this is the sense of distinct in soft domains). Now consider another example (illustrating the sense of distinct in hard domains): A student takes a class in chemistry and a class in history; study for one class is little help in preparing for the exam in the other; the subject matters of the two classes are entirely different. Whereas the distinctiveness in soft domains asserts a difference among ideas but defines each part in terms of their shared relationship, in contrast, distinctiveness in hard domains implies that the ideas are separated and independent (even though bridges might later be erected across the separate islands).

So how are the distinct domains of morality and social convention related: in the soft sense or in the hard sense? The verdict on this question has important implications for how we regard Kohlberg's theory. If the answer is that morality and social convention are distinct in the hard sense, then Kohlberg proposed a developmental theory that was a hodgepodge of markers that don't make any sense to add together. If the hard version of domains is true for social cognition, then Kohlberg's measure was like adding assessments of the visual module to assessments of the motor module.

Combining such things together is gibberish—no one should use this mess for anything, but should start afresh, keeping the parts separated. Recall the quote from Turiel (1978b): Both Piaget and Kohlberg assumed that "development progresses from a state of conformity to the conventions of the social system to a state of autonomous and principled moral reasoning. . . . I [Turiel] have proposed an alternative view of social convention. Convention is part of the individual's conceptualization of nonmoral aspects of the social interaction and develops alongside the development of justice concepts" (pp. 58–59). Accordingly, one should not expect to find the key moral advance of adolescence to be the "discovery of the system", as our maintaining norms schema assumes, nor to characterize adolescence as a time of increasing authoritarianism (Adelson, 1971), nor to talk about the conventionality in thinking about human rights as a cognitively limited orientation (McClosky & Brill, 1983). Although Turiel did not claim that domains are genetically determined as did Pinker (1997), he did stress the separation of domains, and Kohlberg's mistake of viewing development as a progression from conventionality to postconventionality—both claims that make a Kohlbergian analysis inappropriate.

On the other hand, if morality and social convention are related in the soft sense of domains, then one may discriminate morality and social convention in some senses, realizing that the two distinguishable parts make up a larger reality, and that the two parts have meaning by being defined in terms of their relation to each other. And, therefore, in the soft-domain sense it is all right to use Kohlbergian assessment tools (until better ones come along), because they are not fundamentally flawed (in the sense of combining things that don't belong together). Furthermore (according to the soft sense of distinct domains), one might expect that the decision making of a person might focus on one aspect or another of some larger whole—that is, some people, when confronting a social situation, may activate Kohlbergian-like ideas, whereas some other people may activate other networks of ideas. In soft domains, the distinguishability of aspects does not imply that they ought to be kept separate. Moreover, in a soft domain view, development can be portrayed as conventional thinking giving way to postconventional thinking.

The Argument for "Hard" Domains
in Social Cognition

Turiel made a programmatic statement about the research strategy of his approach in 1986 (Turiel & Davidson, 1986). We summarize Turiel's programmatic statement in terms of four points (the footnote cites quotations from Turiel's article that excerpt statements from the article showing that he does make these points).[2]

- In cognitive science, the postulation of domains is a promising line of research. Domain theory denies that there is a single, unitary cognitive process that applies to all experience and all human cognitive functioning. Specialized cognition occurs in distinct domains, each operating to perform a delimited job with reference to specific kinds of experiences. One major job of research in social cognition is to define the domains.
- Research that separates the distinct strands of development into domains has as its priority the clarification of within-domain development. The age-related developmental sequences that comprise each domain must be the first discovery of psychologists.
- There will be empirical evidence that it is better to separate domains than to study phenomena more globally. The within-domain sequences of development will have greater consistency than the more global sequences.

---

[2]Quotes from Turiel and Davidson (1986) regarding the research program for a domain approach (corresponding to the points in the text) are as follows:

There is a growing body of research, in addition to our own, showing that children's thinking includes separate systems. . . ." (1986, p. 114)

Descriptions of within-domain concepts and their development are, at the least, more fundamental than analyses of between-domain developments. (p. 112)

It is not possible to attempt a description of linkages between cognitive domains, until domains have been isolated and accurately described. (p. 112)

Prior to considering between-domain coordinations, it is necessary to isolate domains and accurately describe judgments within domains. (p. 122)

Studies guided by this strategy, which examined within-domain concepts and domain distinctions, illustrate how heterogeneous and inconsistent or opposing judgments can reflect coherence within domains. (p. 122)

A lack of systematicity with regard to age-related changes would seem to be the rule from the perspective of global characterization of vertical organization. . . . If, however, the findings are considered from the perspective of domains of knowledge, then it becomes apparent that along with the between-domain heterogeneity, there is coherence within domains. (p. 124)

The locus of developmental transformations lies within domains and that analyses of within-domain development should account for three factors: structural discontinuity (qualitative differences on the vertical dimension; e.g., developmental changes in justification categories), functional continuity (the criteria by which the qualitatively different judgments are in the same domain; e.g., commonalities across ages in criterion judgments), and the processes of change from one level to the next (involving deformation of one form of reasoning in concurrence with the formation of a subsequent form). (p. 137)

- Separating out each domain, using data on *justifications*, researchers will find sequences of social cognitive development that are empirically more powerful than global sequences. In short, the payoff of domain research is to be found in the age-related sequences that will be demonstrated in each separate domain. Many inconsistencies and anomalies in Kohlberg's theory and data will be clarified by newly defined domain sequences. (We interpret Turiel to be claiming here that the domain-defined sequences of morality will empirically outperform the global, Kohlberg-defined sequences.)

It is important to appreciate the strategic importance of Turiel's programmatic statement. Turiel recognized that to claim to have discovered domains (in the hard sense) in social cognition, there must be more evidence than simply demonstrating that humans make distinctions among social phenomena or that there is an architecture to long-term memory. Some cognitive science researchers make the case for the existence of domains by citing physiological evidence (Hirschfeld & Gelman, 1994). For instance, they demonstrate that blood flows to different parts of the brain when people are performing different tasks; or that people who suffer injury to specific parts of the brain lose specific functions but not others. However, physiological evidence is hard to come by in *social* cognition, and Turiel instead contended that the existence of domains in social cognition depends on a two-step strategy: People make functional distinctions in social experience (shown by "domain analysis," the horizontal dimension); and the developmental sequences within the newly defined moral domain are more empirically powerful than are Kohlberg's stages (the vertical dimension).

The significance of having to establish both of these points in order to claim hard domains can be seen by recognizing the insufficiency of only demonstrating the first point: that people make discriminations among social phenomena. In order to make a logical point, we use facetious examples: Suppose, for example, that we find that children consistently discriminate hitting acts from stealing acts. Does that imply that there are different domains (in the hard sense) of hitting and stealing? Furthermore, suppose children discriminate the differences of hitting someone smaller and younger from those of hitting someone bigger and more powerful—do we then infer that there are separate hard domains of "bullying" and "courageous self-defense"? Suppose that children discriminate between hitting someone small so hard that it breaks the skin from hitting someone small so lightly that it doesn't really hurt—do we then have more separate domains? Therefore, supposing a new domain for every distinction made by children gets us lots of domains, if only the horizontal dimension is involved. But then invoking domain theory doesn't explain, clarify, or add anything to the original observation that people make distinctions among social phenomena.

Orlando Lourenço wryly remarked that children distinguish between forks and knives, but that doesn't imply that we have discovered a "fork domain" distinguished from a "knife domain."[3] The problem is that distinctions are not sufficient grounds for arguing for hard domains. According to Turiel's own research strategy, without producing evidence for the *two* points, one cannot claim to have found hard domains in social cognition.

We expected to find discussion of the two points in Turiel's latest review of morality (1997) in the *Handbook of Child Psychology*. Surprisingly, despite the chapter title, "The Development of Morality," Turiel did not discuss evidence for developmental sequences of morality. Therefore, we consulted a recent review of domain research by Smetana (1995). In a section titled, "Development Within the Moral Domain," Smetana listed only five studies as the total evidence for development sequences within the two domains of morality and social convention (evidence for the vertical dimension): Davidson, Turiel, and Black (1983); Tisak and Turiel (1988); Damon (1977); and Turiel (1978b, 1983). Let us consider these studies one by one, in some detail. Note that only the first two references are relevant to the new Turiel-defined *moral* domain; the others refer to the nonmoral conventional domain.

Davidson et al. (1983) described a cross-section of 61 subjects of 6, 8, and 10 years of age. Justifications are classified into nine categories. Using ANOVA, two of the justification categories show statistical significance for age-group differences ("personal choice" at $p < .0001$; and "appeal to authority" at $p < .05$; the remaining seven categories of justification do not show significant age trends. Therefore, this study does give some support for having discovered a new age-related sequence for the Turiel-defined moral domain.

Referring to Tisak and Turiel (1988), Smetana (1995, p. 97) stated that this study "found similar age differences in moral reasoning." But in our reading of this study, we could not find any evidence for age differences in moral reasoning that suggest a developmental sequence. Instead, Tisak and Turiel claimed (p. 352), "Justifications differed by domain at *all* ages"[our emphasis], but not *by* age. No age differences appear in Table 2 of that study. Although this is evidence relevant to the horizontal dimension, the study appears to be a disconfirmation of Turiel-defined, age-related developmental sequences (the vertical dimension).

---

[3]Lourenço, personal communication, October 14, 1996.

Damon (1977) was cited by Smetana as support for Turiel's moral domain. Sometimes other non-Kohlbergian moral sequences are cited as evidence for Turiel's moral domains (e.g., Nucci & Weber, 1991), but any and every non-Kohlbergian developmental scheme is no confirmation for Turiel's moral sequence, nor support for there being hard domains. Damon's moral stage scheme bears no resemblance to the Davidson et al. (1983) scheme. Just as Kohlberg's scheme stands or falls independently of Piaget's moral judgment work, the Turiel/Davidson scheme stands independently of the Damon morality scheme.[4]

As Smetana mentioned, the Turiel reference in 1978b is not to the *moral* domain but to the *social-conventional* domain. (A stage scheme about social conventional thinking does not describe Turiel's scheme of moral thinking as an alternative to Kohlberg's moral stages.) In support of a social-conventional stage sequence, Turiel (1978b) cited one cross-sectional study of eight groups, ranging from first grade to postcollege. In all, there were 109 participants. The correlation of stage with age in this sample was an impressive .90. In any case, this study is not relevant to describing sequences in Turiel's moral domain.

Turiel (1983) reiterated the findings of the 1978b cross-sectional study on his seven-stage scheme of the social-conventional domain—and thus that reference does not contain any new cross-sectional data. There was, however, one new longitudinal study (1983) on social conventional stages: a longitudinal study of 60 participants is reported (25 subjects were tested over 1 year, gains were statistically nonsignificant; 24 subjects were tested over 2 years, significant at the .001 level; 11 subjects were tested over 3 years, significant at the .025 level]. Again, this study did not address Turiel's claims about a newly defined *moral* stage sequence.

---

[4]There are several additional arguments for why research on non-Kohlbergian sequences is not evidence for hard domains. First the existence of developmental sequences (such as in Damon, 1977) would only be evidence against the Kohlbergian sequence (in particular, the claim that in adolescence and adulthood, postconventional thinking develops from conventional thinking) if Kohlbergians claimed that their sequence was the only one possible, or if the non-Kohlbergian sequence demonstrated that it outperformed the Kohlbergian sequence (as on the criteria discussed in chap. 4). The first point is not true (that Kohlbergians claim that there are no other sequences). And the second point is not documented by point-by-point comparison of rival sequences (the only empirical study that we know of that lays out point-by-point comparisons on relevant validity criteria is in Rest, Thoma, & Edwards, 1997). The comparative work documenting the superiority of non-Kohlbergian sequences simply hasn't been done.

Second, because the Damon (1977) scheme (and other schemes cited in Nucci & Weber, 1991) applies to young children —and is not addressed to concepts of the morality of society —they can hardly be tests of the Kohlbergian hypothesis of conventionl-postconventional shift in adolescence. Earlier (chap. 2) , we acknowledged that Kohlberg's early stages may need modification. But our particular claim in this book concerns development in the later years.

Third, the opposing side needs to make the case that it is specifically the separation of the social/conventional domain from the moral domain that gives their sequences greater consistency and empirical power over Kohlbergian sequences. This has not been done in the studies cited.

In sum, the evidence for age-related developmental sequences in the new Turiel-defined *moral* domain (as distinct from Kohlberg's stages) seems to be slim. From Smetana's list, the support for the vertical dimension of the moral domain consists of only one cross-sectional study (Davidson et al., 1983) of 61 subjects. Perhaps we have missed some studies, or perhaps domain research has some more recent studies to report. Nevertheless, compared to the evidence cited in chapter 4 in support of a Kohlbergian developmental sequence, we do not think Turiel made his second point about the vertical dimension, that newly defined sequences of morality that separate conventionality from morality produce clearer sequences than do Kohlberg's.

Nevertheless, Turiel and other domain theorists have documented well the first point, the horizontal dimension (Helwig et al., 1990, list over 40 studies on the horizontal dimension). Thus, there is good evidence for soft domains but not for hard domains. Before examining the implications of soft domains for a neo-Kohlbergian approach, let us consider the moral, philosophical implications of separating morality from convention.

THEORETICAL IMPLICATIONS OF SEPARATING MORALITY FROM SOCIAL CONVENTION

Turiel stated that the anomalies and inconsistencies in Kohlberg's data would be cleaned up by separating morality from social convention. How does Turiel conceive of morality separate from social convention? For Turiel, the prototype of the social conventional domain seems to be phenomena like etiquette and traffic rules. Think for a minute about traffic rules: Traffic rules could prescribe that cars drive on the left-hand side of the road or on the right-hand side; there is no moral preference for left or right, it is just a matter of social convenience that one or the other choice be conventionally followed. Different societies may choose different sides of the road; there is no moral necessity nor moral universal about this convention. Furthermore, any society can switch from one side to the other, if there is group consensus to do so.

With this idea in mind, now consider Turiel's description of the domain of social convention (1983, p. 34):

> Social conventions are . . . behavioral uniformities which coordinate interactions of individuals within social systems. Individual members of the society have shared knowledge about conventions. . . . Consequently, conventions (e.g., modes of greeting, forms of address) provide people with means of knowing what to expect of each other and thereby serving to coordinate interactions between people. . . . Conventions involve coordinations at the level of social

organization; they are uniformities that coordinate the stable interactions of individuals functioning within a social system and the ends are social organizational. . . . [T]he acts are arbitrary and alternative courses of action can serve similar functions. . . . Conventions are validated by consensus and, therefore, are relative to the society context. In addition to the variability of conventions, from one social order to another, they may be altered by consensus or general usage within a social system.

On the other hand, in defining the *moral* domain, Turiel seemed to have in mind what many moral philosophers refer to as the special class of "natural duties." Natural duties are those acts of direct help or of avoiding harm to another person that anyone in any society would empathically see as a duty, regardless of cultural teachings (Rawls, 1971). For instance, a natural duty would be the sense that it is wrong to starve innocent children to death. The main idea is that everyone would judge—regardless of one's culture—that it is naturally wrong to starve innocent children to death. What is important to note here is that the concept of natural duties covers only part of morality, in contrast to obligations that are taken on by assuming roles, by contracts, or by promises. And yet Turiel defined the whole domain of morality as if *all* morality were "natural duties":

> In contrast with convention, moral prescriptions are not perceived to be alterable by consensus. . . . The individual's moral prescriptions (e.g., regarding killing and the value of life) are determined by factors inherent to social relationships, as opposed to particular forms of social organization. An individual's perception of an act such as the taking of a life as a transgression is not contingent on the presence of a rule, but rather stems from factors intrinsic to the event (e.g., from the perception of the consequences to the victim). This means that moral issues are not perceived as relative to the societal context. (1983, p. 35)

Therefore, Turiel made the separation of the moral domain from the social convention domain by delimiting the meaning of "social convention" essentially to etiquette, and delimiting "moral" to be essentially "natural duties." Delimiting the essential nature of the two domains in this way leaves out a lot of morality and social conventional issues (e.g., those having to do with contracts, covenants, treaties, constitutions, institutional role systems, and promises). For instance—as cited earlier in chapter 2—Walzer (1983) discussed how Jews in medieval Europe differed from the people of Athens in the fifth and fourth centuries B.C. to provide for the welfare and security of their people. Each community had very different social institutions and agreements about this provision—the ways in which each dealt with moral problems were very much dependent on their societal contexts.

In Turiel's 1983 book, excerpts from the philosophers John Rawls and Aristotle are quoted to support the separation of morality from social convention, as if these philosophers regard matters of morality as separate from matters of group agreements/social organization. But the chief goal of Rawls' 1971 book was to argue for a theory of justice by which social organizations can be evaluated: "Justice is the first virtue of social institutions. . . . A society is a cooperative venture for mutual advantage. . . . [T]he principles of social justice provide a way of assigning rights and duties in the basic institutions of society and they define the appropriate distribution of the benefits and burdens of social cooperation" (pp. 3ff.).

Regarding Aristotle, Alasdair MacIntyre (1981), one of the foremost neo-Aristotelian scholars, characterized Aristotle's position on the societal embeddedness of morality this way:

> I am someone's son or daughter, someone else's cousin or uncle; I am a citizen of this or that city, a member of this or that guild or profession; I belong to this clan, that tribe, this nation. Hence what is good for me has to be the good for one who inhabits these roles. As such, I inherit from the past of my family, my city, my tribe, my nation, a variety of debts, inheritances, rightful expectations and obligations. These constitute the givens of my life, my moral starting point. (p. 220)

> [T]he self has to find its moral identity in and through its membership in communities such as those of the family, the neighborhood, the city and the tribe. . . . The notion of escaping from it into a realm of entirely universal maxims which belong to man as such, whether in its eighteenth-century Kantian form or in the presentation of some modern analytical moral philosophies, is an illusion and an illusion with painful consequences. (p. 221)

If this represents Aristotle's moral philosophy, he can hardly be invoked as supporting the idea that morality is separate from alterable, nongeneral social organization. Furthermore, chapter 2 discussed the arguments of many contemporary moral philosophers who view morality as a *social* construction, not solely the *individual* construction of a person reflecting on his or her own interpersonal experiences and having moral intuitions based on empathy or reversibility. Along with the idea of morality as socially constructed goes the idea of negotiated agreements contingent on the participants, and alterability and nongenerality due to historical circumstances.

Turiel's Conventionality and Kohlberg's Conventionality.   Turiel uses the term *Conventional* in a way different than Kohlberg. For Turiel, the conventional domain concerns matters of social organization and social agreement that are alterable and contingent; they are relative and needn't generalize to other countries or cultures, and are not matters of moral importance. In contrast, Kohlberg uses the term *conventional*, to refer to a developmental stage in which the person wants to maintain conventions as a sign of moral solidarity with the collective, wants to perform the traditional duties expected of him or her, and views him or herself as under the law (civil or religious). Kohlberg stated that the term *conventional*, is a "focus on socially shared moral norms and roles as the basis for making *morally* prescriptive judgments of rights, responsibilities and so on" (Colby et al., 1987, p. 11). In short, maintaining conventions at this stage is very moralistic. As examples of conventional thinking, Kohlbergians have in mind the law and order of George Wallace, the anti-Communism of McCarthyism, the "Silent Majority" of Richard Nixon.[5] The Kohlbergian use of the term is almost the exact opposite of Turiel's—the hallmark of McCarthyism, the Silent Majority, and Wallace's law and order orientation is the *fusing* of conventionality with morality, not their separation.

From the perspective of postconventional thinking we agree that one can conceptually distinguish between, on the one hand, natural duties, and, on the other hand, the rules and practices of social institutions. This is not the perspective of the maintaining norms schema. Indeed, at the postconventional level, these distinguishable notions are different elements that philosophers try to put in reflective equilibrium—elements in tension with each other. However, our argument throughout this book has been that, at the maintaining norms level, the two are not so separate. To start off a theory of social cognition by separating morality and social convention into independent modules obscures their relationships, even if one tries to build bridges between the two later on.

EVIDENCE FOR "SOFT DOMAINS"

The following citation of studies does not undertake to be a complete review of the domain literature, but only illustrative in order to indicate possible convergence between our neo-Kohlbergian approach and a soft domain approach. Research indicates the following:

First, people of various ages and from various cultures distinguish—on the one hand—natural duties based on empathy (intuitions based on the intrinsic consequences of acts for others) from—on the other hand— social arrangements that are alterable, contingent on agreement, and are not universal. Helwig et al., (1990) cited many studies that distinguish transgressions using the criteria of alterability, contingency, generality, and

---

[5]The Silent Majority were the Americans who worked hard, paid their taxes, were law abiding, supported authorities, did not participate in protest demonstrations, were offended by the hippies, and who put bumper stickers on their cars reading "America: Love it or leave it."

seriousness. This consistent finding tells us something about the architecture of social knowledge as it is stored in long-term memory—in other words, it tells us something about soft domains. From these data we are not sure what exactly people understand as social convention (it does not give evidence that 2-year-olds have concepts of society in mind or that they are concerned with how to create a moral order in society), but it is evidence that natural duties based on empathic intuitions are very widespread and occur at surprisingly early ages.

There is no reason to think that there are only three soft domains in social cognition. The architecture of a human's social cognition may be organized into many domains (associated networks of ideas/schemas): For example, there may be a domain for religious beliefs/spirituality; a domain of thinking oriented to career/corporate culture/employer; a domain of thinking oriented to family/spouse/parents/kin; and a domain for race/class/caste/sexual identity. Given that people identify themselves in various ways, and that various networks of ideas are uppermost in their minds, there are likely to be many networks (more than three) that are activated in interpreting experience and making decisions. The architecture of social cognition is likely to be much more complex than having only three divisions.

Second, young children are portrayed in domain research as more complex than Piaget or Kohlberg suggested—children do not follow the simple rule of "obey authority." Children will defy authority and the demands of powerful others for the sake of fulfilling natural duties; children distinguish contexts of authority and the scope of legitimate authority (e.g., Damon, 1977; Weston & Turiel, 1980). Does this complexity exceed the cognitive capacities of children? Taking cues from research in language development, for example, we note that the very same creatures (young children) are able to discern many intricacies of language (e.g., recognizing that the general rule for past tense is to add "-ed" to the verb; but they also recognize that irregular verbs don't follow this general rule). So, likewise, even young children seem able to recognize intricacies of morality where general rules are overruled by specific circumstances. The implication of these studies for moral judgment research in general is that the full representation of social/moral knowledge cannot be represented by simple characterizations, but needs to provide for many intricacies. It provides evidence for the view that there is more to moral reasoning than six stages or three schemas.

Third, parents tailor their verbal admonitions in anticipating the domains that are likely to be activated in their children (e.g., Nucci & Nucci, 1982a, 1982b). For instance, parents admonish with "that would hurt" to moral domain transgressions by their children; they admonish with "that's against the rules" to conventional transgressions. This is evidence that parents intuitively have a sense of which domains their children are regarding as relevant in decision making.

Fourth, decision making is embedded within domains. That is, decision making and the reasons for action are connected to the lines of thinking within a domain of thinking. For instance, Smetana (1982) studied women's thinking about abortion, determining whether abortion was viewed as a moral issue (taking another's life) or as a personal issue (no moral issue). She found that for women who viewed abortion as a moral issue, their thinking about abortion was related to Kohlbergian moral judgment scores, whereas for women who viewed it as a personal issue, their thinking on abortion was unrelated to Kohlbergian moral judgment scores. In other words, the Kohlbergian assessments were connected to decision making only for women who placed the issue in the moral domain. This is consistent with the soft domain view, that social cognition is subdivided into networks of ideas, each providing distinctive schema for interpretation and decision making. It is not consistent with a hard domain view because Smetana used *Kohlbergian* assessment to represent the moral domain. (According to a hard notion of domains, Kohlbergian assessment confuses the separate domains, and is too fundamentally flawed to be used.)

Smetana's study is reminiscent of Taylor and Crocker's point #7 (1981, p. 111), "Schemas provide a basis for anticipating the future, setting goals, making plans, and developing behavioral routines to deal with them." Schemas don't just describe and catalogue experience; schemas also suggest prescriptions for action and guide decision making. If certain schemas are activated, then certain decision making may ensue that would be different if other schema were activated that suggested different decision making. If we understand the word *domain* to refer to certain networks of schemas, then Smetana made the same point as Taylor and Crocker.

Smetana's study is also consistent with Thoma's (1994a) research on the Utilizer score. Thoma supposed that when decision making is placed in a Kohlbergian framework (activating Kohlbergian schemas), then DIT scores are more strongly related to decision making and behavior than when the subject places the issue in a different framework (a non-Kohlbergian network of ideas), in which case the decision making and the behavior are not so related to DIT scores. As mentioned in chapter 5, the utilizer score is a measure of the degree to which subjects are utilizing Kohlbergian moral concerns or not. As a moderator variable between DIT and external behavioral measures, the U score improves the predictability of moral judgment to behavior. When the U score is high (signifying that the subject is making decisions using Kohlbergian schema), then the DIT items predict to behavior better than when the U score is low (signifying that the subject is making decisions not using Kohlbergian schema). In the cases of both Smetana's and Thoma's studies, the subject's placement of issues in the moral domain (thus activating the moral schema) increases the predictability of decision making from Kohlbergian assessment. Thus, we must recognize that all problems dealing with questions of right and wrong are not always placed in a domain defined by Kohlbergian characteristics—different people invoke different networks of associated ideas in decision making.

Both Smetana's work and Thoma's work is reminiscent of research in social cognition on "schematics" versus "aschematics " (general discussion in Fiske & Taylor, 1991). On issues on which a person is "schematic," the domain is regarded as especially important and is chronically used. Also, the person is likely to have activated the schemas of that domain in attending to certain dimensions of experience, and to use the schemas of that domain in organizing experience and in decision making. On issues on which a person is "aschematic," the domain is not considered important—those schemas are not activated, nor are they likely to be well developed.

Fifth, educational interventions designed to prime certain domains can stimulate growth in the relevant domains, but do not necessarily stimulate growth in other domains. For instance, Nucci and Weber (1991) designed one intervention to stimulate thinking in the moral domain, another intervention to stimulate thinking in the conventional domain, and a third intervention that mixed both moral and conventional thinking. They found that increases on the DIT were greater when the moral intervention was employed, and increases on Turiel's conventional stage assessment were greater when the conventional intervention was employed. As in the Smetana study, this study supported the notion of soft domains but not hard domains, for the same reasons given earlier. Nucci and Weber's findings are also reminiscent of the review of college effects by Pascarella and Terenzini (1991), who reported that physical science majors in college learn more physical science and humanities majors learn humanities (p. 65). The generalization is that the domain of growth is related to the emphasis of the educational intervention; bodies of knowledge are internally represented by different structures. Nucci and Weber's study is also consistent with the meta-analytic review of DIT studies by Schlaefli, Rest, and Thoma (1985), which reported that educational interventions that emphasize moral issues have greater increases on the DIT than do those that emphasize the academic subjects of history, humanities, or literature.

Sixth, moral judgments are highly contextualized. Wainryb (1997) argued against broad generalizations of whole cultures—like, for example, Triandis' (1995) characterization of collectivistic cultures as being duty oriented in their morality in contrast to individualistic cultures, which are rights oriented. Wainryb argued that individuals vary within a culture and in different situations. This position is consistent with a soft domain view, deemphasizing the highly generalized between-culture differences in ideology and emphasizing the particular cognitive schema within a person that gives rise to acts and interpretation. The work also suggests that the network of ideas (of a domain) cannot be characterized by a few generalizations, but that there is much intricacy in people's knowledge structures. Social knowledge structures are not simple, single-rule schema; rather, they are complicated and intricate.

The concern with greater specification of knowledge structures (more intricacy) seems to be both on the agenda for our neo-Kohlbergian approach and research in the domain tradition. There are at least five arenas in our current research endeavors that look for greater intricacies in moral thinking: (a) the four-component model; (b) acknowledging various levels of abstraction (the developmental schema, intermediate concepts, and concrete prescriptions and proscriptions)—in particular, recent research into intermediate concepts (discussed in chap. 5); (c) research with the utilizer score; (d) the study of discourse processing; and (e) interactions with cultural ideologies (see the next chapter for further discussion). At the same time, it should be said that we are also impressed with the usefulness in a broader level of analysis, as exemplified in our three schemas that attend more to the *commonalities* in thinking than to *specificities*. Such broad-gauge characterizations are useful in illuminating phenomena such as the hippie rejection of American society, the zealous support of American society in McCarthyism, George Wallace's law and order orientation, Nixon's Silent Majority, and the culture wars between orthodoxy and progressivism. The findings of the DIT as discussed in chapters 4 and 5 attest to the usefulness of analyzing group trends with the general characterizations of merely three schema. It is not inconsistent to move in both directions: looking for specificity and looking for commonalities.

Is Religion a Domain or a Schema?

Our recognition of soft domains has mentioned religion as one candidate as a possible soft domain (as a network of interconnected ideas distinguishable from other networks of ideas that, if activated, may offer distinct interpretations of experience and distinct decision making). But previously (chap. 3), we discussed the morality schema of maintaining norms as possibly conceptualized in terms of religious norms. This raises the question "Is religion a *domain* or a developmental *schema* of moral thinking?" Our answer is "Both."

Religion in the broad sense deals with distinctive questions: Is the universe governed by chance, or from design by a transcendent being? Why is there something rather than nothing? What relationship can I have with a transcendent being? Is there life after death? Do I have a special destiny in God's plan? And, Kohlberg's favorite: Why should I be moral in an immoral world? Religious questions are distinguishable from questions of morality such as the following: What are the possibilities and conditions of cooperation? How can we organize a just society? What kind of relationships can I have with my co-participants in life? What do I owe to others, and what do others owe to me? How can I have fulfilling relationships with others? (Other questions cut across both domains: e.g., What is a good life? What sort of person ought I to be? What values are worth having?)

Religions have various answers to the religious questions; they propose various metaphysics, rituals, traditions, and holy literatures to inform mortals about the transcendent. In this sense, religion is a domain distinct from morality. But religions also prescribe moral relationships. Most religions deal with how humans are to get along with each other in this world. Insofar as religious prescriptions are regarded as divine commands from a transcendental authority—as being beyond scrutiny and human understanding in principle, and as prescribing the law or norms that are established and binding on humans (without fuss or questioning by humans)—then that religious thinking is understood in terms of the maintaining norms schema.

Simply put, we might say that morality deals with this world; religion deals with the transcendent; but when religion defines how we in this world are to relate to each other, then religion serves to define morality. In other words, the questions of one domain (e.g., how can people organize cooperation?) are answered by another domain (be faithful to the transcendent being's will!). A person who is primed to be thinking in terms of transcendent matters (the religious domain is activated) may answer the moral questions in terms of thinking from the religious domain. Crossing the special province of domains has been the subject of much discussion—for instance, in the case of religion attempting to answer historic and scientific questions. There are dangers in crossing domains, in science trying to answer religious questions and vice versa. The basic point, however, is that questions about how people ought to relate to each other are answered in terms of many domains.

Our theory of moral development does not automatically relegate religion to the maintaining norms schema. If religious directives are understood as messages from transcendent beings that are interpreted in the light of human experience and understanding, the fact that those ideals are from a transcendental source does not preclude them from being postconventional ideals. Religion answers moral questions to the extent that it guides (either as the maintaining norms schema or the postconventional schema) the interrelationships of worldly participants. Note that the DIT poses dilemmas about people in civil society (a school principal, police, students in a university, a doctor), not about religious figures and transcendent beings. Therefore, the domain of the DIT is social justice, even if some people respond as if a religious question had been asked.

RESEARCH IMPLICATIONS
OF A WIDER NOTION OF DOMAINS

In order to be more concrete about the implications of a wider notion of domains—with the understanding that we mean soft domains, not hard-wired modules in Pinker's sense of modules—we offer an example of future research in soft domains.

We suggest that the network of ideas that a person has about religion/spirituality might be studied as a domain ("domain" in the sense of a network of ideas, a distinct set of schemas that can be activated in interpretation of social experience and in decision making). Recall Lawrence's study (1987) of radically fundamentalist seminarians who stated that they were responding to the DIT not in terms of human intuitions about fairness, but in terms of being faithful to divine revelation. Recall Richards and Davison (1992), who contended that religious conservatives see matters of right and wrong not in terms of justice, but in terms of "living in harmony with divine law" (p. 469). Recall the cross-cultural finding of Gielen and Markoulis (1994) that the DIT doesn't work well in Arab/Moslem countries, indicating perhaps that people in those countries are by and large not responding to moral questions in Kohlbergian categories (i.e., in terms of conceptions of organizing societywide cooperation, the domain of social justice thinking), but, instead, perhaps they are defining issues of right and wrong in terms of a religious domain (e.g., What would God want? What religious teachings tell us what to do?).

Like Nucci (1985, 1991), we might first present subjects with a list of acts such as ordaining women, receiving communion without confession, ridiculing a cripple, or masturbation. Second—diverging from Nucci—we might ask subjects questions that treat religion as a distinct domain instead of limiting questions to the usual three domains (morality, social convention, and personal); including questions such as: Would God care about this act? Would this act affect you after death? Is it important to consider religious teachings on this matter? Would this act be strongly disapproved of by the people of your religious faith? Does their approval or disapproval matter to you? Instead of grouping subjects in terms of mainline denominations (e.g., Roman Catholics, Jews), we might seek contrasting groups of subjects who are strongly orthodox or progressive in worldview (e.g., Narvaez, Getz, Thoma, & Rest, in press). Third, analyze the data to determine if there is a religious domain distinct from morality, social convention, and the personal, or if the religious domain melds into these domains. If separate, we could determine if thinking in a religious domain is a consistent individual difference (e.g., following the orthodoxy/progressive classification), or whether it depends on the act. We could also further assess how Thoma's U index is related to a non-Kohlbergian domain.

Researchers have much to do in mapping the domains of social cognition. The enterprise involves no less than finding answers to this question: What was the person thinking about when he or she committed the act? Interpreting domains in terms of social cognition (rather than in terms of hard-wired modules) implies the following: (a) that social cognition is organized into associative networks of ideas/schema—entailing that the entire contents of social cognition are not accessed or activated every time one interprets the social world or makes a social decision, but instead only parts (or domains) of social cognition; (b) that the ideas in one domain might interpret a particular social experience in a way different than another domain; (c) that for a particular social experience, different people may activate different domains as a function of situational circumstance, consistent individual difference, subgroup difference, cultural difference, and so on.

To progress in social domain research, we need to find answers to the following: How do we identify the various domains (e.g., moral, social conventional, personal, religious, career, racial/caste/class identity, kin, etc.)? Within each domain, what are the basic epistemological categories (e.g., the elements of meaning, such as "duty," "full reciprocity," or "societywide system of cooperation"; or what are the domain criteria, such as alterability, contingency, or generality)? What determines how different people at different times activate the various domains (e.g., a self-identity defined in terms of being a caring person that makes certain schema chronically accessible, or is it some characteristic of the situation, or something about the stimulus that activates a domain)? What experiences are interpreted by domains (e.g., abortion, drug use, aggression)? How do different domains influence decision making? When we collect information on domains, is the data biased by demand characteristics of the test situation, willingness of subjects to disclose or self-present, a priori theories about how they are supposed to respond, misrepresentative sampling, and so on? Judging from research in social cognition (e.g., Fiske

& Taylor, 1991; Wyer & Srull, 1994), there is much work to do in defining the architecture of social/moral knowledge.

BOTTOM LINE

First, there may be *hard* domains in social cognition, but we don't believe anyone has found them yet. Second, mapping the architecture of social cognition (into soft domains—networks of associated ideas) is a gigantic undertaking. Third, the search for specificity (within cultures, within subgroups, within individuals, or within individuals in particular circumstances) will inform us how complicated morality really is. Nevertheless, at the same time we also want to search for commonalities.

8

֍ ✦ ֎

Integrating With the Cultural Psychology Approach

THE BASIC STORY

Richard Shweder has championed "cultural psychology" (Shweder, 1991)—essentially an approach emphasizing anthropological study, focusing on the way local cultural traditions shape the "ethnic divergences in mind, self, and emotion" (p. 73). Shweder, Mahapatra, and Miller (1987, 1990) reported a study comparing participants from Hyde Park, Illinois (American sample), with participants from the Hindu temple town of Bhubaneswar, India (Indian sample). Shweder started with the procedure of Turiel's domain analysis. First, he compiled a list of acts that transgressed social norms. The list was based on careful preliminary field work and included some transgressions that are particular to India (e.g., a widow eating fish, the eldest son having a haircut the day after his father's death, eating beef) and also acts that were not particular to India (ignoring an accident victim, a father breaking a promise to his son, cutting in the line for a movie). Second, he asked the questions for separating domains of morality from convention (seriousness of the transgression, alterability, contingency, generality). Shweder reported findings that were contrary to those reported by Turiel:

- In India, many of the social convention transgressions were considered more serious than the moral transgressions.
- In India, the social conventions were not considered alterable or contingent.
- The Indians did not make the distinction between the moral and the social conventional domains that Turiel said is universal—instead, the Indians said their social conventions should be obeyed universally.

167

- Young Indians were like older Indians, young Americans were like older Americans.

Therefore, *cultural* difference seemed to account more for the variance in moral thinking than Turiel's domains or Kohlberg's stages.

The differences in moral beliefs between the people of the Hindu temple town of Bhubaneswar and Hyde Park, Illinois, were vividly described (Shweder et al., 1987, 1990; Shweder & Much, 1991; Shweder, Much, Mahapatra, & Park, in press). Shweder agreed with one premise of cognitive constructivists—that people construct reality cognitively, but much of the way a person perceives, understands, thinks, and acts is gradually and cumulatively shaped by the multitude of instructions, explanations, and daily practices of one's culture rather than by reading a manifesto or studying ideological treatises. Cumulatively, over centuries, cultures come to create "realities" in very different ways (Shweder, 1991). Shweder challenged both Turiel (about domains) and Kohlberg (about stages) in the same study (Shweder et al., 1987). And, in other articles, Shweder criticized Kohlberg's universal developmental sequence that is postulated to proceed from conventional to postconventional thinking (Shweder, 1982; Shweder & Much, 1991). From Shweder's point of view, Kohlberg's notion of only one universal developmental pathway for morality is ethnocentric and uninformed about cultural differences. Shweder argued that fundamental differences in human intentions and actions can be accounted for in terms of cultural differences, which vary greatly over the world. People in different cultures build different conceptions of the world, including different moral realities.

TAKING A CLOSER LOOK AT SHWEDER'S POSITION

In the following section we make these points: We argue that Shweder confused Kohlberg's stages with Turiel's definitions of domains, and we discuss some conceptual confusions stemming from equating Turiel's notions with Kohlberg's (regarding natural law, conventionality, and postconventional reasoning); we discuss Kohlberg's and Shweder's comments on religion; we discuss the issue of moral relativism and the social/cultural construction of morality by a community, not by the individual isolated in his or her own reflections and intuitions.

Equating Kohlberg's Stages With Turiel's Domains

Shweder discussed Kohlberg's theory in a number of places (e.g., Shweder, 1982; Shweder et al., 1987; 1990; Shweder & Much, 1991). Shweder equated Kohlberg's distinctions among three developmental levels (pre-conventional, conventional, and postconventional) with Turiel's three domains (personal, conventional and moral). According to Shweder (Shweder et al., 1990, p. 152): "Turiel's social interactional domain theory of moral development turns Kohlberg's scheme . . . on its side. . . . Turiel, Nucci and Smetana accept Kohlberg's proposed criteria for distinguishing moral understandings from conventional ones. . . . " In short, Shweder believed that Kohlberg's distinctions among three developmental levels are essentially the same as Turiel's distinctions among three domains, only with a 90-degree twist. Compounding this error, Shweder suggested that Kohlberg's theory is tested by showing that *Turiel's* notion of convention-ality (arbitrary, alterable social contrivances) does not come before *Turiel's* notion of morality (natural duties); and finding no evidence for develop-mental sequence in his data using Turiel's conceptions, he concluded that *Kohlberg* was wrong.

Furthermore, Shweder (Shweder et al., 1990) believed that Turiel's method of domain analysis assesses the same construct that Kohlberg tried to study with his interview, except that Turiel's interview is better:

> Kohlberg's interview methodology requires subjects to access verbally their moral concepts, produce moral arguments, and talk like a moral philosopher. Several researchers [including Turiel and Shweder] . . . have relaxed the demand characteristics of the moral dilemma interview situation, requiring only that subjects be consistent in their responses to direct probes about the objective versus consensual status of moral versus conventional obligations. (p. 144)

Thus, Shweder assumed that the relaxed interview with more direct probes is simply a better way to get at the same construct as Kohlberg's, not making the distinction in level of abstraction between asking participants about the wrongness of specific acts (e.g., should widows eat fish—Turiel's and Shweder's interest) and asking them to morally justify the structure of society (Kohlberg's interest).

Natural Law. Shweder affirmed the idea that there is an objective morality based on natural law. For instance, it is natural for people to think that starving innocent children to death is wrong, regardless of whether the culture has prohibitions against it or not. But Shweder seemed to assume that Kohlberg confined objective, natural, universal morality to postconventional stages (as if Kohlberg's position would be that people at his earlier stages might not be so sure about starving innocent children to death). Shweder faulted Kohlberg for waiting until the postconventional level to acknowledge natural law (Shweder et al., 1987).

Our interpretation of Kohlberg is that he does *not* wait until postconventional morality to acknowledge natural law, but instead regards his whole sequence as natural (not depending on specific cultural teachings, but instead arrived at through responding to social experience and making sense of the logic of cooperation). Kohlberg followed Piaget on this point. Piaget said, "Morality is the logic of action" (1932/1965, p. 398). This implies that as people reflect on the consequences of their actions on others, and reflect on how to build reciprocal relationships on which cooperation is organized, certain naturally occurring solutions occur to those people (i.e., the stages of morality). In short, Kohlberg did not confine "natural" morality to the postconventional stages. It begins in preconventional morality, and continues on to conventional and postconventional moral thinking. For Kohlberg, natural law applies to all levels.

The Conventional.   Shweder assumed that Turiel's notion of the conventional (alterable, contingent, and relative social contrivances, little importance) means the same as Kohlberg's notion of Conventional. In contrast —as we have argued—Kohlberg meant almost the opposite of Turiel's conventionality. Kohlberg's law and order orientation regards established social convention as what is morally right, and for which one should be ready to do holy battle with the enemy.

Shweder (Shweder et al., 1987) did not find evidence for Turiel's conventionality in his Indian sample (i.e., that transgressions are relativistic, alterable, contingent, unimportant, social contrivances), but instead does find Kohlbergian conventionality (in the sense of an orientation that is dutiful to role, authoritarian/hierarchical, and good of society rather than good of the individual). Shweder believed this to be evidence that the Indian moral world exists apart from the American moral world, each having different moral epistemologies and separate moral realities. Shweder characterized the fundamental difference between the moral worlds in terms of a distinction between rights-based morality (American) and duty-based morality (Indian). This is reminiscent of other cross-cultural psychologists, such as Triandis (1995), who emphasized global cultural differences: individualist versus collectivistic societies having, respectively, rights-based versus duty-based moralities. Kohlberg proposed that we account for the fundamental difference between duty-based and rights-based moral orientation in terms of a *developmental* shift from conventional to postconventional morality. If Kohlberg was correct, Shweder need not have gone halfway around the world to the temple town of Bhubaneswar to find duty-oriented morality. The law and order orientation is alive and flourishes in the United States. According to Kohlberg, the shift from duty-based morality to rights-based is not a contrast between the American culture and the Indian culture, but occurs as a matter of individual development.

Consider how a *developmental* explanation can undercut a *cultural* explanation. If it is true that individuals actually shift *developmentally* from conventional morality to postconventional morality, *culture* has been held constant. The individual who has changed from conventional to postconventional has done so with the same childhood upbringing and with the same cultural influences. If the developmental explanation is true, we need not then invoke centuries of differential cultural evolution to explain differences between duty-based and rights-based moral orientation. Although not denying a role to cultural influence in explaining all the differences in moral thinking, Kohlberg accounted for the fundamental differences in the moralities (duty based vs. Rights based) in terms of how thoughts are organized in the individual head rather than by centuries of differential cultural evolution. Kohlberg's proposal is so bold that we surely need much empirical evidence to believe it. (Hence the relevance of the chapters on DIT findings that provide the evidence.)

Shweder recently expanded his taxonomy of moral thinking from two categories (rights based and duty based) to three basic moral orientations (Shweder et al., 1997): autonomy (which is essentially rights-based thinking), community (which is essentially duty-based), and divinity (which is religious-based thinking). Jensen (1996) used the threefold classification system in a recent doctoral dissertation under Shweder's supervision. Jensen found Shweder's three fundamental moral orientations *both* in India and in America, but used Hunter's (1991) terms, *orthodox* and *progressive* to describe the fundamental differences in world view. In her dissertation, Jensen stated: "Orthodox Indians and Americans resembled each other more in their moral reasoning than they resembled their progressivist compatriots and coreligionists" (Jensen, 1996, p. 171). And so the duty-based moral orientation (orthodoxy) can be found in the United States as well as in India. Although Jensen emphasized that some differences are due to local cultural differences, her dissertation suggested that the fundamental differences in worldview (rights-based, duty-based, and religion-based morality; orthodoxy vs. progressivism) occur within both India and the United States. Hence, *culture* per se does not account for this within-culture difference nor between-culture similarity.

Postconventional Morality.   Shweder described the Hindu concept of *dharma* (one must do one's duty to fulfill one's role, because sin is always punished in this life or the next; the natural and supernatural world guarantees that everyone gets what they deserve). He proposed that *dharma* is an alternative form of postconventional reasoning (e.g., Shweder, 1991). Shweder reported and interpreted an Indian's discussion of Kohlberg's well-known dilemma of "Heinz and the drug" (Shweder & Much, 1991). Shweder presented mostly his own interpretation of what the Indian interviewee really meant to say but didn't articulate as well as Shweder articulated for him. Leaving the validity of such a method aside, Shweder did succeed in making the point that this Indian interview is very different from typical American interviews, and different from the examples in Kohlberg's scoring guides. Because the discussion of "Heinz in Orissa" is so different (talking about *dharma*), Shweder argued that there must be different forms of postconventional thinking, and the interview with the Babaji is one instance.

But let us consider what postconventional means. Kohlberg did use the label *postconventional* to signify the most developed form of thinking, and so there is, by implication, an honorific quality to the term (e.g., "most advanced," "highest developed"). But the term is not simply a term of respect (i.e., meaning "You are a great debater," or "I respect your right to your religious views"); it is more than an honorific label. (We explain the details of our definition of postconventionality in chap. 3.) The Hindu doctrine of *dharma* is not postconventional because (a) it does not recognize the rights of all participants (i.e., the Untouchables do not have equal rights, and therefore *dharma* does not have the element of full reciprocity), and (b) moral authority is placed outside the bounds of human critique or scrutiny (moral authority resides in the Hindu metaphysic, which is beyond scrutiny).

In Shweder's interview with the Babaji, the Indian interviewee, no grounds are given for why another Indian who happens to be Muslim would want to share the Hindu moral order described by the Babaji. The Hindu description of how the supernatural world works would not carry moral authority for an Indian Muslim. The history of India is full of clashes of Hindu and Muslim followers who did not see eye to eye regarding the supernatural world, and the doctrine of *dharma* is currently being disputed and challenged by spokespersons for the Untouchable castes (Crossette, 1996). These Indian critics (representing nearly a quarter of a billion people in India and Nepal) regard Hinduism as fostering a kind of Indian apartheid. They certainly do not accept *dharma* as a satisfactory, sharable moral vision for all people. Shweder's version of the Babaji might reflect the particular views of certain orthodox Hindu upper castes, but their views are not generally sharable ideals.

Religion

Shweder stated that Kohlberg's moral theory is "secularism that rejects divine authority" (Shweder et al., 1987, p. 24). Shweder said that Kohlberg assigned religious expressions to Stage 4 rather than at the higher stages, because "Kohlberg does not believe in superior beings who have privileged access to truths about natural laws" (p. 24).

Regardless of Kohlberg's private views on religion (about which we have no privileged information), he did in his public writings acknowledge that religious belief often influences moral thinking in powerful ways. But Kohlberg did not have too much to say about the role of religion, and his scoring guides contain few references to religious thinking. Nevertheless, he did regard religious belief as not just a single, unitary, homogeneous set of notions; Kohlberg viewed religious thinking as taking many forms. Religious thinking changes with development. In this regard, Kohlberg was influenced by research on faith development by Fowler (1981), Oser (1980), and Snarey (1991).

Moral thinking that is influenced by religious thinking can be scored at every Kohlbergian stage. A very brief description of Kohlberg's speculations on different stages of religious thinking is given here to make the point that religious thinking is not of just one kind (see Kohlberg & Power, 1981). We give examples for monotheistic religions. At Stage 1, God is awesomely powerful as creator and miracle worker, and commands obedience. At Stage 2, you offer sacrifices to God and abide by His commandments so that God will be good to you. At Stage 3, God is a friend and benefactor who is interested in you and knows your every thought and deed; therefore, you want to be your best because you don't want to disappoint God. At Stage 4, religious law supersedes civil law and is also the law of nature. At Stage 5, God is seen as the "energizer" of a just society and a force for autonomous personhood. After Stage 5, religious faith becomes Kohlberg's "Stage 7" (skipping stage 6), answering the question "Why be moral?" (Kohlberg, 1984). At Stage 7, the person is affirmed in leading the moral life and religious faith confirms moral thinking. Regardless of the specific characterizations of the stages of religious thinking, the main point here is that Kohlberg believed that religious thinking was not one single thing, but instead that it changes with development. Therefore, it is incorrect to suggest that Kohlberg automatically relegated all religious thought to Stage 4. Furthermore, Kohlberg's speculations about a religious "Stage 7" hardly evinces hostility toward religion.

However, Shweder made a good point in attending to the role of religion in moral thinking. Other current theorists (e.g., Colby & Damon, 1992; Walker, Pitts, Henning, & Matsuba, 1995) agree with the point that religious thinking is a major influence in moral thinking, underplayed in

Kohlberg's work. Shweder proposed that moral thinking can be analyzed in terms of being rights based (autonomy), duty based (community), or religion based (divinity). These are what Shweder called the "Big Three."[1]

But this analysis is faulty for a number of reasons. First, if one looks at the Big Three definition of autonomy, Shweder's conception still relies too much on Turiel's definition of the morality domain (underemphasizing concepts about the moral basis of society and social order, such as the maintaining norms schema and the postconventional schema). Under autonomy, Shweder lumped Kohlbergian Stage 2 ideas together with Stages 5 and 6, without differentiation. In our view, it is important to know whether a person is talking about rights for one's own benefit (a selfish point of view—Stage 2), or whether the person is talking about the rights of everybody in the society and about organizing a system of cooperation that everyone can support (human rights for minorities, for the unfortunate, etc.—an ideal at Stage 5 or 6). Simply to look for "rights talk" (no matter whether selfish or in the service of a humane society) is to miss a major difference in moral orientation. In general, Shweder disregarded the developmental distinctions in moral thinking that we document in this book.

Second, regarding community, Shweder missed the difference between Kohlberg's conventionality and Turiel's conventionality. A Kohlbergian definition of conventionality emphasizes the duty to perform one's role, the society's good as opposed to the individual's good, and endorses authoritarian and hierarchical role structures. Shweder described duty-based morality as if it were unique to India and Kohlberg had not described it in terms of his conventionality. Again, there are developmental distinc-

---

[1]Shweder's three moral orientations were defined in a recent dissertation by Jensen (1996):

The Ethic of Autonomy.   Moral discourse within the ethic of autonomy defines the person as an autonomous individual who is free to make choices, with few limits. Justifications within this ethic center on an individual's rights, needs, feelings, and well-being. What restricts a person's behavior is mainly a prohibition on inflicting harm to oneself and others, and encroaching upon the rights of other people. The ethic also includes a concern for equality. (p. 230)

The Ethic of Community.   Moral discourse within the ethic of community describes the person in terms of her membership in groups, such as the family, the community, or the nation. Persons are described as acting in terms of their social roles, such as mother, scout leader, or American. The view is that our roles bind us together in intricate relations of differing obligations. The ethic also includes a concern with promoting the welfare, goals, needs, and interests of social groups. (p. 234)

The Ethic of Divinity.   Moral discourse within the ethic of divinity envisions the person as a spiritual entity. A person's behaviors are to be in accordance with the guidelines rendered by a given spiritual or natural order. Thus the person avoids degradation and comes closer to moral purity. (p. 237)

tions that we think should be made. "Community" should be separated into an authoritarian conventionality on the one hand, and into a post-conventional communitarianism on the other (such as that of Walzer, 1983).

Third, regarding divinity, Kohlberg noted the diversity of religious thought (as did Fowler, Oser, and Snarey, cited previously). Kohlberg's more differentiated approach seems more appropriate than treating all religious thinking the same, as Shweder did. In our research on orthodoxy-progressivism, we think there are important discriminations to be made within thinking that is religious (e.g., as seen in the contrasts between two congregations of religious believers—orthodox and progressive—as Jensen [1996] recognized).

Fourth, Shweder's method of sorting ethical statements into "underlying metaphor" or "discourse family" seems arbitrary and overly dependent on language (Shweder et al., in press). In terms of discourse families or underlying metaphors, why are there only *three* classes of discourse? People also do talk about acts "being disgusting," "as polluting," "behavior that stinks"—and as otherwise offensive aesthetically—so why not an "aesthetic" category in addition to the "Big Three"? Additional categories also seem possible (a sports metaphor? a war metaphor?). But what do we have once moral verbiage is sorted according to underlying metaphor and discourse categories? The theoretical or empirical usefulness of such sortings remains to be demonstrated.

Fifth, by emphasizing the differences between the three orientations, Shweder missed identifying particular elements in religious thinking that combine with elements of political ideology and moral judgment development. Our study of orthodoxy and progressivism (chap. 5) provided more powerful explanations than any we have seen with a "Big Three" analysis.

Relativism

Discounting developmental differences in morality, Shweder emphasized differences due to culture. He pointed to the anthropological fact that different cultures of the world have different moral values. Shweder (1991) stated:

> In our social construction approach to the analysis of cross-cultural variation . . . the way individuals perceive, describe, and explain each other's behavior is decisively influenced by received conceptualizations of the person in relationship to the moral-social order and the natural order. We have assumed that even though each society viewed its own moral code . . .as "natural," there is no logical, prudential, or evidential grounds for selecting one type of moral order over the other. (p. 174)

Shweder seemed to be arguing here that, because of the fact of cultural diversity, each society ought to be regarded as ethically equivalent; morality is relative to whatever society in which one happens to be. The de facto norms of a social order constitute the moral standards for the group. This seems to be the relativism that Kohlberg was so eager to counteract (recall Kohlberg's caricature of moral relativism as implying that, in cannibalistic societies, it's right to eat people; that in Aztec society it's right to sacrifice people; etc.).

Surely Shweder could not take the view of simple relativism, as implied in the previous extract. Consider some of the difficulties to which a simple relativistic view leads: In the temple town of Bhubaneswar, the Indian government has designated the Untouchable caste as a "scheduled" class (i.e., scheduled for affirmative action, to further integrate the Untouchables into Indian society). According to simple relativism, don't the people of Bhubaneswar have a moral duty to resist the Indian government because, according to Hindu teachings, contact with the Untouchables is unclean and sinful (Shweder, 1991)? Furthermore, might not people in the town of Bhubaneswar regard Shweder's interaction with the Untouchables as polluting the town—and therefore the people have the moral duty to resist participation in Shweder's study? A further implication is that if there were another culture that believes itself to be superior to Hinduism (like the Indian Muslims in the tradition of the conqueror, Mahmud of Ghazni), wouldn't the people of the expansionist culture have a duty to militarily invade the town of Bhubaneswar?

Given the anthropological fact that there are many moral orientations in the world that are incompatible with each other, what in the relativist's view prevents people from being at war with each other endlessly? The simple relativist view (i.e., that there are no grounds for selecting one moral order over another; that morality is whatever the norms of a group happen to be) provides no grounds for the principle of tolerance, nor for human rights, and no rationale for organizing cooperation in a pluralistic society like India or the United States. To note that different people all over the world think differently does not supply the grounds for believing that we ought to respect other cultures, show tolerance for religious differences, or protect peoples's rights to their differences. Moral respect for diversity entails a very different kind of theory than that there are no grounds for selecting one moral order over another.

Shweder, however, is not the simple relativist that Kohlberg castigated in his criticisms of cultural and ethical relativism on behalf of moral universalism. In other writings, Shweder (1990, p. 206) affirmed that "rightness and goodness are (in some 'good enough' sense), 'objective' things. . . . [M]oral values are not simply arbitrary figments of the imagination or whimsical made-up things." What Shweder had in mind by these qualifications of simple relativism is not clear. It is not clear whether or not Shweder had in mind the points discussed in chapter 2 made by contemporary moral philosophers (about morality being a social construction; about the development of a common morality for a community of participants; that the common morality is subject to constant scrutiny and debate by the community involving the necessity of justification by invoking sharable ideals; and putting community standards in reflective equilibrium with the practices, principles, analysis of specific cases, and moral intuitions). However we still are left with this question: What is the relation of cultural ideology (a preexisting group product) to an individual's cognitive construction of the epistemology of morality?

HETERONOMY AND AUTONOMY

Theorists have debated the relative importance of cultural ideology and the individual's construction of meaning in terms of "heteronomy" versus "autonomy." Heteronomy and autonomy are the Yin and Yang of moral theorists. They are the ubiquitous bipolar opposites that moral theorists put in tension. Simply stated, autonomy is the self-initiated, agentic side of morality; heteronomy is the external, conforming side of morality. Theorists differ in emphasizing one or the other, and in hypothesizing developmental orders or oscillations of heteronomy and autonomy.

Let us do a quick inventory of theorists. Piaget depicted heteronomy as the early stage of moral development, and autonomy as the later stage. For the young child, parents and authorities demand heteronomous obedience; the older child learns to negotiate with similar-status peers and to develop autonomously chosen agreements. In contrast, Freud depicted the id as the agentic, self-initiated, self-serving side of personality, whereas the superego represented at first the external demands of parents, to be gradually replaced by the demands of society. Social learning theory (and character education) has championed the heteronomous side of morality (whereby children are to learn the morality that is handed down to them). Cognitive developmental psychology has championed the self-initiated, self-constructed side (whereby children discover what the possibilities and conditions of cooperation are).

Kohlberg had two suggestions for the relationship between heteronomy and autonomy. The first formulation depicted the self-constructed side as moral "structure" and the heteronomous side as "content"—the basic idea is that autonomous, self-constructive processes establish the skeleton and the heteronomy of cultural teachings supply the filling. Later, Kohlberg introduced A and B substages, which combined Piaget's notion that heteronomy was earlier and autonomy was later with the notion that heteronomy oscillates with autonomy as one moves through the stages. The A substage reflects the type of external norm at each stage (e.g., threatening demands, deals, stereotypes, laws, principles), and the B substage reflects how the subject conceives of reciprocity with others (e.g., market exchanges, good friends, law-abiding citizens, humans governed by moral principles).

Which do we favor: heteronomy or autonomy? We think that both processes codetermine moral thinking. We recognize both the formative power of culture (the heteronomy side) and the meaning-making, constructive side of the individual cognizer (moral judgment, the autonomous side). Although granting the constructive aspect of the individual, each individual does not completely invent him or herself anew. (This point is dramatically presented in Jared Diamond's 1997 Pulitzer Prize-winning book, *Guns, Germs, and Steel.*)

Furthermore, in our view, the two processes do not oscillate or shift with development, but co-occur to produce moral thinking. Inspiration for this dual-process idea comes from text comprehension research (e.g., Kintsch & van Dijk, 1978), in the proposal that the comprehending of text involves two processes carried out in parallel (not serially), by the reader, and that they synergistically interact with each other to produce reading comprehension. (The two processes of text comprehension are not analogous to our two processes of moral thinking, but we borrow the main idea that humans process information in parallel, not always serially.) Therefore, we don't ask if heteronomy come before autonomy, or if they oscillate. In our parallel-processing formulation, moral thinking is made up of moral judgment (the autonomous element) and cultural ideology (the heteronomous element).

Support for our parallel-process proposal comes from our studies of orthodoxy and progressivism (Narvaez, Getz, Thoma, & Rest, in press; Rest, Narvaez, Thoma, & Bebeau, 1998). Recall that in the orthodoxy/progressivism studies, moral judgment was measured by the DIT, cultural ideology was measured by a scale of religious fundamentalism and political identification, and moral thinking was assessed by positions on 40 controversial public policy issues (measured by the ATHRI).[2]

Recall from chapter 5 that the major findings of the studies were that scores on the ATHRI are powerfully predicted by a *combination* of moral judgment and cultural ideology. We speculated that moral judgment and

---

[2]Note that our use of the term *cultural ideology* focuses only on religious fundamentalism and identity in partisan party politics, not everything that could be included as cultural ideology.

cultural ideology combine in the formation of orthodoxy/progressivism, which in turn determines moral thinking about abortion, religion in schools, rights of homosexuals, women's roles, and so on. We speculated that at the time of development in which the maintaining norms schema is in ascendance, people are especially appreciative of fundamentalist religion because such religious ideologies supply clear and strong norms and unambiguous authorities. (For the person who is coming to the dawning realization that society must have some norms and authorities, an ideology that supplies clear norms and strong authorities is especially appreciated.) Furthermore, fundamentalist religions that discourage questioning of their authority also block further development in moral judgment (whereas postconventional morality invites questioning and debate). Thus, we have two processes that are reciprocating and mutually shaping each other: Moral judgment creates the conceptual bedrock in which religious fundamentalism makes sense (moral judgment serves to select and interpret cultural ideology); and, in turn, cultural ideology affects the progress of moral judgment.

Cultural psychology and our neo-Kohlbergian approach might ally to pursue these leads. We can imagine several kinds of studies. First, one type of study is identifying and describing the experience out of which moral judgment categories develop—as, for instance, in Shweder (1990). Daily experiences present the basic material for the work of meaning-making of moral judgment. A diet of certain cultural peculiarities and daily practices is likely to affect the epistemological categories of the human cognizer. Presumably, most people do not form their moral thinking by reading treatises on ideology. This, then, is the study of how cultural ideology is transmitted.

Second, another type of study (according to this parallel-processing idea) is that moral judgment development constrains the selection and interpretation of cultural ideology. Presumably, the developmental capacities of the individual make one more or less receptive to aspects of one's cultural ideology. One's particular experiences and how one reflects on them influence the moral thinking that is formulated.

Third, cultural ideologies might limit or facilitate the development of moral judgment. As one instance of this influence, we have cited orthodox ideologies that cast as sinful and heretical the questioning and scrutiny of morality. Presumably, this has a limiting effect on the individual's movement into postconventional thinking. A different instance of the limiting influence of cultural ideology on moral judgment is described by Banfield (1958) of a region in southern Italy (Lucania). In this region, cooperation is so meager, solidarity so weak, and public spirit so corrupt that people there rarely rise above the personal interest schema (or Kohlberg's Stage 2). In fact, Banfield described the time under facism (Mussolini) as an improvement in community cooperation. Furthermore, we might ask, "Do cultural ideologies that have clear norms and strong authorities foster development out of personal interests into maintaining norms?" (This brings to mind the recent condemnation in the American press of the brutality and primitiveness of Singapore, because of the practice of caning law violators; yet, Singapore has an enviable lack of crime compared with the United States) Are orthodox ideologies more efficient at fostering development into conventionality than are progressive ideologies?

This view of the reciprocal dynamics of culture and cognitive development is different from Kohlberg's structure-content view, in that moral judgment is viewed as being shaped by cultural ideology, not just providing the skeleton for cultural content to fill in. Our view is also different from Shweder's (1990), which doesn't credit a place for Kohlbergian-type development in selecting and interpreting cultural ideology. In sum, we argue for the place of Kohlbergian moral judgment, realizing that there is more to the psychology of morality than moral judgment.

9

ᕳ ◆ ᕲ

Summary

THE MAJOR POINTS

There are five major points we made in this book:

1. Many criticisms of Kohlberg's approach have been made over the years; some of them (from both psychologists and philosophers) require modifications in the classic Kohlberg approach. After an analysis of various criticisms, we presented our version of a neo-Kohlbergian approach based on DIT research.

2. We proposed a seven-part operationalization of construct validity for a test of moral judgment and review studies done over the past 25 years on the DIT. We concluded that the supporting evidence is plentiful and consistent.

3. DIT research has led to many new issues, new theorizing, and new findings, and is continuing to provide a platform for widening research. At the same time, we realize that the DIT is due for some updating, now that a full cycle of research has been completed with the original version. We are now experimenting with new dilemmas, new items, and new indexes—and encourage others to experiment with DIT2.

4. Schema theory offers new ideas for research, as well as a reconceptualization of how the DIT works.

5. The approaches of domain theory and of cultural psychology can be integrated with our neo-Kohlbergian approach; the merging suggests many new lines of research.

Now we briefly summarize the major supporting arguments for each of these five points developed in this book.

Criticisms by Psychologists,
and Philosophers and the DIT Proposal

Sifting through the many criticisms of Kohlberg's own approach made in the past 3 decades, several criticisms by psychologists and philosophers seem to us to be valid, requiring modifications in theory and method (chap. 2). *Psychological* research presents four major problems: the staircase model of stage development (and the definition of stages in terms of justice operations); the interview method that is overreliant on verbal articulation; the underestimation of young children's empathic capacities; and the lack of postconventional thinking in Kohlberg's studies. *Philosophical* problems demanding change are: Kohlberg's adoption of the assumptions of foundational principlism and deductivism; failure to recognize bottom-up morality (induction from specific cases) and the process of consensus building found in common morality; and conceptions of the social construction of morality entailing embeddedness in historical/communal context (instead of the lonely individual decision maker with only his or her own cognitive rationality as a guide).

Given these problems, DIT research proposes modifications in theory and method (chap. 3). We use a model of development that conceptualizes change in terms of shifting distributions instead of the staircase stage model—defining developmental stages not in terms of operations but more in terms of the content of schemas. We don't rely on verbal explanation given in interviews (and on its face validity); instead, we use a recognition task for data collection and establish construct validity in terms of seven criteria. We are open to redefinitions of the early stages of young children's thinking, but because DIT research isn't addressed to young children, we remain focused on adolescent and adult moral thinking. We redefine theoretically the notion of "postconventional schema" so that it does not presume a deontological, Kantian/Rawlsian, deductivistic moral philosophy. We renounce the claim to advance a specific normative moral theory, although we do maintain a psychological developmental theory (and the general claim that postconventionality is more philosophically adequate than is conventionality). The redefinition of postconventionality involves distinguishing content from structure in a different way than Kohlberg's approach. Our definition incorporates more "content" than does Kohlberg's notion of justice operations. We also redefine the distinction between relativism and universalism. There are not just two positions on this issue—simple relativism (mindless conformity to the group) and universalism. In the concept of common morality—a morality that builds both bottom-up and top-down in reflective equilibrium, open to public scrutiny—we have a third position that is not mindless conformity, but central to the notion of democracy.

Validity and Reliability Studies of the DIT

We operationalize construct validity in terms of seven criteria:

- *Discrimination of more expert groups from less expert groups.* This involves the familiar cross-sectional study in age/educational trends, much used in developmental research. The traditional problem with cross-sectional studies is that unknown confounds may be causing the group differences instead of developmental differences. This problem is ameliorated by having large composite samples (into the thousands of subjects) of diverse groups, collected by diverse researchers, under diverse conditions, with many replications.
- *Upward trends in longitudinal data.* Although many of the longitudinal studies are conducted with college students (freshmen to seniors), there are studies of other groups as well. Colleges seem to do an especially good job in shifting conventional thinking to postconventional thinking.
- *Sensitivity to educational interventions.* This is another type of study of intra-individual developmental change (testing and retesting the same subjects), and there are many instances of this type. The literature offers many ideas for educational programs.
- *Developmental hierarchy (higher is better).* As discussed in chapter 4, one line of study is to relate the DIT to separate assessments of moral comprehension (higher DIT scorers comprehend and recall more of the moral arguments). Another approach is to relate the DIT to other developmental measures (higher DIT scorers tend to be higher developed on the other measures).
- *Links to real-life behavior.* Behavior has been studied with a vast array of measures (many contents, naturalistic and experimental, and based on self-report, observations, and ratings by others). The theoretical brunt of these studies is to affirm that the set of dilemmas and items that we use in the DIT—despite their limitedness in scope and in everyday realism—do predict to significant measures outside themselves and, therefore, are not tapping an insignificant, irrelevant, or useless psychological dimension. It remains to be seen if other data-gathering procedures illuminate better the phenomena of micromorality and macromorality.

- *Links to political attitude and choice.* In our interpretation of the DIT, we have emphasized how the construct of moral judgment measures concepts of the morality of society (macro-morality). It is consistent with this interpretation that the DIT should have high predictability to controversial public policy issues—matters of political choice that are of foremost relevance today.
- *Reliability and internal consistency.* There are a number of subissues that we report on here, including some very recent developments in indexing. Our conclusion is that the DIT has adequate reliability.

Chapter 4 presented data from both "classic" early studies and recent studies, and also cited hundreds of studies conducted over the past 25 years involving thousands of subjects. The general conclusion is that the DIT has consistent and general usefulness. A conceptual thread running throughout hundreds of studies is their relevance to the seven validity criteria.

New Issues, New Theories, New Findings

Although the validity studies speak to the stability and usefulness of research with the DIT, many new issues and controversies have been the focus of other studies (chap. 5). Empirical findings have led to consideration of new issues and new research beyond the original conceptions of the DIT. We have responded to critics. Recent years have been particularly fruitful; there are not signs that this research is winding down from exhaustion. The new research discussed in Chapter 5 includes the following:

The four-component model (and ideas for moral education programs).
Intermediate concepts.
The utilizer moderator.
Threats to validity (verbal ability, political attitude, sex/gender).
Religion, and the orthodoxy/progressive construct.
Life experiences (and the larger picture of adult development).
Cross-cultural studies.
Merging moral judgment research with discourse comprehension research.
New indexes, new dilemmas, and new items (DIT2).

Schema Theory

We refer to the cognitive structures studied by the DIT as *schemas* rather than *stages,* to signal our differences with some of the classic formulations by Kohlberg; however, we recognize that the cognitive structures we talk about are somewhere between cognitive developmental stages and social cognition's schemas. Social cognition research suggests many new leads for moral judgment research, especially with regard to hypotheses about memory and the processing of information, both efficiently and with errors. Furthermore, schema theory provides new ways to understand how the DIT works as a procedure: The DIT can be regarded as a device for activating moral schemas. Patterns of ratings and rankings indicate the degree to which a subject has developed moral schemas. DIT items are written to encourage top-down (concept-driven) processing, so as to assess the schema that the subject brings to moral situations. Moral schemas function in the encoding of social situations, in filling in missing information, in supplying the logical linkages among stimulus elements, and in guiding action and problem solving.

Integrating Our Neo-Kohlbergian Approach With Turiel's Domain Approach and With Shweder's Cultural Psychology Approach

Turiel began the domain approach as an alternative to Kohlberg's approach, contending that Kohlberg's notion of a developmental sequence from conventional to postconventional morality mixed up the separate domains of morality and convention. We distinguish two senses of the term *Domain*: a hard or strong interpretation, and a soft or weak interpretation. Cognitive science has been successful in advancing the notion of hard domains: hard-wired modules for information processing that have evolved, pre-programmed to carry out specialized information processing operations. The notion of soft domains is that the architecture of social knowledge is organized into networks of connected or associated ideas, and that only part of social knowledge is activated by particular social experiences. We argue that Turiel has been unsuccessful in demonstrating the existence of hard domains in social cognition (by his own criteria); however, there is much evidence for soft domains. Part of the evidence for soft domains is corroborated by DIT research, and we propose further investigation into the architecture of social knowledge in intermediate concepts, the Utilizer score, and the investigation of more soft domains than those now studied.

Shweder also starts out his approach as an alternative to both Turiel's domains and to Kohlberg's stages. But Shweder's research omits the developmental distinctions that we have found useful. We agree with some of the directions that Shweder suggests: considering morality as a social construction and embedded in the particulars of life, studying the everyday influences that convey ideologies, and studying the influence of religion upon moral thinking. Based on our research on the orthodoxy/progressive construct, we suggest an alliance with cultural psychology that combines moral judgment (the self-construction of epistemological categories) with cultural ideology (interpretations that are external to the individual, and culturally-derived), viewing both as reciprocally influencing the other in the formation of moral thinking.

Throughout this book we do not claim that the moral judgment construct (or the DIT) is all there is to the psychology of morality, nor that the DIT is the ultimate instrument of moral judgment. But we do claim that the development of moral judgment is an important part of the psychology of morality, especially the transition from conventional to postconventional thinking in adolescence and adulthood, as originally stated by Lawrence Kohlberg.

Appendix A

ATHRI

Attitudes about public policies

Your Identification number

|_|_|_|_|_|

*[**Directions:** For each of the following statements, circle the number which best expresses your opinion: 1=Strongly Agree (SA), 2=Agree (A), 3=Uncertain (U), 4=Disagree (D), 5=Strongly Disagree (SD).]*

SA	A	U	D	SD	
1	2	3	4	5	1. Counselors should encourage girls to consider training to become pilots, carpenters, military officers, truck drivers, and other usually male occupations.
1	2	3	4	5	2. Laws should be passed to regulate the activities of religious cults that have come here from Asia.
1	2	3	4	5	3. Citizens should be allowed to voice their opinions if they disagree with their government.
1	2	3	4	5	4. Welfare assistance should be limited to those who are really needy and not given to those who refuse to work.
1	2	3	4	5	5. Freedom of speech should be a basic human right.
1	2	3	4	5	6. The government should find ways to insure a good food supply for poor children in our large inner-cities.
1	2	3	4	5	7. Teenagers should be allowed to receive medical treatment without parental consent.
1	2	3	4	5	8. Occasionally it is reasonable to deny the right to vote to some groups; for instance to persons involved in un-American activities or to members of the Communist party.
1	2	3	4	5	9. If we let religious fundamentalists teach in our schools they will try to indoctrinate our children.*
1	2	3	4	5	10. Our nation should work toward liberty and justice for all.
1	2	3	4	5	11. If some of its students don't speak English, a school should add bilingual teachers even if doing so is expensive.

Appendix A continued on next page

Appendix A continued

SA	A	U	D	SD	
1	2	3	4	5	12. All people should have food, clothing, and shelter
1	2	3	4	5	13. Professors in state-run universities should be granted academic freedom in their teaching, even if they teach marxist ideas.
1	2	3	4	5	14. Books should be banned if they are written by people who have been involved in right-wing White Supremacy groups.*
1	2	3	4	5	15. Churches should not change American Indians' beliefs.
1	2	3	4	5	16. It is fair to put to death a person who has willfully taken the life of another.
1	2	3	4	5	17. In a democratic country, the press should be free from government censorship.
1	2	3	4	5	18. If an Equal Rights Amendment were adopted, it would disrupt society and the division of labor between males and females.
1	2	3	4	5	19. If unemployed people cannot find work, they just are not looking hard enough
1	2	3	4	5	20. Teachers who are homosexuals can be good role models for our children, just like anyone else.
1	2	3	4	5	21. People from Fascist countries should not be allowed to come here and spread their propaganda.*
1	2	3	4	5	22. Publishers of school books should use inclusive language like person or people, and avoid man or men when appropriate.
1	2	3	4	5	23. The basic rights in the constitution (the right to vote, to be presumed innocent until proven guilty, etc.) Should be upheld for all citizens.
1	2	3	4	5	24. The full range of birth control information should be made available to the public at large.
1	2	3	4	5	25. People who oppose the government's taxation policies should not be allowed to organize demonstrations.*
1	2	3	4	5	26. People should have freedom of religion (worship as they choose) and freedom of belief (believe as they choose).
1	2	3	4	5	27. Homosexuals shouldn't be hired for jobs requiring considerable contact with the public.
1	2	3	4	5	28. We should not waste time having costly trials for people we are 100% sure are guilty.

Appendix A continued on next page

Appendix A continued

SA	A	U	D	SD	
1	2	3	4	5	29. People should not be discriminated against because of their race, sex, religion, or handicap in a democratic country like ours.
1	2	3	4	5	30. People who oppose the government's military policies should not be allowed to organize demonstrations.
1	2	3	4	5	31. Teachers who are fundamentalist Christians can be good role models for our children, just like anyone else.*
1	2	3	4	5	32. A terminally ill and suffering patient should be able to have the doctor "pull the plug."
1	2	3	4	5	33. Police should not have to get search warrants when they are pursuing suspects with known criminal records.
1	2	3	4	5	34. People from Communist countries should not be allowed to come here and spread their propaganda.
1	2	3	4	5	35. Books should be banned if they are written by people who have been involved in un-American activities.
1	2	3	4	5	36. Professors in state-run universities should be granted academic freedom in their teaching, even if they teach male superiority.*
1	2	3	4	5	37. If they are quiet and well-behaved, students should be allowed to wear black armbands in school to protest a governmental policy or action with which they disagree.
1	2	3	4	5	38. Abortion is any woman's right.
1	2	3	4	5	39. People in a free country should not have to worry about unwarranted intrusions by the government into their private lives.
1	2	3	4	5	40. Loyal citizens should be given full constitutional rights but disloyal citizens should not expect to be given all those rights.
1	2	3	4	5	41. It is legitimate for authorities to curtail the activities of groups protesting a governmental policy or action.
1	2	3	4	5	42. If we let atheists teach in our schools they will try to indoctrinate our children.
1	2	3	4	5	43. Occasionally it is reasonable to deny the right to vote to some groups; for instance to persons involved in militia groups with stockpiles of weapons.*

Appendix A continued on next page

Appendix A continued

SA	A	U	D	SD	
1	2	3	4	5	44. The Roman Catholic Church should work toward allowing women to enter the priesthood.
1	2	3	4	5	45. People should be able to have a voice in how they deal with their own physical well-being, with their health and their illnesses.
1	2	3	4	5	46. Wire-tapping and surveillance are necessary, even if they violate the law, when danger to the public is suspected.
1	2	3	4	5	47. If busing is the best way to ensure that black students have the same educational opportunities as white students, it should be encouraged.
1	2	3	4	5	48. Gun ownership is every citizen's right.*

Note: This version has eight additional items to Getz's (1985) original 40 items. Additional items are marked by an asterisk; Items 9, 14, 21, 25, 31, 36, 43, and 48 were not in original.

Appendix B

Services and Materials Available
From the Minnesota Center

"Info Pack" is a 20+ page package of information about the center. Included are a copy of the DIT, and availability of other instruments; a list of recent papers and publications by center staff and affiliates (often the prepublication papers are available years before the work gets published and listed in bibliographies); description of the Scoring Service of DITs from the center; announcements of new indexes and new forms; and prices and ordering information of materials from the center. This packet is *free* from:

The Center for the Study of Ethical Development
206-A Burton Hall/178 Pillsbury Drive SE
University of Minnesota
Minneapolis, MN 55455
(Phone: 612-624-0876; FAX: 612-624-8241)
E-mail:narvaez@tc.umn.edu
Internet: http://edpsy.coled.umn.edu/PSYCHF/CSED/

DIT Files is a collection of over 1,500 reports, dissertations, journal articles, and books housed in Burton Hall, University of Minnesota. It is the most extensive collection of DIT research reports in existence. Visitors are invited to come to use the files and make personal copies. (Call the center for further details.)

DitKit is a 3 1/2" computer diskette with over 1,500 references on it. It is a listing of the contents of the DIT files. Being in ASCII format allows electronic searches of authors or topics using a word processor or data base program. (Available from center for $5.00.)

Ideas for Research With the DIT is a 60+ page booklet plus a demonstration diskette for DIT researchers, students, and advisors, and for faculty teaching courses in morality and methodology. This booklet describes types of studies with the DIT; how to put the data file from the Scoring Service into the statistical package program of SPSS®; how to generate various graphs and statistical analyses, norming data for the items of the DIT, and various tips and tricks in data analysis. The diskette contains DitKit. (Available from the center for $20.)

Summer institutes are 4-day summer sessions at Minnesota for researchers and students to demonstrate the services of the center, present an overview of DIT research, discuss current research of center staff and affiliates, and consult on your project (regarding references and past research or the mechanics of data analysis and design). Call the center for details.

REFERENCES

Note: Published articles and books on the DIT are indicated by an asterisk ("*") in front of the author's name.

*Adamson, T. E., Baldwin, D. C., Sheehan, T. J., & Oppenberg, A. A. (1997). Characteristics of surgeons with high and low malpractice claim rates. *West Journal of Medicine, 166,* 37–44.

Adelson, J. (1971). The political imagination of the young adolescent. *Daedalus, 100,* 1013–1050.

Adelson, J., & Beall, L. (1970, May). Adolescent perspectives on law and government. *Law and Society Review,* pp. 495–504.

Adelson, J., Green, B., & O'Neil, R. (1969). The growth of the idea of law in adolescence. *Developmental Psychology, 1,* 327–332.

Adelson, J. & O'Neil, R. (1966). The development of political thought in adolescence: The sense of community. *Journal of Personality and Social Psychology, 4,* 295–306.

*Armstrong, M. (1987, Spring). Moral development and accounting education. *Journal of Accounting Education,* 27–43.

*Armstrong, M. (1993, Spring). Ethics and professionalism in accounting education. *Journal of Accounting Education,* 1–14.

*Arnold, D., & Ponemon, L. (1987, April). Moral judgment perspective for the various auditing judgment issues. *Proceedings of the British Accounting Association,* 47–57.

*Arnold, D., & Ponemon, L. (1991). Internal auditors' perceptions of whistle-blowing and the influence of moral reasoning. *Auditing: A Journal of Practice & Theory, 10*(2),1–15.

Baab, D. A., & Bebeau, M. J. (1990). The effect of instruction on ethical sensitivity. *Journal of Dental Education, 54*(1), 44.

*Bagarozzi, D. (1982). The effects of cohesiveness on distributive justice. *Journal of Psychology, 110,* 267–273.

*Bakken, L., & Ellsworth, R. (1990). Moral development in adulthood: Its relationship to age, sex, and education. *Educational Research Quarterly, 14*(2), 2–9.

*Bakken, L., & Romig, C. (1994). The relationship of perceived family dynamics to adolescents' principled moral reasoning. *Journal of Adolescent Research, 9*(4), 442–457.

*Baldwin, D. C., Adamson, T. E., Self, D. J., Sheehan, T. J., & Oppenberg, A. A. (1996). Moral reasoning and malpractice: A pilot study of orthopedic surgeons. *The American Journal of Orthopedics,* 481–486.

*Baldwin, D., Daugherty, S., & Self, D. (1991). Changes in moral reasoning during medical school. *Academic Medicine, 66*(9), 51–53.

Banfield, E. C. (1958). *The moral basis of a backward society.* New York: Free Press.

Bargh, J. A. (1989). Conditional automaticity: Varieties of automatic influence on social perception and cognition. In J. S. Uleman & J. A. Bargh (Eds.), *Unintended thought* (pp. 3–51). New York: Guilford.

*Barnett, R., Evens, J., & Rest, J. (1995). Faking moral judgment on the Defining Issues Test. *British Journal of Social Psychology, 34,* 267–278.

Bartlett, F. A. (1932). *A study in experimental and social psychology.* New York: Cambridge University Press.

*Baxter, G. D., & Rarick, C. A. (1987). Education for the moral development of managers: Kohlberg's stages of moral development and integrative education. *Journal of Business Ethics, 6,* 243–248.

Beauchamp, T. L., & Childress, J. F. (1994). *Principles of biomedical ethics (4th ed.).* New York: Oxford University Press.

*Bebeau, M. J. (1983a). Professional responsibility curriculum report: American College fellows serve as expert assessors. *The Journal of the American College of Dentists, 50*(2), 20–30.

*Bebeau, M. J. (1983b, September/October). Teaching professional ethics. *Encounters* (the magazine of The Science Museum of Minnesota) pp. 19–20.

*Bebeau, M. J. (1985). Teaching ethics in dentistry. *Journal of Dental Education, 49*(4), 236–243.

*Bebeau, M. J. (1988). The impact of a curriculum in dental ethics on moral reasoning and student attitudes. *Journal of Dental Education, 52*(1), 49.

*Bebeau, M. J. (1991). Can ethics be taught? A look at the evidence. *Journal of the American College of Dentists, 58*(1), 5, 10–15.

*Bebeau, M. J. (1993a). Dental ethics comes of age. Review. *Journal of the American College of Dentists, 60*(2), 51–53.

*Bebeau, M. J. (1993b). Designing an outcome-based ethics curriculum for professional education: Strategies and evidence of effectiveness. *Journal of Moral Education, 22*(3), 313–326.

*Bebeau, M. J. (1993c). Social and ethical empowerment of the profession. *Pennsylvania Dental Journal, 60*(6), 14–19.

*Bebeau, M. J. (1994a). Can ethics be taught? A look at the evidence: Revisited. *The New York State Dental Journal, 60*(1), 51–57.

*Bebeau, M. J. (1994b). Influencing the moral dimension of dental practice. In J. Rest & D. Narvaez (Eds.), *Moral development in the professions* (pp. 121–146). Hillsdale, NJ: Lawrence Erlbaum Associates.

Bebeau, M. J., Born, D. O., & Ozar, D. T. (1993). The development of a professional role orientation inventory. *The Journal of the American College of Dentists, 60*(2), 27–33.

*Bebeau, M. J., & Brabeck, M. M. (1987). Integrating care and justice issues in professional moral education: A gender perspective *Journal of Moral Education, 16*(3), 189–203.

*Bebeau, M. J., & Brabeck, M. M. (1989). Moral reasoning and ethical sensitivity among men and women in the professions. In M. M. Brabeck (Ed.), *Who cares? Theory, research, and educational implications of the ethic of care* (pp. 144–164.) New York: Praeger.

*Bebeau, M. J., Rest, J., & Narvaez, D. (in press). Beyond the promise: A perspective for research in moral education. *Educational Researcher,*

*Bebeau, M. J., Rest, J. R., & Yamoor, C. M. (1985). Measuring the ethical sensitivity of dental students. *Journal of Dental Education, 49*(4), 225–235.

*Bebeau, M. J., & Thoma, S. J. (1994). The impact of a dental ethics curriculum on moral reasoning. *Journal of Dental Education, 58*(9), 684–692.

Bebeau, M. J., & Thoma, S. J. (1998, April). *Designing and testing a measure of intermedate level ethical concepts.* Paper presented at the annuel meeting of the American Educational Research Association, San Diego, CA.

*Bebeau, M. J., & Thoma, S. J. (in press). Intermediate concepts and the connection to moral education. *Educational Psychology Review,*

Bennett, W. (1993). *The book of virtues.* New York: Simon & Schuster.

*Benor, D. E., Notzer, N., Sheehan, T. J., & Norman, G. R. (1984). Moral reasoning as a criterion for admission to medical school. *Medical Education, 18,* 423–428.

*Berg, G., Watson, C., Nugent, B., & Gearhart, L. (1994). A comparison of combat's effects on PTSD scores in veterans with high and low moral development. *Journal of Clinical Psychology, 50*(5), 669–676.

*Bergem, T. (1986). Teachers' thinking and behavior: An empirical study of the role of social sensitivity and moral reasoning in the teaching performance of student teachers. *Scandinavian Journal of Educational Research, 30,* 193–203.

*Berkowitz, M. (1980). Book review of James Rest's *Development in judging moral issues. Moral Education Forum, 50*(1), 8–11.

*Bernardi, R. A. (1994). Validating research results when Cronbach's Alpha is below .70: A methodological procedure. *Educational and Psychological Measurement, 54*(3), 766–775.

*Bernardi, R. A., & Arnold, D. F., Sr. (1994). The influence of client integrity and competence and auditor characteristics on materiality estimates. *Irish Accounting Review, 1,* 1–23.

*Bernier, J. (1980). Training and supervising counselors: Lessons learned from deliberate psychological education. *Personnel and Guidance Journal, 59,* 15–20.

*Bertin, B., Ferrant, E., Whiteley, J., & Yokata, N. (1985). Influences on character development during the college years: The retrospective view of recent graduates. In J. Dalton (Ed.), *Promoting values education in student development* (pp. 29–41). Washington, DC: National Association of Student Personnel Administrators.

*Biggs, D., & Barnett, R. (1981). Moral judgment development of college students. *Research in Higher Education, 14,* 91–102.

*Biggs, D., Schomberg, S., & Brown, J. (1977). Moral judgment development of freshmen and their precollege experiences. *Research in Higher Education, 7,* 329–339.

*Black, H., & Phillips, S. (1981). An intervention program for the development of empathy in students. *The Journal of Psychology, 112,* 159–168.

Blasi, A. (1990). How should psychologists define morality? In T. Wren (Ed.), *The moral domain* (pp. 38–70). Cambridge, MA: MIT Press.

*Blizek, W., Cederblorn, J., & Finkler, D. (1981). The humanities and criminal justice. *L.E.A. : The Journal of the American Criminal Justice Association.*

*Bloom, R. (1976). Morally speaking, who are today's teachers? *Phi Delta Kappan, 57,* 624–625.

Bloom, R. (1977). *Resistance to faking on the Defining Issues Test of moral development.* Unpublished manuscript, College of William and Mary, Williamsburg, VA.

*Bloom, R. (1978). Discipline: Another face of moral reasoning. *College Student Journal, 12*(4), 356–359.

*Bloomberg, M. (1974). On the relationship between internal-external control and morality. *Psychological Reports, 35,* 1077–1078.

Blum, L. A. (1980). *Friendship, altruism, and morality.* Boston: Routledge & Kegan Paul.

*Bode, J. R., & Page, R. A. (1980). The ethical reasoning inventory. In L. Kuhmerker, M. Mentkowski, & V. L. Erickson (Eds.), *Evaluating moral development* (pp. 139–150). Schenectady, NY: Character Research Press.

*Boom, J., & Molenaar, P. (1989). A developmental model of hierarchical stage structure in objective moral judgements. *Developmental Review, 9*(2), 133–145.

*Boss, J. A. (1994). The effect of community service work on the moral development of college ethics students. *Journal of Moral Education, 23*(2), 183–198.

*Bouhmama, D. (1984a). Assessment of Kohlberg's stages of moral development in two cultures. *Journal of Moral Education, 13,* 124–132.

*Bouhmama, D. (1984b). A study of the relationship between moral judgment and religious attitude of Algerian university students. *British Journal of Religious Education,* 81–85.

*Bouhmama, D. (1987). Relation of formal education to moral judgment development. *Journal of Psychology, 122,* 155–158.

*Boyes, M., & Allen, S. (1993). Styles of parent–child interaction and moral reasoning in adolescence. *Merrill Palmer Quarterly, 39*(4), 551–570.

*Brabeck, M. (1983). Moral judgment: Theory and research on differences between males and females. *Developmental Review, 3,* 274–291.

*Brabeck, M. (1984). Ethical characteristics of whistle blowers. *Journal of Research in Personality, 18,* 41–53.

Braine, M. D. S. (1959). The ontogeny of certain logical operations. *Psychological Monographs, 73* (5, Whole No. 475).

Brainerd, C. J. (1973). Judgments and explanations as criteria for the presence of cognitive structures. *Psychological Bulletin, 79,* 172–179.

Brainerd, C. J. (1977). Response criteria in concept development research. *Child Development, 48,* 360–366.

Brandt, R. B. (1959). *Ethical theory.* Englewood Cliffs, NJ: Prentice-Hall.

*Bredemeier, B. J., & Shields, D. L. (1984a). Divergence in moral reasoning about sport and life. *Sociology of Sport Journal, 1,* 348–357.

*Bredemeier, B. J., & Shields, D. L. (1984b). The utility of moral stage analysis in the investigation of athletic aggression. *Sociology of Sport Journal, 1,* 138–149.

*Bredemeier, B. J. L., & Shields, D. L. L. (1994). Applied ethics and moral reasoning in the context of sport. In J. R. Rest & D. Narvaez (Eds.), *Moral development in the professions: Psychology and applied ethics* (pp. 173–188). Hillsdale, NJ: Lawrence Erlbaum Associates.

Bridges, C., & Priest, R. (1983). *Development of values and moral judgment of West Point Cadets* (Project report, USMA-OIR-83-002). West Point, NY: United States Military Academy.

*Brown, D., & Annis, L. (1978). Moral development and religious behavior. *Psychological Reports, 43*(3), 1230.

Brown, D. G., & Lowe, W. L. (1951). Religious beliefs and personality characteristics of college students. *Journal of Social Psychology, 33,* 103–129.

Brown, F. (1976). *Principles of educational and psychological testing.* New York: Holt, Rinehart & Winston.

*Bruggeman, E., & Hart, K. (1996). Cheating, lying, and moral reasoning by religious and secular high school students. *Journal of Educational Research, 89*(6), 340–344.

Bruner, J. S. (1964). The course of cognitive growth. *American Psychologist, 19,* 1–14.

*Buier, R. M., Butman, R. E., Burwell, R., & Van Wicklin, J. (1989). The critical years: Changes in moral and ethical decision making in young adults at three Christian liberal arts colleges. *Journal of Psychology and Christianity, 8* (3), 69–78.

Callahan, J.C. (Ed.). (1988). *Ethical issues in professional life.* New York: Oxford University Press.

*Candee, D., Sheehan, T. J., Cook, C. D., & Husted, S. D. (1979). Moral reasoning and physicians' decisions in cases of critical illness. *Proceedings of the 18th Annual Conference of Research in Medical Education, 18,* 93–98.

*Candee, D., Sheehan, T. J., Cook, C. D., Husted, S. D., & Bargen, M. (1982). Moral reasoning and decisions in dilemmas of neonatal care. *Pediatric Research, 16,* 846–850.

*Carroll, J., & Rest, J. (1981). Development in moral judgment as indicated by rejection of lower stage statements. *Journal of Research in Personality, 15,* 538–544.

*Carroll, J., & Rest, J. (1982). Moral development. In J. Wolman & G. Stricker (Eds.), *Handbook of developmental psychology* (pp. 434–451).Englewood Cliffs, NJ: Prentice-Hall.

*Cartwright, C., & Simpson, L. (1990). The relationship of moral judgment development and teaching effectiveness of student teachers. *Education, III,* 139–144.

*Cassells, J., & Redman, B. (1989). Preparing students to be moral agents in clinical nursing practice: Report of a national study. *Nursing Clinics of North America, 24*(2), 463–473.

*Castleberry, S., French, W., & Carlin, B. (1993). The ethical framework of advertising and marketing research practitioners: A moral development perspective. *Journal of Advertising, 22*(2), 39–46.

*Cauble, M. (1976). Formal operations, ego identity and principled morality: Are they related? *Developmental Psychology, 12,* 363–364.

*Chang, F. Y. (1994). School teachers' moral reasoning. In J. R. Rest & D. Narvaez (Eds.), *Moral development in the professions: Psychology and applied ethics* (pp. 71–84). Hillsdale, NJ: Lawrence Erlbaum Associates.

Chase, W. & Simon, H. (1973). Perception in chess. *Cognitive Psychology, 4,* 55–81.

*Chiu, L. (1990). A comparison of moral reasoning in American and Chinese school children. *International Journal of Adolescence and Youth, 2*(3), 185–198.

*Chovan, W., & Freeman, N. (1993). Moral reasoning and personality components in gifted and average students. *Perceptual and Motor Skills, 77*(3, Pt. 2), 1297–1298.

*Clay, M. (1983). Moral reasoning and the student nurse. *Journal of Advanced Nursing, 8*(4), 297–302.

*Clouse, B. (1985). Moral reasoning and Christian faith. *Journal of Psychology and Theology, 13*(3), 190–198.

*Clouse, B. (1991). Religious experience, religious belief and moral development of students at a state university. *Journal of Psychology and Christianity, 10*(4), 337–349.

Clouser, K. D., & Gert, B. (1990). A critique of principlism. *The Journal of Medicine and Philosophy, 15,* 219–236.

Coder, R. (1975). *Moral judgment in adults.* Unpublished doctoral dissertation, University of Minnesota.

*Cognetta, P. (1977). Deliberate psychological education: A high school cross-age teaching model. *The Counseling Psychologist, 4,* 22–24.

*Cohen, E. (1982). Using the Defining Issues Test to assess stage of moral development among sorority and fraternity members. *Journal of College Personnel, 23,* 324–328.

Colby, A., & Damon, W. (1992). *Some do care: Contemporary lives of moral commitment.* New York: Free Press.

Colby, A., Kohlberg, L., Gibbs, J., & Lieberman, M. (1983). A longitudinal study of moral judgment. *Society for Research in Child Development: Monograph Series.* Chicago.

Colby, A., Kohlberg, L., Speicher, B., Hewer, A., Candee, D., Gibbs, J., & Power, C. (1987). *The measurement of moral judgment* (Vols. 1 and 2). New York: Cambridge University Press.

*Connolly, J., & McCarrey, M. (1978). The relationship between levels of moral judgment maturity and locus of control. *The Canada Journal of Behavoral Science, 10*(2), pp. 162–175.

*Conry, E. J., & Nelson, D. R. (1989). Business law and moral growth. *American Business Law Journal, 27*(1), 1–39.

*Cook, C. D. (1978). Influence of moral reasoning on attitudes toward treatment of the critically ill. *Proceedings of the 17th Annual Conference of Research in Medical Education, 17,* 442–443.

*Cook, C. D., & Margolis, C. Z. (1974). Rating pediatric house officer performance. *Pediatric Research, 8,* 472.

*Cook, J. (1985). *The influence of guided group interaction, positive peer culture on ego development and moral judgment of juvenile offenders.* Council for Exceptional Children Secondary Behavioral Disorders.

*Copeland, T., & Parish, T. (1979). An attempt to enhance moral judgment of offenders. *Psychological Reports, 45,* 831–843.

*Cortese, A. (1982). Moral development in Chicano and Anglo children. *Hispanic Journal of Behavioral Sciences, 4*(3), 353–366.

*Crisham, P. (1981). Measuring moral judgment in nursing dilemmas. *Nursing Research, 30*(2), 104–110.

Crossette, B. (1996, October 20). Caste may be India's moral Achilles' heel. *The New York Times,* p. 3.

Crowder, J. W. (1978). *The Defining Issues Test and correlates of moral judgment.* Unpublished master's thesis, University of Maryland.

*Curtis, J., Billingslea, R., & Wilson, J. (1988). Personality correlates of moral reasoning and attitudes toward authority. *Psychological Reports, 63,* 947–954.

Damon, W. (1977). *The social world of the child.* San Francisco: Jossey-Bass.

Damon, W. (1988). *The moral child.* New York: Free Press.

*Daniels, M. H., & Baker, G. L. (1979). Assessing the moral development of medical students: An empirical study. *Proceedings of the 18th Annual Conference of Research in Medical Education, 18,* 87–92.

Davidson, P., Turiel, E., & Black, A. (1983). The effect of stimulus familiarity on the use of criteria and justifications in children's social reasoning. *British Journal of Developmental Psychology, 1,* 49–65.

*Davison, M. L. (1979). The internal structure and the psychometric properties of the Defining Issues Test. In J. Rest (Ed.), *Development in judging moral issues* (pp. 223–245). Minneapolis: University of Minnesota Press.

*Davison, M. L., & Robbins, S. (1978). The reliability and validity of objective indices of moral development. *Applied Psychological Measurement, 2*(3), 391–403.

*Davison, M. L., Robbins, S., & Swanson, D. (1978). Stage structure in objective moral judgments. *Developmental Psychology, 14*(2), 137–146.

*Day, J. (1993). Moral development and small-group processes: Learning from research. *Journal for Specialists in Group Work, 18*(2), 55–66.

*de Casterle, B. D., Jansses, P. J., & Grypdonck, M. (1996). The relationship between education and ethical behavior of nursing students. *Western Journal of Nursing Research, 18*(3), 330–350.

*DeConinck, J. B., & Good, D. J. (1989). Perceptual differences of sales practitioners and students concerning ethical behavior. *Journal of Business Ethics, 8,* 667–676.

Deemer, D. (1986). *Moral judgment and life experience.* Unpublished doctoral dissertation, University of Minnesota.

*Deemer, D. (1989). Moral judgment and life experience. *Moral Education Forum, 14*(2), 11–21.

DeGrazia, D. (1992). Moving forward in bioethical theory: Theories, cases, and specified principlism. *The Journal of Medicine and Philosophy, 17,* 511–539.

*Deka, N., & Broota, K. (1988). Relation between principled moral judgement among four religious communities in India. *Journal of Personality and Clinical Studies, 4*(2), 151–156.

*Dewolfe, T., & Jackson, L. (1984). Birds of a brighter feather: Level of moral reasoning and attitude similarity as determinants of interpersonal attraction. *Psychological Reports, 54,* 303–308.

Diamond, J. (1997). *Guns, germs, and steel: The fates of human societies.* New York: Norton.

*Dickinson, V., & Gabriel, J. (1982). Principled moral thinking (DIT P percent score) of Australian adolescents—sample characteristics and family correlates. *Genetic Psychology Monographs, 106*(1), 25–29.

*Dirks, D. H. (1988). Moral development in Christian higher education. *Journal of Psychology and Theology, 16,* 324–331.

*Dispoto, R. (1977). Moral valuing and environmental variables. *Journal and Research in Science Teaching, 14*(4), 273–288.

Döbert, R. (1990). Against the neglect of content in the moral theories of Kohlberg and Habermas. In T. Wren (Ed.), *The moral domain* (pp. 71–108). Cambridge, MA: MIT Press.

*Dobrin, A. (1989). Ethical judgments of male and female social workers. *Social Work, 34,* 451–455.

*Duckett, L., Rowan-Boyer, M., Ryden, M. B., Crisham, P., Savik, K., & Rest, J. (1992). Challenging misperceptions about nurses' moral reasoning. *Nursing Research, 41,* 323–331.

*Duckett, L. J., & Ryden, M. B. (1994). Education for ethical nursing practice. In J. R. Rest & D. Narvaez (Eds.), *Moral development in the professions: Psychology and applied ethics* (pp. 51–70). Hillsdale, NJ: Lawrence Erlbaum Associates, Inc.

*Duckett, L., Ryden, M., Waithe, M. E., Schmitz, K., Caplan, A., & Crisham, P. (1990). Teaching ethics in professional education. *The NEA Higher Education Journal, 6*(1), 77–84.

Edelstein, W., & Nunner-Winkler, G. (1990). From the introduction to the German edition. In T. Wren (Ed.), *The moral domain* (pp. xvii–xxix). Cambridge, MA: MIT Press.

Educational Leadership (1993). *Educational Leadership* Nov. 1993.

Eisenberg, N. (1986). *Altruistic emotion, cognition and behavior.* Hillsdale, NJ: Lawrence Erlbaum Associates.

Eisenberg, N., Shea, C. L., Carlo, G., & Knight, G. P. (1991). Empathy-related responding and cognition: A chicken and the egg dilemma. In W. M. Kurtines & J. L. Gewirtz (Eds.), *Handbook of moral behavior and development* (Vol. 2, pp. 63–88). Hillsdale, NJ: Lawrence Erlbaum Associates.

*Emler, N., Heather, N., & Winton, M. (1978). Delinquency and the development of moral reasoning. *British Journal of Social Clinical Psychology, 17,* 325–331.

*Emler, N., Palmer-Canton, & St. James, (in press). Politics, moral reasoning and the Defining Issues Test: A reply to Barnett et al. (1995). *British Journal of Social Psychology;*

*Emler, N., Resnick, S., & Malone, B. (1983). The relationship between moral reasoning and political orientation. *Journal of Personality and Social Psychology, 45,* 1073–1080.

*Enright, R., Lapsley, D., Harris, D., & Shawver, D. (1983). Moral development interventions in early adolescence. *Theory into Practice, 22*(1), 134–144.

*Erickson, V. L., Colby, S., Libbey, P., & Lohman, G. (1976). The young adolescent: A curriculum to promote psychological growth. In D. Miller (Ed.), *Developmental education: And oher emerging alternatives in secondary guidance programs* (pp. 73–128) St. Paul: Minnesota Department of Education.

Ericsson, K. A., & Smith, J. (Eds.). (1991). *Toward a general theory of expertise.* New York: Cambridge University Press.

Erikson, E. (1968). *Identity, youth and crisis.* New York: Norton.

*Ernsberger, D., & Manaster, G. (1981). Moral development, intrinsic/extrinsic religious orientation and denominational teachings. *Genetic Psychology Monographs, 104,* 23–41.

Evens, J. (1995). *Indexing moral judgment using multidimensional scaling.* Unpublished doctoral dissertation, University of Minnesota.

*Eyler, J. (1980). Citizenship education for conflict: An empirical assessment of the relationship between principled thinking and tolerance for conflict and diversity. *Theory and Research in Social Education, 8*(2), 11–26.

*Eyler, J. (1982). Test of a model relating political attitudes to participation in high school activities. *Theory and Research in Social Education, 10,* 43–62.

*Eyler, J., & Halteman, B. (1981). The impact of a legislative internship on students' political skill and sophistication. *Teaching Political Science, 9,* 27–34.

*Faucett, J., Morgan, E., Poling, T., & Johnson, J. (1995). MBTI type and Kohlberg's postconventional stages of moral reasoning. *Journal of Psychological Type, 34,* 17–23.

*Felton, G. M., & Parsons, M. A. (1987). The impact of nursing education on ethical/moral decision making. *Journal of Nursing Education, 26*(1), 7–11.

*Fincham, F., & Barling, J. (1979). Effects of alcohol on moral functioning in male social drinkers. *The Journal of Genetic Psychology, 134,* 79–88.

*Finger, W., Borduin, C., & Baumstark, K. (1992). Correlates of moral judgment development in college students. *Journal of Genetic Psychology, 153*(2), 221–223.

Fiske, S. T., & Kinder, D. R. (1981). Involvement, expertise, and schema use: Evidence from political cognition. In N. Cantor & J. Kihlstrom (Eds.), *Personality, cognition, and social interaction* (pp. 171–190). Hillsdale, NJ: Lawrence Erlbaum Associates.

Fiske, S. T., Lau, R. R., & Smith, R. A. (1990). On the varieties and utilities of political expertise. *Social Cognition, 8*, 31–48.

Fiske, S. T. & Taylor, S. E. (1991). *Social cognition* (2nd ed.). New York: McGraw-Hill.

Flavell, J. H. (1963). *The developmental psychology of Jean Piaget.* Princeton, NJ: Van Nostrand.

Flavell, J. H. (1970). Concept development. In P. Mussen (Ed.), *Carmichael's manual of child psychology* (pp. 983–1059). New York: Wiley.

Flavell, J. H. (1985). *Cognitive development.* Englewood Cliffs, NJ: Prentice-Hall.

Flavell, J. H., & Wohlwill, J. F. (1969). Formal and functional aspects of cognitive development. In D. Elkind & J. H. Flavell (Eds.), *Studies in cognitive development: Essays in honor of Jean Piaget* (pp. 60–120). New York: Oxford University Press.

*Fleetwood, R., & Parish, T. (1976). The relationship between moral development test scores of juvenile delinquents and their inclusion in a moral dilemma discussion group. *Psychological Reports, 39*, 1075–1080.

*Ford, J. B., Latour, M. S., Vitrell, S. J., & French, W. A. (1997). Moral judgment and market negotiations: A comparison of Chinese and American managers. *Journal of International Marketing, 5*(2), 57–76.

*Forsyth, D., & Berger, R. (1982). The effects of ethical ideology on moral behavior. *Journal of Social Psychology, 117*, 53–56.

*Foster, V., & Sprinthall, N. (1992). Developmental profiles of adolescents and young adults choosing abortion: Stage sequence, decalage, and implications for policy. *Adolescence, 27*(107), 655–673.

Fowler, J. (1981). *Stages of faith: The psychology of human development and the quest for meaning.* San Francisco: Harper & Row.

*Friedman, W., Robinson, A., & Friedman, B. (1987). Sex differences in moral judgments? A test of Gilligan's theory. *Psychology of Women Quarterly, 11*, 37–46.

*Frish, N. C. (1987). Value analysis: A method for teaching nursing ethics and promoting the moral development of students. *Journal of Nursing Education, 26*(8), 328–332

*Froming, W. J., & McColgan, E. B. (1979). Comparing the Defining Issues Test and the Moral Dilemma Interview. *Developmental Psychology, 15*, 658–659.

*Furnham, A., & Barratt, L. (1988). Moral judgment and personality differences in 'problem children' and delinquents. *Personality and Individual Differences, 9*(1), 187–188.

*Gaertner, K. (1991). The effects of ethical climate on managers' decisions. In M. Sharpe (Ed.), *Morality, rationality and efficiency: Perspectives in socio-economics 1990* (pp. 211–226). New York: Armonk.

Gallatin, J., & Adelson, J. (1970, July). Individual rights and the public good. *Comparative Political Studies*, 226–242.

*Galotti, K., Kozberg, S., & Farmer, M. (1991). Gender and developmental differences in adolescents' conceptions of moral reasoning. *Journal of Youth and Adolescence, 20*(1), 13–30.

*Garwood, S. C., Levine, D. W., & Ewing, L. (1980). Effect of protagonist's sex on assessing gender differences in moral reasoning. *Developmental Psychology, 16*, 677–681.

Gates, H. L. (1998, March 9). The end of loyalty. *The New Yorker*, pp. 34–44.

Gelman, R., & Baillargeon, R. (1983). A review of some Piagetian concepts. In J. H. Flavell & E. M. Markman (Eds.), *Manual of child psychology, Vol. 3, Cognitive development* (pp. 167–230). New York: Wiley.

*Getz, I. (1984). The relation of moral reasoning and religion: A review of the literature. *Counseling and Values, 28*(3), 94–116.

Getz, I. (1985). *The relation of moral and religious ideology to human rights.* Unpublished doctoral dissertation, University of Minnesota.

Gibbs, J. C. (1979). Kohlberg's moral stage theory. A Piagetian revision. *Human Development, 22*, 89–112.

Gibbs, J. C. (1991). Towards an integration of Kohlberg's and Hoffman's theories of morality. In W. M. Kurtines & J. L. Gewirtz (Eds.), *Handbook of moral behavior and development (Vol. 1: Theory)* (pp. 183–222). Hillsdale, NJ: Lawrence Erlbaum & Associates.

*Gielen, U. (1987). Studying moral development with the Defining Issues Test: A progress report from James Rest. *Moral Education Forum, 12*(2),

*Gielen, U., Ahmed, R., & Avellani, J. (1992). The development of moral reasoning and perceptions of parental behavior in students from Kuwait. *Moral Education Forum, 17*(3), 20–37.

*Gielen, U., Cruckshank, H., Johnston, A., Swanzey, B., & Avellani, J. (1986). The development of moral reasoning in Belize, Trinidad-Tobago,and the U.S.A. *Behaviour Science Research, 20*(1–4), 178–207.

*Gielen, U. P., & Markoulis, D. C. (1994). Preference for principled moral reasoning: A developmental and cross-cultural perspectives. In L. L. Adler & U. P. Gielen (Eds.), *Cross-cultural topics in psychology* (pp. 73–87). Westport, CT: Greenwood.

Gilligan, C. (1977). In a different voice: Women's conceptions of the self and of morality. *Harvard Educational Review, 47*, 481–517.

Gilligan, C. (1982). *In a different voice.* Cambridge, MA: Harvard.

Gilligan, C., & Murphy, J. M. (1979). Development from adolescence to adulthood: The philosopher and the 'Dilemma of the Fact.' In D. Kuhn (Ed.), *Intellectual development beyond childhood* (pp. 85–100). San Francisco: Jossey–Bass.

*Givner, N., & Hynes, K. (1983). An investigation of change in medical students' thinking. *Medical Education, 17*, 3–7.

Glass, G. V. (1977). Integrating findings: The meta-analysis of research. *Review of Research in Education, 5*, 351–379.

*Glazer-Waldman, H., Hedl, J., & Chan, F. (1990). Impacting moral reasoning in allied health students. *Journal of Allied Health, 19*(4), 351–362.

*Glover, R. (1994). Using moral and epistemological reasoning as predictors of prejudice. *Journal of Social Psychology, 134*(5), 633–640.

*Glover, R. J. (1997). Relationships in moral reasoning and religion among members of conservative, moderate, and liberal religious groups. *The Journal of Social Psychology, 137*(2), 247–254.

*Goolsby, J., & Hunt, S. (1992). Cognitive moral development and marketing. *Journal of Marketing, 56*(1), 55–68.

*Graham, K., Turnbull, W., & La Rocque, L. (1979). Effects of alcohol on moral judgment. *Journal of Abnormal Psychology, 88*(8), 442–445.

*Green, L. (1980). Safety need resolution and cognitive ability as interwoven antecedents to moral development. *Social Behavior and Personality, 9*(2), 139–145.

*Griffore, R. (1978). Characteristics of teachers' moral judgment. *Educational Research Quarterly, 3*, 20–30.

Gross, P. R., & Levitt, N. (1994). *Higher superstition.* Baltimore: Johns Hopkins University Press.

*Gunzburger, D., Wegner, D., & Anooshian, L. (1977). Moral judgment and distributive justice. *Human Development, 20*, 160–170.

*Gutkin, D., & Suls, J. (1979). The relation between the ethics of personal conscience-social responsibility and principled moral reasoning. *Journal of Youth and Adolescence, 8*, 433–441.

Guttmann, A., & Thompson, D. (1997). *Democracy and disagreement.* Cambridge, MA: Harvard University Press.

Habermas, J. (1990). Justice and solidarity. In T. Wren (Ed.), *The moral domain* (pp. 224–251). Cambridge, MA: MIT Press.

Hart, H. L. A. (1961). *The concept of law.* London: Oxford University Press.

*Hartwell, S. (1990). Moral development, ethical conduct and clinical education. *New York Law School Review, 107.*

*Hartwell, S. (1995). Promoting moral development through experiential teaching. *Clinical Law Review, 1*(3), 505–539.

*Hau, K. (1990). Moral development and the ability to fake in a moral judgement test among Chinese adolescents. *Psychologica, An International Journal of Psychology in the Orient, 33*(2), 106–111.

*Hay, J. (1983). A study of principled moral reasoning within a sample of conscientious objectors. *Moral Education Forum, 3*, 1–8.

Helwig, C. C., Tisak, M. S., & Turiel, E. (1990). Children's social reasoning in context: Reply to Gabennesch. *Child Development, 61*, 2068–2078.

*Hendel, D. (1991). Evidence of convergent and discriminant validity in three measures of college outcomes. *Educational and Psychological Measurement, 51*(2), 351–358.

*Henderson, B., Gold, S., & Clarke, K. (1984). Individual differences in IQ, daydreaming and moral reasoning in gifted and average adolescents. *International Journal of Behavioral Development, 7*, 215–230.

*Henkel, S., & Earls, N. (1985). The moral judgment of physical education teachers. *Journal of Teaching in Physical Education, 4*, 178–189.

*Hernandez, J., & DiClemente, J. (1991). Moral reasoning and unprotected sex among young men. *Journal of Health Education, 23*(6), 347–351.

Hess, R., & Torney, J. (1967). *The development of political attitudes in children.* Chicago, IL: Aldine.

*Heyns, P., Van Niekerk, H., & Le Roux, J. (1981). Moral judgment and behavioral dimensions of juvenile delinquency. *International Journal of Advanced Counselling, 4*, 139–151.

*Hilbert, G. (1988). Moral development and unethical behavior among nursing students. *Journal of Professional Nursing, 4*(3), 163–167.

Hirschfeld, L. A., & Gelman, S. A. (1994). *Mapping the mind: Domain specificity in cognition and culture.* New York: Cambridge University Press.

Hoffman, M. (1991). Empathy, social cognition, and moral action. In W. Kurtines & J. Gewirtz (Eds.), *Handbook of moral behavior and development* (Vol. 1, pp. 275–302). Hillsdale, NJ: Lawrence Erlbaum Associates.

*Holley, R. (1991). Assessing potential bias: The effects of adding religious content to the Defining Issues Test. *Journal of Psychology and Christianity, 10*(4), 323–336.

Holmes, S. (1993). *The anatomy of antiliberalism.* Cambridge, MA: Harvard University Press.

*Holt, L., Kauchak, D., & Person, K. (1980). Moral development, educational attitudes and self-concept in beginning teacher education students. *Educational Research Quarterly, 5*(3), 50–56.

Holyoak, K. J. (1994). Symbolic connectionism: Toward third-generation theories of expertise. In K. A. Ericsson & J. Smith (Eds.), *Toward a general theory of expertise* (pp. 301–336). New York: Cambridge University Press.

*Hood, A. (1984). Student development: Does participation affect growth? *Bulletin of the Association of College Unions–International, 54*, 16–19.

*Houston, J. (1983). Kohlberg-type moral instruction and cheating behavior. *College Student Journal, 17*, 196–204.

*Howard-Hamilton, M. (1994). An assessment of moral development in gifted adolescents. *Roeper Review, 17*(1), 57–59.

*Howard-Hamilton, M., & Franks, B. (1995). Gifted adolescents: Psychological behaviors, values, and developmental implications [Special issue: The psychology of the gifted]. *Roeper Review, 17*(3), 186–191.

Hunter, J. D. (1991). *Culture wars: The struggle to define America.* New York: Basic.

*Hurt, B. (1977). Psychological education for teacher education students: A cognitive-developmental curriculum. *The Counseling Psychologist, 6*, 57–60.

*Hustead, S. D. (1978). Assessment of moral reasoning in pediatric faculty, house officers, and medical students. *Proceedings of the 17th Annual Conference of Research in Medical Education, 17*, 439–441.

*Icerman, R., Karcher, J., & Kennelley, M. (1991, Winter). A baseline assessment of moral development: Accounting, other business and nonbusiness students. *Accounting Educator's Journal, 46*–62.

*Iozzi, L. A., & Paradise-Maul, J. (1980). Issues at the interface of science, technology and society. In L. Kuhmerker, M. Mentkowski, & V. L. Erickson (Eds.), *Evaluating moral development* (pp. 131–138). Schenectady, NY: Character Research Press.

Iyengar, S., & Ottati, V. (1994). Cognitive perspective in political psychology. In R. S. Wyer & T. K. Srull (Eds.), *Handbook of social cognition* (2nd ed., pp. 143–189). Hillsdale, NJ: Lawrence Erlbaum Associates.

*Jasinska-Kania, A. (1989). Moral values and political attitudes. In N. Eisenberg, J. Reykowski, & E. Staub (Eds.), *Social and moral values. Individual and societal perspectives.* Hillsdale, NJ: Lawrence Erlbaum Associates.

*Jeffrey, C. (1993, Spring). Ethical development of accounting students, business students, and liberal arts students. *Issues in Accounting Education, 26*–40.

Jensen, L. A. (1996). *Different habits, different hearts: Orthodoxy and progressivism in the United States and India.* Unpublished doctoral dissertation, University of Chicago.

Jensen, L. A. (1997a). Culture wars: American moral devisions across the adult lifespan. *Journal of Adult Development, 4,* 107–121.

Jensen, L. A. (1997b). Moral divisions with countries between Orthodoxy and Progressivism: India and the United States. *Journal for the Scientific Study of Religion,*

*Jessee, P., Cecil, C., & Jessee, J. (1991). Pediatric family home visitors: Effectiveness in problem solving. *Children's Health Care, 20*(3), 179–184.

*Johnston, M. (1985). How elementary teachers understand the concept of on-task: A developmental critique. *Journal of Classroom Interaction, 21,* 15–24.

*Johnston, M. (1989). Moral reasoning and teachers' understanding of individualized instruction. *Journal of Moral Education, 18,* 45–59.

*Johnston, M., & Lubomudrov, C. (1987). Teachers' level of moral reasoning and their understanding of classroom rules and roles. *The Elementary School Journal, 88,* 64–77.

*Johnston, M., Lubomudrov, C., & Parsons, M. (1982). The cognitive development of teachers: Report on a study in progress. *Moral Education Forum, 7*(4), 24–36.

*Kalle, R. (1978). The relationship between Kohlberg's moral judgment stage and emotional empathy. *Bulletin of Psychological Society, 1*(3), 191–192.

*Kaseman, T. (1980). *A longitudinal study of moral development of the West Point class of 1981.* West Point, NY: United States Military Academy, Department of Behavioral Sciences and Leadership.

*Kay, S. (1982). Kohlberg's theory of moral development: critical analysis of validation studies with the Defining Issues Test. *International Journal of Psychology, 17,* 27–42.

*Keating, D. (1978). A search for social intelligence. *Journal of Educational Psychology, 70*(2), 218–223.

*Keef, S. P. (1992). The diamond dilemma: A case study. *Accounting Education, 1,* 185–200.

*Keen, C. (1991). Effects of a public issues program on adolescents' moral and intellectual development. In J. Kendall & Assoc. (Eds.), *Combining service and learning, a resource book for community and public service* (Vol. I, pp. 393–404).

*Ketefian, S. (1981a). Critical thinking, educational preparation, and development of moral judgment. *Nursing Research, 30*(2), 98–103.

*Ketefian, S. (1981b). Moral reasoning and moral behavior among selected group of practicing nurses. *Nursing Research, 30*(3), 171–176.

*Ketefian, S. (1989). Moral reasoning and moral education. *Annual Review of Nursing Research, 7,* 173–195.

*Kilgannon, S., & Erwin, T. (1992). A longitudinal study about the identity and moral development of Greek students. *Journal of College Student Development, 33*(3), 253–259.

Killen, M., & Hart, D. (1995). *Morality in everyday life.* New York: Cambridge University Press.

Kilpatrick, W. K. (1993). *Why Johnny can't tell right from wrong.* New York: Simon & Schuster.

Kim, V., & Berry, J. W. (Eds.). (1993). *Indigenous psychologies: Research and experience in cultural context.* Newbury Park, CA: Sage.

*King, P. M., & Kitchener, K. S. (1994). *Developing reflective judgment.* San Francisco: Jossey-Bass.

*King, P., Kitchener, K., Wood, P., & Davison, M. (1989). Relationships across developmental domains: A longitudinal study of intellectual, moral, and ego development. In M. L. Commons, C. armon, L. Kohlberg, F. A. Richards, J. D. Sinrott (Eds.), *Comparisons and applications of developmental models.* (pp. 57–72). New York: Praeger.

Kintsch, W., & van Dijk, T. A. (1978). Toward a model of text comprehension and production. *Psychological Review, 85,* 363–394.

*Kitchener, K., King, P., Davison, M., Parker, C., & Wood, P. (1984). A longitudinal study of moral and ego development in young adults. *Journal of Youth and Adolescence, 13*(3), 197–211.

*Kitchener, K., King, P., Wood, P., & Davison, M. (1989). Sequentiality and consistency in the development of reflective judgment: A six-year longitudinal study. *Journal of Applied Developmental Psychology, 10,* 73–95.

Kohlberg, L. (1958). *The development of modes of moral thinking and choice in the years 10–16.* Unpublished doctoral dissertation, University of Chicago.

Kohlberg, L. (1968). The child as a moral philosopher. *Psychology Today, 7,* 25–30.

Kohlberg, L. (1969). Stage and sequence: The cognitive developmental approach to socialization. In D. A. Goslin (Ed.), *Handbook of socialization theory* (pp. 347–480). Chicago: Rand McNally.

Kohlberg, L. (1971). From is to ought: How to commit the naturalistic fallacy and get away with it in the study of moral development. In T. Mischel (Ed.), *Cognitive development and epistemology* (pp. 151–236). New York: Academic.

Kohlberg, L. (1976). Moral stages and moralization: The cognitive developmental approach. In T. Lickona (Ed.), *Moral development and behavior* (pp. 31–53), New York: Holt, Rinehart & Winston.

Kohlberg, L. (1981). *Essays on moral development: The philosophy of moral development: Moral stages and the idea of justice (Vol. 1).* San Francisco: Harper & Row.

Kohlberg, L. (1984). *Essays on moral development: The psychology of moral development: The nature and validity of moral stages* (Vol. 2). San Francisco: Harper & Row.

Kohlberg, L. (1986a). A current statement on some theoretical issues. In S. Modgil & C. Modgil, (Eds.), *Lawrence Kohlberg: Consensus and controversy* (pp. 485–546). Philadelphia: Falmer.

Kohlberg, L. (1986b). My personal search for universal morality. *Moral Education Forum, 11*(1), 4–10.

Kohlberg, L., Boyd, D. R., & Levine, C. (1990). The return of Stage 6: Its principle and moral point of view. In T. Wren (Ed.), *The moral domain: Essays in the ongoing discussion between philosophy and the social sciences* (pp. 151–181). Cambridge, MA: MIT Press.

Kohlberg, L., & Candee, D. (1984). The relationship between moral judgment to moral actions. In L. Kohlberg (Ed.), *Essays on moral development: The nature and validity of moral stages* (Vol. 2, pp. 498–581). San Francisco: Harper & Row.

Kohlberg, L., & Power, C. (1981). Moral development, religious thinking, and the question of a seventh stage. In L. Kohlberg (Ed.), *Essays on moral development. Vol. 1: The philosophy of moral development* (pp. 311–372). New York: Harper & Row.

Kramer, R. (1968). *Moral development in young adulthood.* Unpublished doctoral dissertation, University of Chicago.

Kramer, S. N. (1967). *The cradle of civilization.* New York: Time–Life.

*Krawczck, R. M. (1997). Teaching ethics: Effect on moral development. *Nursing Ethics, 4*(1), 57–65.

Krebs, D., Vermeulen, S., Carpendale, J., & Denton, K. (1991). Structural and situational influences on moral judgment: The interaction between stage and dilemma. In W. Kurtines & J. Gewitz (Eds.), *Handbook of moral behavior and development,* (Vol. 2, pp. 139–170). Hillsdale, NJ: Lawrence Erlbaum Associates.

*Lampe, J., & Finn, D. (1992). A model of auditors' ethical decision process. *Auditing: A Journal of Practice and Theory* (Supplement), 1–21.

Lapsley, D. K. (1996). *Moral psychology.* Boulder, CO: Westview Press.

Lapsley, D. K., Sison, G. C., & Enright, R. D. (1976). *A note concerning moral judgment, authority biases and the Defining Issues Test.* Unpublished manuscript, University of New Orleans.

*Lawrence, J. A. (1980). Moral judgment intervention studies using the Defining Issues Test. *Journal of Moral Education, 9,* 14–29.

*Lawrence, J. (1987). Verbal processing of the Defining Issues Test by principled and non-principled moral reasoners. *Journal of Moral Education, 16*(2),117–130.

*Leahy, R. L. (1981). Parental practice and the development of moral judgment and self-image disparity during adolescence. *Developmental Psychology, 17,* 580–594.

*Leahy, R., & Eiter, M. (1980). Moral judgment and the development of real and ideal androgynous self-image during adolescence and young adult. *Developmental Psychology, 16,* 302–370.

*Leming, J. (1978). Cheating behavior, situational influence, and moral development. *Journal of Educational Research, 71,* 214–217.

Leming, J. (1997). Research and practice in character education: A historical perspective. In A. Molnar & K. J. Rehage (Eds.), *The construction of children's character* (pp. 31–44). Chicago: University of Chicago Press.

Letchworth, G. A., & McGee, D. (1981). *Influence of ego-involvement, attitude and moral development on situational moral reasoning.* Unpublished manuscript, University of Oklahoma.

Levinson, D. J., Darrow, C. N., Klein, E. B., Levinson, M. H., McKee, B. (1978). *The seasons of a man's life.* New York: Ballantine.

Lewicki, P. (1986). *Non-conscious social information processing.* New York: Academic.

Lickona, T. (1991). *Educating for character.* New York: Bantam.

Lind, G. (1995, April). *The meaning and measurement of moral competence revisited.* Paper presented at the Annual Meeting of the American Educational Research Association, San Francisco.

*Lippitt, M., & Day, V. (1982). A comparison of moral reasoning of group and individuals on the Defining Issues Test. *Academy of Management Journal, 25*(1), 201–208.

Locke, D. (1986). A psychologist among the philosophers: Philosophical aspects of Kohlberg's theories. In S. Modgil & C. Modgil (Eds.), *Lawrence Kohlberg: Consensus and controversy* (pp. 21–38). Philadelphia: Falmer.

*Loeb, S. E. (1991). The evaluation of outcomes of accounting ethics education. *Journal of Business Ethics, 10,* 77–84.

*Lonky, E., Kaus, C., & Roodin, P. (1984). Life experience and mode of coping: Relation to moral judgment in adulthood. *Developmental Psychology, 20*(6), 1159–1167.

*Lonky, E., Reihman, J. M., & Serlin, R. C. (1981). Political values and moral judgment in adolescence. *Youth & Society, 12*(4), 423–441.

*Lonky, E., Roodin, P., & Rybash, J. (1988). Moral judgment and sex role orientation as a function of self and other presentation mode. *Journal of Youth and Adolescence, 17*(2), 189–194.

Lourenço, O., & Machado, A. (1996). In defense of Piaget's theory: A reply to 10 common criticisms. *Psychological Review, 103*(1), 143–164.

*Loxley, J., & Whiteley, J. (1986). *Character development in college students* (Vol. 2). Schenectady, NY: Character Research Press.

*Lutwak, N., & Hennessy, J. (1985). Interpreting measures of moral development. *Measurement and Evaluation in Counseling and Development, 18,* 26–31.

*Lupfer, M. B., Cohen, R. & Bernard, J. L. (1987). The influence of level of moral reasoning on the decisions of jurors. *Journal of Social Psychology, 13,* 78–87.

*Ma, H. (1985a). Consistency of stage structure in objective moral judgment across differential samples. *Psychological Reports, 57,* 987–990.

*Ma, H. (1985b). Cross-cultural study of the development of law-abiding orientation *Psychological Reports, 57,* 967–974.

*Ma, H. (1988a). The Chinese perspectives on moral judgment development. *International Journal of Psychology, 23,* 201–227.

*Ma, H. (1988b). Objective moral judgment in Hong Kong, mainland China and England. *Journal of Cross-Cultural Psychology, 19*(1), 78–95.

*Ma, H. (1989). Moral orientation and moral judgment in adolescents in Hong Kong, mainland China and England. *Journal of Cross-Cultural Psychology, 20*(2), 152–177.

*Ma, H. K. (1992). The relation of altruistic orientation to human relationships and moral judgment in Chinese people. *International Journal of Psychology, 27*(6), 377–400.

*Ma, H., & Chan, W. (1987). The moral judgments of Chinese students. *Journal of Social Psychology, 127*(5), 491–497.

*Maccallum, J. A. (1993). Teacher reasoning and moral judgement in the context of student discipline situations. *Journal of Moral Education, 22*(1), 3–18.

MacIntyre, A. (1981). *After virtue.* Notre Dame, IN: University of Notre Dame Press.

MacIntyre, A. (1988). *Whose justice? Which rationality?* Notre Dame, IN: University of Notre Dame Press.

Marcus, G. E., Sullivan, J. L., Theiss-Morse, E., & Wood, S. L. (1995). *With malice toward some: How people make civil liberties judgments.* New York: Cambridge University Press.

*Marlowe, A., & Auvenshine, C. (1982). Greek membership: Its impact on the moral development of college freshmen. *Journal of College Student Personnel, 23,* 53–57.

*Marron, J., & Kayson, W. (1984). Effects of living status, gender, and year in college on college students. *Psychological Reports, 55,* 811–814.

*Martin, R. M., Shafto, M., & Vandeinse, W. (1977). The reliability, validity, and design of the Defining Issues Test. *Developmental Psychology, 13*(5), 460–468.

Marty, M. E., & Appleby, R. S. (1993). *Fundamentalism and the State*. Chicago: University of Chicago.

*Mason, M., & Collison, B. (1995). Adolescent substance abuse treatment incorporating 'rites of passage.' *Alcoholism Treatment Quarterly,13*(3), 69–79.

*Maul, J. (1978). A high school with intensive education: Moral atmosphere and moral reasoning. *Journal of Moral Education, 10*(1), 9–17.

*Mayton, D., Diessner, R., & Granby, C. (1993). Nonviolence and moral reasoning. *Journal of Social Psychology, 133*(5), 745–746.

*McClelland, D., Constantine, C., & Regalado, D. (1978). Effects of child rearing practices and adult maturity. *Psychology Today, 12*(1), 42–53.

McClosky, H., & Brill, A. (1983). *Dimensions of tolerance: What Americans believe about civil liberties*. New York: Russell Sage.

*McColgan, E., Rest, J., & Pruitt, D. (1983). Moral judgment and antisocial behavior in early adolescence. *Journal of Applied Developmental Psychology, 4*, 189–199.

*McCrae, R. (1985). Review of the Defining Issues Test. In J. V. Mitchell, Jr. (Ed.), *The ninth mental measurements yearbook* (pp. 439– 440). Lincoln: University of Nebraska Press.

*McCullough, L. (1985). Ethics in dental medicine: A framework for moral responsibility in dental practice. *Journal of Dental Education, 49*(4), 219–224.

*McGeorge, C. (1975). The susceptibility to faking of the Defining Issues Test of moral development. *Developmental Psychology, 11*, 108.

*McGeorge, C. (1976). Some correlates of principled moral thinking in young adults. *Journal of Moral Education, 5*, 265–273.

*McGraw, K., & Bloomfield, J. (1987). Social influence on group moral decisions: The interactive effects of moral reasoning and sex role orientation. *Journal of Personality and Social Psychology, 53*(6), 1080–1087.

*McNeel, S. P. (1991). Christian liberal arts education and growth in moral judgment. *Journal of Psychology and Christianity, 10*, 311–322.

*McNeel, S. P. (1994a). Assessment of dimensions of morality in Christian college students. In D. J. Lee & G. G. Stronks (Eds.), *Assessment in Christian higher education: Rhetoric and reality* Lanham, MD: University Press of America.

*McNeel, S. P. (1994b). College teaching and student moral development. In J. Rest & D. Narvaez (Eds.), *Moral development in the professions: Psychology and applied ethics* (pp. 27–50). Hillsdale, NJ: Lawrence Erlbaum Associates.

*McNergney, R., & Satterstrom, L. (1984). Teacher characteristics and teacher performance. *Contemporary Educational Psychology, 9*, 19–24.

*Mentkowski, M. (1980). Creating a mindset for evaluating a liberal arts curriculum where valuing is a major outcome. In L. Kuhmerker, M. Mentkowski, & V. L. Erickson (Eds.), *Evaluating moral development* (pp. 27– 62). Schenectady, NY: Character Research Press.

*Mentkowski, M., & Doherty, A. (1983). Abilities that last a lifetime: Outcome of the Alverno experience. *American Association for Higher Education Bulletin, 36* (6), 3–6.

*Mentkowski, M., & Strait, M. (1983). *A longitudinal study of student change in cognitive development, learning styles, and generic abilities in an outcome-centered liberal arts curriculum*. Milwaukee, WI: Alverno College, Office of Research and Evaluation.

*Meyer, P. (1977). Intellectual development: Analysis of religious content. *Counseling Psychologist, 6*, 47–50.

*Miceli, M., Dozier, J., & Near, J. (1991). Blowing the whistle on data fudging: A controlled field experiment. *Journal of Applied Social Psychology, 21*(4), 271–295.

Miller, J. G. (1997). Agency and context in cultural psychology: Implications for moral theory. In H. D. Saltzstein (Ed.), *Culture as a context for moral development: New perspectives on the particular and the universal, new directions for child development* (pp. 69–86). San Francisco: Jossey-Bass.

Modgil, S., & Modgil, C. (Eds.). (1986). *Lawrence Kohlberg: Consensus and controversy*. Philadelphia: Falmer.

Moon, Y. L. (1985, April). *A review of cross-cultural studies on moral judgment development using the Defining Issues Test*. Paper presented at AERA annual meeting, Chicago.

*Moreland, K. (1985). Review of the Defining Issues Test. In J. V. Mitchell, Jr. (Ed.), *The ninth mental measurements yearbook* (pp. 440–442). Lincoln: University of Nebraska Press.

*Muehleman, T., & Barrett, T. (1983). Conflict compromise theory on preference for stages of moral reasoning. *Psychological Reports, 53,* 1015–1018.

Munsey, B. (Ed.). (1980). *Moral development, moral education and Kohlberg.* Birmingham, AL: Religious Education Press.

*Murk, D., & Addleman, J. (1992). Relations among moral reasoning, locus of control, and demographic variables among college students. *Psychological Reports, 70*(2), 467–476.

Murphy, J. M., & Gilligan, C. (1980). Moral development in late adolescence and adulthood: A critique and reconstruction of Kohlberg's theory. *Human Development, 23,* 77–104.

*Mustapha, S., & Seybert, J. (1990). Moral reasoning in college students: Effects of two general education curricula. *Educational Research Quarterly, 14*(4), 32–40.

*Nardi, P., & Tsujimoto, R. (1978). The relationship of moral maturity and ethical attitude. *Journal of Personality, 7,* 365–377.

*Narvaez, D. (1991). Counseling for morality: A look at the four–component model. *Journal of Psychology and Christianity, 10*(4), 358–365.

*Narvaez, D. (1993a). High achieving students and moral judgment. *Journal for the Education of the Gifted, 16*(3), 268–279.

*Narvaez, D. (1994). Opening a new window into the moral mind: Recall for moral stories. *Moral Education Forum, 19*(3), 2–13.

*Narvaez, D. (1998). The influence of moral schemas on the reconstruction of moral narratives in eighth graders and college students. *Journal of Educational Psychology, 90,* 13–24.

Narvaez, D. (1999). *Expertise differences in comprehending moral narratives: Recall, think aloud, importance ratings and giving advice.* Manuscript submitted for publication.

*Narvaez, D. (in press). Using discourse processing methods to study moral thinking. *Educational Psychology Review.*

*Narvaez, D., Bentley, J., Gleason, T., & Samuels, S. J. (1998). Moral theme comprehension in third grade, fifth grade and college students. *Reading Psychology, 19*(2), 217–241.

*Narvaez, D., Getz, I., Thoma, S. J., & Rest, J. (in press). Individual moral judgment and cultural ideology. *Developmental Psychology,*

Narvaez, D., Gleason, T., Mitchell, C., & Bentley, J. (1999). *Moral theme comprehension in children.* Manuscript submitted for publication.

Narvaez, D., Mitchell, C., & Linzie, B. (1998). *Cultural influences on online text elaborations.* Paper presented at the Annual meeting on the Society for Text and Discourse, Madison, WI.

*Narvaez, D., & Rest, J. (1990). Morality: A common concern. *Counseling and Human Development, 22*(8), 1–12.

*Narvaez, D., & Rest, J. (1995). The four components of acting morally. In W. Kurtines & J. Gewirtz (Eds.), *Moral behavior and moral development: An introduction* (pp. 385–400). New York: McGraw-Hill.

*Nevin, K. J., & McNeel, S. P. (1992). Facilitating student moral development through faculty development. *Moral Education Forum, 17*(4), 12–18.

*Newell, K., Young, L., & Yamoor, C. (1985). Moral reasoning in dental hygiene students *Journal of Dental Education, 49*(2), 79–84.

Newsweek (1994, June 13). *Newsweek, 52.*

*Nichols, K., Isham, M., & Austad, C. (1977). A junior high school curriculum to promote psychological growth and moral reasoning. In G. D. Miller (Ed.), *Developmental theory and its application in guidance programs* (pp. 93–122). St. Paul: Minnesota Department of Education.

*Nichols, M., & Day, V. (1982). A comparison of moral reasoning of groups and individuals on the Defining Issues Test. *Academy of Management Journal, 25*(1), 201–208.

Niebuhr, R. (1943). *The nature and destiny of man: A Christian interpretation* (Vols. 1 & 2). New York: Scribner's Sons.

Nietzsche, F. (1886/1968). Beyond good and evil. In W. Kaufman (Trans.), *The portable Nietzsche* (pp. 443–447). New York: Viking.

Nisbett, R. E.. & Wilson, T. D. (1977). Telling more than we can know: Verbal reports on mental processes. *Psychological Review, 84*(3), 231–259.

*Nokes, K. M. (1989). Rethinking moral reasoning theory. *Image: Journal of Nursing Scholarship, 21,* 172–175.

Nozick, R. (1974). *Anarchy, state, and utopia.* New York: Basic.

Nucci, L. P. (1985). Children's conceptions of morality, social convention, and religious prescription. In C. Harding (Ed.), *Moral dilemmas* (pp. 137–174). Chicago: Precedent.

Nucci, L. P. (1991). Doing justice to morality in contemporary values education. In J. S. Benninga (Ed.), *Moral, character, and civic education in the elementary school* (pp. 21–42). New York: Teachers College Press.

Nucci, L. P., & Nucci, M. P. (1982a). Children's responses to moral and social conventional transgressions in free-play settings. *Child Development, 53,* 403–412.

Nucci, L. P., & Nucci, M. P. (1982b). Children's social interactions in the context of moral and conventional transgressions. *Child Development, 53,* 403–412.

*Nucci, L., & Pascarella, E. (1987). The influence of college on moral development. In J. Smart (Ed.), *Higher education. Handbook of theory and research,* (Vol. 3, pp. 271–326). New York: Agathon.

*Nucci, L., & Weber, E. K. (1991). The domain approach to values education: From theory to practice. In W. M. Kurtines & J. L. Gewirtz (Eds.), *Handbook of moral behavior and development, Volume 3: Application* (pp. 251–266). Hillsdale, NJ: Lawrence Erlbaum Associates.

*Oja, S. (1977). A cognitive-structural approach to adult conceptual, moral and ego development through in-service education. In G. D. Miller (Ed.), *Developmental theory and its application in guidance program* (pp. 291–298). St. Paul: Minnesota Department of Education.

*Oja, S., & Sprinthall, N. (1978). Psychological and moral development for teachers: Can you teach old dogs? *Character Potential: A Record of Research, 8,* 218–255.

*O'Kane, A., Fawcett, D., & Blackburn, R. (1996). Psychopathy and moral reasoning: Comparison of two classifications. *Personality and Individual Differences, 20*(4), 505–514.

Okin, S. M. (1989). *Justice, gender, and the family.* New York: Basic.

*Olejenik, A. (1980). Adult's moral reasoning with children. *Child Development, 51,* 1205–1238.

*Olsen, D. (1997). Development of an instrument to measure the cognitive structure used to understand personhood in patients. *Nursing—Research, 46* (2), 78–84.

*Oordt, M. (1991). The role of empathy in moral judgment and its application to psychotherapy. *Journal of Psychology and Christianity, 10*(4), 350–357.

*Orchowsky, S., & Jenkins, L. (1979). Sex biases in the measurement of moral judgment. *Psychological Reports, 44,* 1040.

Oser, F. (1980). Stages of religious judgment. In J. Fowler & A. Vergote (Eds.), *Toward moral and religious maturity* (pp. 277–315). Morristown, NJ: Silver Burdett.

*Overvold, M. C., & Konrad, A. R. (1983). Moral reasoning and the public schools. *The Educational Forum, XLVII* 393–409.

*Ozar, D., & Hockenberry, K. (1985). Professional ethics in dentistry: the PEDNET bibliography. *Journal of Dental Education, 49*(4), 244–249.

*Page, R., & Bode, J. (1980). Comparison of measures of moral reasoning and development of a new objective measure. *Educational and Psychological Measurement, 40,* 317–329.

*Page, R., & Bode, J. (1982). Inducing changes in moral reasoning. *Journal of Psychology, 112,* 113–119.

*Paisley, R., Gerler, E., & Sprinthall, N. (1990). The dilemma in drug abuse prevention. *School Counselor, 38*(2), 113–122.

*Parish, T. (1980). The relationship between factors associated with father loss and individual's level of moral judgment. *Adolescence, XV*(59), 535–541.

*Parish, T., & Copeland, F. (1981). The impact of father absence on moral development in females. *Sex Roles, 7*(6), 635–636.

*Parish, T., Rosenblatt, R., & Kappes, B. (1980). The relationship between human values and moral judgment. *Quarterly Journal of Human Behavior, 16*(4), 1–5.

*Park, J., & Johnson, R. (1984). Moral development in rural and urban Korea. *Journal of Cross-Cultural Psychology, 15,* 35–46.

*Parr, G., & Ostrovsky, M. (1991). The role of moral development in deciding how to counsel children and adolescents. *The School Counselor, 39*(1), 14–19.

*Parsons, M., Holt, L., Kauchak, D., & Peterson, K. (1983). A developmental study of levels of moral judgment and perception of ideal teacher roles. *Focus on Learning, 9*, 25–31.

*Pascarella, E. T., & Terenzini, P. (1991). *How college affects students: Findings and insights from twenty years of research.* San Francisco: Jossey-Bass.

Pence, G. (1980). *Ethical options in medicine.* Oradell, NJ: Medical Economics Co.

*Penn, W. (1990). Teaching ethics—a direct approach. *Journal of Moral Education, 19*(2), 124–138.

*Perez-Delgado, E., Garcia-Ros, R., & Clemente-Carrion, A. (1992). The influence of formal education and sex variables on the development of sociomoral reasoning. *Revista de Psicologia Universitas Tarragonensis, 14*(2),63–92.

Phillips, D., & Nicolayev, J. (1978). Kohlbergian moral development: A progressing or degenerating research program. *Educational Theory, 28*, 286–301.

Piaget, J. (1932/1965). *The moral judgment of the child* (M. Gabain, Trans.). New York: Free Press.

Pinker, S. (1997). *How the mind works.* New York: Norton.

*Plueddemann, J. (1989). The relationship between moral reasoning and pedagogical preference in Kenyan and American college students. *Religious Education, 84*, 506–520.

*Ponemon, L. (1990). Ethical judgments in accounting: A cognitive-developmental perspective. *Critical Perspectives on Accounting,* 191–215.

*Ponemon, L. (1992a). Auditor underreporting of time and moral reasoning: An experimental-lab study. *Contemporary Accounting Research, 9*, 171–189.

*Ponemon, L. (1992b, April/May). Ethical reasoning and selection-socialization in accounting. *Accounting, Organizations and Society,* 239–258.

*Ponemon, L. (1993a, Fall). Can ethics be taught in accounting? *Journal of Accounting Education,* 1–29.

*Ponemon, L. (1993b). The influence of ethical reasoning on auditors' perceptions of management's competence and integrity. *Advances in Accounting,* 1–29.

*Ponemon, L., & Gabhart, D. (1990). Auditor independence judgments: A cognitive developmental model and experimental evidence. *Contemporary Accounting Research, 7*, 227–251.

*Ponemon, L. A., & Gabhart, D. (1994). The accounting and auditing profession: An application of ethical reasoning research. In J. R. Rest & D. Narvaez (Eds.), *Moral development in the professions* (pp. 101–120). Hillsdale, NJ: Lawrence Erlbaum Associates.

*Ponemon, L., & Glazer, A. (1990). Accounting education and ethical development: The influence of liberal learning on students and alumni in accounting practice. *Issues in Accounting Education, 5*(2), 195–207.

*Potter, R. E. (1997). Considering moral sensitivity in media ethics courses and research. *Journal of Mass Media Ethics, 12*(1), 51–64.

*Powell, R. E., Locke, D. C., & Sprinthall, N. A. (1991). Female offenders and their guards: A programme to promote moral and ego development of both groups. *Journal of Moral Education, 20*, 191–203.

Power, C., Higgins, A., & Kohlberg, L. (1989). *Lawrence Kohlberg's approach to moral education.* New York: Columbia University Press.

*Pratt, M., Golding, G., & Hunter, W. (1983). Aging as ripening: Character and consistency of moral judgment in young, mature and older adults. *Human Development, 26*(9–10), 277–288.

*Pratt, M., Golding, G., & Hunter, W. (1984). Does morality have a gender?: Sex, sex role, and moral judgment relationships across the adult life span. *Merrill-Palmer Quarterly, 30*(4), 321–348.

*Pratt, M., & Royer, J. (1982). When rights and responsibilities don't mix: Sex and sex-role patterns in moral judgment orientation. *Canadian Journal of Behavioral Science, 14*(3), 190–204.

*Prawat, R. (1976). Mapping the affective domain in young adolescents. *Journal of Educational Psychology, 68*(5), 566–572.

*Prentice, J., Mueller, D., & Golab, A. (1989). Assessing moral judgment by selective recall: A review. *Journal of Research and Development in Education, 22*(4), 47–50.

*Presley, S. (1985). Moral judgment and attitudes toward authority of political resisters. *Journal of Research in Personality, 19*, 135–151.

*Pressley, M., Hogse, D., & Schmierer, D. (1980). Adults' judgment about adolescents' moral judgment. *Child Development, 51,* 1289–1291.

*Priest, B., Kordinak, S., & Wynkoop, T. (1991). Type of offense and level of moral development among adult male inmates. *Journal of Addictions and Offender Counseling, 12*(1), 2–11.

Pritchard, M. S. (1991). *On becoming responsible.* Lawrence: University of Kansas Press.

Puka, B. (1990). The majesty and mystery of Kohlberg's Stage 6. In T. Wren (Ed.), *The moral domain: Essays in the ongoing discussion between philosophy and the social sciences* (pp. 182–223). Cambridge, MA: MIT Press.

Puka, B. (1991). Toward the redevelopment of Kohlberg's theory: preserving essential structure, removing controversial content. In W. Kurtines & J. Gewirtz (Eds.), *Handbook of moral behavior and development,* (Vol. 1, pp. 373–394). Hillsdale, NJ: Lawrence Erlbaum Associates.

Rawls, J. (1971). *A theory of justice.* Cambridge, MA: Harvard University Press.

Rawls, J. (1993). *Political liberalism.* New York: Columbia University Press.

*Redford, J., McPherson, R., Frankiewicz, R., & Gaa, J. (1995). Intuition and moral development. *Journal of Psychology, 129*(1), 91–101.

Reed, D. R. C. (1997). *Following Kohlberg: Liberalism and the practice of the democratic community.* Notre Dame, IN: University of Notre Dame Press.

*Reiman, A., & Parramore, B. (1993). Promoting preservice teacher development through extended field experience. In M. O'Hair & S. Odell (Eds.), *Diversity and teaching: Teacher education yearbook* (pp. 111–121) Forth Worth, TX: Association of Teacher Educators.

*Reiman, A., & Thies-Sprinthall, L. (1993). Promoting the development of mentor teachers: Theory and research programs using guided reflection. *Journal of Research & Development in Education, 26,* 179–185.

*Renwick, S., & Emler, N. (1984). Moral reasoning and delinquent behaviour among students. *British Journal of Social Psychology, 23,* 281–283.

Resnick, L. B., Levine, J. M., & Teasley, S. D. (Eds.). (1991). *Perspectives on socially shared cognition.* Washington, DC: American Psychological Association.

Rest, G. (1979). *Development in moral reasoning, liberal-conservative ideology, and conceptualizing politics.* Unpublished manuscript, Stanford University.

Rest, J. (1969). *Hierarchies of comprehension and preference in a developmental stage model of moral thinking.* Unpublished doctoral dissertation, University of Chicago.

Rest, J. (1973). The hierarchical nature of stages of moral judgment. *Journal of Personality, 41,* 86–109.

*Rest, J. (1974a). The cognitive-developmental approach to morality: The state of the art. *Counseling and Values, 18,* 64–68.

*Rest, J. (1974b). Recent research on the Defining Issues Test. In D. DePalma & J. Foley (Eds.), *Moral development: Current theory and research* (pp. 75–94). Hillsdale, NJ: Lawrence Erlbaum Associates.

*Rest, J. (1975a). Longitudinal study of the Defining Issues Test: A strategy for analyzing developmental change. *Developmental Psychology, 11,* 738–748.

*Rest, J. (1975b). The validity of tests of moral judgment. In J. Meyer, B. Burnham, & J. Cholvat (Eds.), *Values education* (pp. 103–116). Waterloo, Ontario: Wilfred Laurier University Press.

*Rest, J. (1976a). An assessment for moral judgment. *Moral Education Forum, 1*(3), 1–4.

*Rest, J. (1976b). The cognitive-developmental approach to morality: The state of the art. In D. Biggs, C. Beck, & C. Pulvina (Eds.), *Counseling and values* (pp. 225–269). Washington, DC: American Personnel and Guidance Association Press Reprints Series.

*Rest, J. (1976c). New approaches in the assessment of moral judgment, In T. Lickona (Ed.), *Moral development and behavior* (pp. 198– 220). New York: Holt, Rinehart and Winston.

*Rest, J. (1976d). The research base of the cognitive-developmental approach to moral education. In T. Hennesy (Ed.), *Moral and ethical issues in education* (pp. 102–119). New York: Fordham.

*Rest, J. (1979). *Development in judging moral issues.* Minneapolis: University of Minnesota Press.

*Rest, J. (1980a). Basic issues in evaluating moral education programs. In L. Kuhmerker, M. Mentkowski, & V. L. Erickson (Eds.), *Evaluating moral development* (pp. 1–12). Schenectady, NY: Character Research Press.

*Rest, J. (1980b). Development in moral judgment research. *Developmental Psychology, 16,* 251–256.

*Rest, J. (1980c). Developmental psychology and value education. In B. M. Mapel (Ed.), *Kohlberg and moral education: Basic issues in philosophy, psychology, religion, and education* (pp. 101–129). Birmingham, AL: Religious Education Press.

*Rest, J. (1980d). The Defining Issues Test: A survey of research results. In L. Kuhmerker, M. Mentkowski, & V. L. Erickson (Eds.), *Evaluating moral development* (pp. 113–120). Schenectady, NY: Character Education Press.

Rest, J. (1980e, May). Psychological research on the basic assumptions of Kohlbergian moral education programs. *Personnel Guidance Journal,* 602–605.

*Rest, J. (1980f). Understanding the possibilities and conditions of cooperation. *Bulletin of the Menninger Clinic, 44*(5), 524–561.

*Rest, J. (1981). Psychological research on morality and programs in prison education. In L. Morin (Ed.), *On prison education* (pp. 245– 271). Ottawa, Canada: Canadian Government Publishing Centre.

*Rest, J. (1982). A psychologist looks at the teaching of ethics: Moral development and moral education. *The Hastings Center Report, 12*(1), 29–36.

*Rest, J. (1983). Morality. In P. H. Mussen (Series Ed.) & J. Flavell & E. Markman (Vol. Eds.), *Handbook of child psychology: Vol. 3, Cognitive Development* (4th ed., pp. 556–629). New York: Wiley.

*Rest, J. (1984). The major components of morality. In W. Kurtines & J. Gewirtz (Eds.), *Morality, moral development and moral behavior* (pp. 24–38). New York: Wiley.

*Rest, J. (1985a). An interdisciplinary approach to moral education. In M. Berkowitz & F. Oser (Eds.), *Moral education: Theory and application* (pp. 9–25). Hillsdale, N.J.: Lawrence Erlbaum Associates.

*Rest, J. (1985b). Research on moral development: Implications for training counseling psychologists. *The Counseling Psychologist, 12*(3), 19–29.

Rest, J. (1986a). *Manual for the Defining Issues Test* (3rd ed.). Minneapolis: Center for the Study of Ethical Development, University of Minnesota.

*Rest, J. (1986b). *Moral development: Advances in research and theory.* New York: Praeger.

*Rest, J. (1986c). Moral development in young adults. In K. Kitchener & R. Mines (Eds.), *Social cognitive development in young adults* (pp. 92–111). New York: Praeger.

*Rest, J. (1987). Basic issues in evaluating moral education programs. *Sathya Sai Journal of Education in Human Values* (10), 1–7.

*Rest, J. (1988a). Is professional school too late to teach ethics? *Ethics: Easier Said than Done, 1*(1), 22–26. Los Angeles, CA: Josephson Institute for the Advancement of Ethics.

*Rest, J. (1988b). Why does college promote development in moral judgment? *Journal of Moral Education, 17,* 183–193.

Rest, J. (1989). With the benefit of hindsight. *Journal of Moral Education, 18*(2), 134–144.

*Rest, J. (1991). Research on moral development in college students. In A. Garrod (Ed.), *Emerging themes in moral development and moral education,* (Chapter 10). New York: Columbia University Press.

Rest, J. (1993). *Guide to using the DIT, revised.* Minneapolis: Center for the Study of Ethical Development, University of Minnesota.

*Rest, J. (1994). Background: Theory and research. In J. R. Rest & D. Narvaez (Eds.), *Moral development in the professions: Psychology and applied ethics* (pp. 1–26). Hillsdale, NJ: Lawrence Erlbaum Associates.

Rest, J. (1997). Epilogue: Larry Kohlberg remembered. *World Psychology, 2,* (3–4), 413–435.

Rest, J., Ahlgren, A., & Mackey, J. (1973). *Minneapolis police report.* Unpublished manuscript, University of Minnesota.

*Rest, J., Barnett, R., Bebeau, M. J., Deemer, D., Getz, I., Moon, Y. L., Spickelmier, J., Thoma, S. J., & Volker, J. (1986). *Moral development: Advances in research and theory.* New York: Praeger.

*Rest, J., Bebeau, M., & Volker, J. (1986). An overview of the psychology of morality. In J. Rest (Ed.), *Moral development: Advances in research and theory* (pp. 1–39). New York: Praeger.

*Rest, J., Cooper, D., Coder, R., Masanz, J., & Anderson, D. (1974). Judging the important issues in moral dilemmas—an objective test of development. *Developmental Psychology, 10*(4), 491–501.

*Rest, J., Davison, M., & Robbins, S. (1978). Age trends in judging moral issues: A review of cross-sectional, longitudinal and sequential studies of the Defining Issues Test. *Child Development, 49,* 263–279.

*Rest, J., Deemer, D., Barnett, R., Spickelmier, J., & Volker, J. (1986). Life experiences and developmental pathways. In J. Rest (Ed.), *Moral development: Advances in research and theory* (pp. 28–58). New York: Praeger.

*Rest, J., & Narvaez, D. (1990). The college experience and moral development. *Korean studies: Its cross-cultural perspective* (pp. 648–661). Seoul, Korea: The Academy of Korean Studies.

*Rest, J., & Narvaez, D. (1991). The college experience and moral development. In W. Kurtines & J. Gewirtz (Eds.), *Handbook of moral behavior and development* (pp. 229–245). Hillsdale, NJ: Lawrence Erlbaum Associates.

*Rest, J. & Narvaez, D. (Eds.). (1994a). *Moral development in the professions: Psychology and applied ethics.* Hillsdale, NJ: Lawrence Erlbaum Associates.

*Rest, J., & Narvaez, D. (1994b). Summary: What's possible? In J. R. Rest & D. Narvaez (Eds.), *Moral development in the professions: Psychology and applied ethics* (pp. 213–224). Hillsdale, NJ: Lawrence Erlbaum Associates.

Rest, J., & Narvaez, D. (1997). *Ideas for research with the DIT.* Manuscript available from the Center for the Study of Ethical Development, University of Minnesota.

Rest, J., & Narvaez, D. (1998). *Guide for DIT-2.* Manuscript available from the Center for the Study of Ethical Development, University of Minnesota.

*Rest, J., Narvaez, D., Bebeau, M. J., & Thoma, S. J. (in press). A neo-Kohlbergian approach. *Educational Psychology Review,*

Rest, J., Narvaez, D., Thoma, S. J. & Bebeau, M. J. (1998). *DIT2: Devising and testing a revised instrument of moral judgment.* Manuscript submitted for publication.

*Rest, J., & Thoma, S. J. (1985a). Evaluating moral development. In J. Dalton (Ed.), *Promoting values development in college students* (Vol. 4, pp. 77–90) Washington, DC: National Association of Student Personnel Administrators, Monograph Series.

*Rest, J., & Thoma, S. J. (1985b). The relation of moral judgment development to formal education. *Developmental Psychology, 21*(4), 709–714.

*Rest, J., & Thoma, S. J. (1986). Educational programs and interventions. In J. Rest (Ed.), *Moral development: Advances in research and theory* (pp. 59–88). New York: Praeger.

*Rest, J., Thoma, S. J., & Edwards, L. (1997). Designing and validating a measure of moral judgment: Stage preference and stage consistency approaches. *Journal of Educational Psychology, 89*(1), 5–28.

*Rest, J., Thoma, S. J., Moon, Y. L., & Getz, I. (1986). Different cultures, sexes, and religions. In J. Rest (Ed.), *Moral development: Advances in research and theory* (pp. 89–132). New York: Praeger.

*Rest, J., Thoma, S. J., Narvaez, D., & Bebeau, M. J. (1997). Alchemy and beyond: Indexing the Defining Issues Test. *Journal of Educational Psychology, 89*(3), 498–507.

Rest, J., Turiel, E., & Kohlberg, L. (1969). Level of moral development as a determinant of preference and comprehension of moral judgments made by others. *Journal of Personality, 37,* 225–252.

*Rholes, W., & Bailey, S. (1982). Experiences that motivate moral development: The role of cognitive dissonance. *Journal of Experimental Social Psychology, 18,* 524–536.

Richards, P. (1988). *The relation between principled moral reasoning and conservative religious ideology: A critical reevaluation.* Unpublished doctoral dissertation, University of Minnesota.

*Richards, P., & Davison, M. (1992). Religious bias in moral development research: A psychometric investigation. *Journal for the Scientific Study of Religion, 31*(4), 467–485.

*Richmond, J. (1989). Legal decisions and the moral judgment of student affairs administrators. *NASPA Journal, 26,* 219–226.

*Rim, Y. (1981). Correlates of moral judgement in married couples. *Personality and Individual Differences, 2,* 247–248.

*Rim, Y. (1992). Moral development and coping styles. *Personality and Individual Differences, 13*(5), 627–629.

Roetz, H. (1996). Kohlberg and Chinese moral philosophy. *World Psychology, 2* (3–4), 335–363.

*Roffey, A., & Porter, D. (1992). Moral decision making and nontoleration of honor code offenses. *Counseling and Values, 36*(2), 135–149.

*Rotenberg, K. J., Hewlett, M. G., and Siegwart, C. M. (1998). Principled moral reasoning and self-monitoring as predictors of jury functioning. *Basic and Applied Social Psychology, 20* (2), 167–173.

*Rowe, I., & Marcia, J. (1980). Ego identity status, formal operations, and moral development. *Journal of Youth and Adolescence, 9,* 87–99.

*Rybash, J., Roodin, P., & Lonky, E. (1981). Young adults' scores on the Defining Issues Test as a function of a self versus other presentation mode. *Journal of Youth and Adolescence, 10*(1), 25–31.

*Ryden, M. B., Duckett, L., Crisham, P., Caplan, A., & Schmitz, K. (1989). Multi-course sequential learning as a model for content integration: Ethics as a prototype. *Journal of Nursing Education, 28,* 102–106.

Saltzstein, H. D., Millary, M. P., Eisenberg, Z., Dias, M. G., & O'Brien, D. P. (1997). Moral heteronomy in context: Interviewer influences in New York City and Recife, Brazil. In H. D. Saltzstein (Ed.), *Culture as a context for moral development: New perspectives on the particular and the universal, New Directions for child development* (pp. 37–50). San Francisco: Jossey-Bass.

Sandel, M. (1982). *Liberalism and the limits of justice.* Cambridge: Cambridge University Press.

*Sanders, C. (1990). Moral reasoning of male freshmen. *Journal of College Student Development, 31*(1), 5–8.

*Sanders, C., Lubinski, D., & Benbow, C. (1995). Does the Defining Issues Test measure psychological phenomena distinct from verbal ability? An examination of Lykken's query. *Journal of Personality and Social Psychology, 69*(3), 498–504.

*Sapp, G., & Gladding, S. (1989). Correlates of religious orientation, religiosity, and moral judgment. *Counseling and Values, 33*(2), 140–145.

Schacter, D. L. (1996). *Searching for memory.* New York: Basic.

Schiller, R. (1997). *The relationship of developmental tasks to life satisfaction, moral reasoning, and occupational attainment at age 28.* Manuscript submitted for publication.

*Schiller, R. (in press). The relationship of developmental tasks to life satisfaction, moral reasoning, and occupational attainment at age 28. *Adult Development,*

*Schlaefli, A., Rest, J., & Thoma, S. (1985). Does moral education improve moral judgment? A meta-analysis of intervention studies using the Defining Issues Test. *Review of Educational Research, 55*(3), 319–352.

Schomberg, S., & Nelson, J. (1976). *Evaluation of a Christian ethics course for seminarians.* Unpublished manuscript, University of Minnesota.

*Schonert, K., & Cantor, G. (1991). Moral reasoning in behaviorally disordered adolescents from alternative and traditional high schools. *Behavioral Disorders, 17*(1), 23–35.

Schultz, E. D. (in preparation). *Relationship between moral judgment and clinical performance in nursing.* Unpublished doctoral dissertation, University of Minnesota.

*Self, D. J. (1991). Study of the influence of veterinary medical education on the moral development of veterinary students. *Journal of the American Veterinary Medical Association, 198,* 782–787.

*Self, D. J. (1993). The moral development of medical students: A pilot study of the possible influence of medical education. *Medical Education, 27,* 26–34.

*Self, D. J. (1996). Clarifying the relationship of veterinary medical education and moral development. *The Journal of the American Veterinary Medical Association, 209*(12), 2002–2004.

*Self, D. J., & Baldwin, D. C. (1994). Moral reasoning in medicine. In J. Rest & D. Narvaez (Eds.), *Moral development in the professions: Psychology and applied ethics* (pp. 147–162). Hillsdale, NJ: Lawrence Erlbaum Associates.

*Self, D., Baldwin, D. C., Jr., & Olivarez, M. (1993). Teaching medical ethics to first-year students by using film discussion to develop their moral reasoning. *Academic Medicine, 68*(5), 383–385.

*Self, D. J., Baldwin, D. C., Jr., & Wolinsky, F. D. (1992). Evaluation of teaching medical ethics by an assessment of moral reasoning. *Medical Education, 26,* 178–184.

*Self, D. J., & Ellison, E. M. (1998). Teaching engineering ethics: Assessment of its influence on moral reasoning skills. *Journal of Engineering Education, 87*(1), 29–34.

*Self, D. J., & Olivarez, M. (1993). The influence of gender on conflicts of interest in the allocation of limited critical care resources: Justice vs. care. *Journal of Critical Care, 8*(1), 64–74.

*Self, D. J., & Olivarez, M. (1996). Retention of moral reasoning skills over the four years of medical education. *Teaching and Learning in Medicine, 8*(4), 195–199.

*Self, D. J., Olivarez, M., & Baldwin, D. C., Jr. (1994). Moral reasoning in veterinary medicine. In J. R. Rest & D. Narvaez (Eds.), *Moral development in the professions: Psychology and applied research* (pp. 163–172). Hillsdale, NJ: Lawrence Erlbaum Associates.

Self, D. J., Pierce, A., & Shadduck, J. A. (1994). A survey of the teaching of ethics in veterinary education. *Journal of the American Veterinary Medical Association, 204*(6), 944–945.

*Self, D. J., Pierce, A. B., & Shadduck, J. A. (1995). Description and evaluation of a course in veterinary ethics. *The Journal of the American Veterinary Medical Association, 207*(12), 1550–1553.

*Self, D. J., Safford, S. K., & Shelton, G. C. (1988). Comparison of the general moral reasoning of small animal veterinarians vs. large animal veterinarians. *The Journal of the American Veterinary Association, 193,* 1509–1512.

*Self, D. J., Wolinsky, F. D. , & Baldwin, D. C., Jr. (1989). The effect of teaching medical ethics on medical students' moral reasoning. *Academic Medicine, 64,* 755–759.

*Shaub, M. (1994, Spring). An analysis of factors affecting the cognitive moral development of auditors and auditing students. *Journal of Accounting Education,* 1–24.

*Shaver, D. (1985). A longitudinal study of moral development at a conservative religious liberal arts college. *Journal of College Student Personnel, 26,* 400–404.

*Shaver, D. (1987). Moral development of students attending a Christian, liberal arts college and a Bible college. *Journal of College Student Personnel, 28,* 211–218.

*Sheehan, T. J., Husted, S. D., Candee, D., Cook, C. D., & Bargen, M. (1980). Moral judgment as a predictor of clinical performance. *Evaluation and the Health Professions, 8,* 379–400.

*Shields, D., & Bredemeier, B. (1994). *Character development and physical activity.* Champaign, IL: Human Kinetics.

*Shulman, H., Sweeney, B., & Gerler, E. (1995). A computer-assisted approach to preventing alcohol abuse: Implications for the middle school. *Elementary School Guidance and Counseling, 30* [Special issue: Applications of computer technology], 63–77.

*Shuman, C., Fournet, G., Zelhart, P., & Roland, B. (1992). Attitudes of registered nurses toward euthanasia. *Death Studies, 16*(1), 1–15.

Shweder, R. A. (1982). Review of Lawrence Kohlberg's *Essays on moral development, Volume I: The philosophy of moral development. Contemporary Psychology,* 421–424.

Shweder, R. A. (1990). In defense of moral realism: Reply to Gabennesch. *Child Development, 61,* 2060–2067.

Shweder, R. A. (1991). *Thinking through cultures.* Cambridge, MA: Harvard University Press.

Shweder, R. A., Mahapatra, M., & Miller, J. G. (1987). Culture and moral development. In J. Kagan & S. Lamb (Eds.), *The emergence of morality in young children* (pp. 1–83). Chicago: University of Chicago Press.

Shweder, R. A., Mahapatra, M., & Miller, J. G. (1990). Culture and moral development. In J. Stigler, R. A. Shweder, & G. Herdt (Eds.), *Cultural psychology: Essays on comparative human development* (pp. 73–112). New York: Cambridge University Press.

Shweder, R. A., & Much, N. C. (1991). Determinations of meaning: Discourse and moral socialization. In R. A. Shweder (Ed.), *Thinking through cultures* (pp. 186–240). Cambridge, MA: Harvard University Press.

Shweder, R. A., Much, N. C., Mahapatra, M., & Park, L. (1997). The big three of morality (autonomy, community, divinity), and the big three explanations of suffering. In A. Brandt & P. Rosin (Eds.), *Morality and health.* New York: Routledge.

Siegler, R. S. (1997). Concepts and methods for studying cognitive change. In E. Amsel & K. A. Renninger (Eds.), *Change and development: Issues of theory, method, and application* (pp. 77–98). Mahwah, NJ: Lawrence Erlbaum Associates.

*Simmons, D. (1982). Is there compassion in principled moral judgment? *Psychological Reports, 50,* 553–554.

Simon, H. (1973). The structure of ill-structured problems. *Artificial Intelligence, 4,* 181–201.

Simpson, E. L. (1974). Moral development research: A case study of scientific cultural bias. *Human Development, 17,* 81–106.

Sisola, S. (1995). *Principled moral reasoning as a predictor of clinical performance in physical therapy.* Unpublished doctoral dissertation, University of Minnesota.

Smetana, J. G. (1982). *Concepts of self and morality: Women's reasoning about abortion.* New York: Praeger.

Smetana, J. G. (1995). Morality in context: Abstractions, ambiguities, and applications. In R. Vasta (Ed.), *Annals of child development* (Vol. 10, pp. 83–139). London: Jessica Kingsley.

*Smith, M. (1990). Christian education and moral development. *Lutheran Education, 126,* 38–45.

Snarey, J. (1985). The cross-cultural universality of social-moral development. *Psychological Bulletin, 97*(2), 202–232.

Snarey, J. (1991). Faith development, moral development, and nontheistic Judaism: A construct validation study. In W. M. Kurtines & J. L. Gewirtz (Eds.), *Handbook of moral behavior and development,* (Vol. 2, pp. 279–306). Hillsdale, NJ: Lawrence Erlbaum Associates.

Snarey, J., & Keljo, K. (1991). In a Gemeinschaft voice: The cross-cultural expansion of moral development theory. In W. M. Kurtines & J. L. Gewirtz (Eds.), *Handbook of moral behavior and development, Vol. I: Theory* (pp. 395–424). Hillsdale, NJ: Lawrence Erlbaum Associates.

*Sprinthall, N. A. (1994). Counseling and social role taking: Promoting moral and ego development. In J. R. Rest & D. Narvaez (Eds.), *Moral development in the professions: Psychology and applied ethics* (pp. 85–100). Hillsdale, NJ: Lawrence Erlbaum Associates.

*Sprinthall, N. A., & Bernier, J. (1979). Moral and cognitive development of teachers. In T. C. Hennessy (Ed.), *Value and moral education* (pp. 119–145). New York: Paulist Press.

*Sprinthall, N. A., Hall, J. S., & Gerler, E. R., Jr. (1992). Peer counseling for middle school students experiencing family divorce: A deliberate psychological education model. *Elementary School Guidance and Counseling, 26,* 279–294.

*Sprinthall, N., & Scott, J. (1989). Promoting psychological development, math achievement, and success attribution of female students through deliberate psychological education. *Journal of Counseling Psychology, 36*(4), 440–446.

*St. Pierre, K., Nelson, E., & Gabbin, A. (1990, Summer). A study of the ethical development of accounting majors in relation to other business and nonbusiness disciplines. *Accounting Educators Journal,* 23–35.

*Stewart, D. W., & Sprinthall, N. A. (1991). Strengthening ethical judgment in public administration. In J. S. Bowmen (Ed.), *Ethical frontiers in public management* (pp. 243–260). San Francisco: Jossey-Bass.

*Stewart, D. W., & Sprinthall, N. A. (1994). Moral development in public administration. In T. L. Cooper (Ed.), *Handbook of administration ethics* (pp. 325–348). New York: Marcel Dekker.

*Stewart, D. W., Sprinthall, N., & Siemienska, R. (1997). Ethical reasoning in a time of revolution: A study of local officials in Poland. *Public Administration Review, 57*(5), 445–453.

Stevenson, C. L. (1937). The emotive meaning of ethical terms. *Mind, XLVI,* 14–31.

*Stevick, R., & Addleman, J. (1995). Effects of short-term volunteer experience on self-perceptions and prosocial behavior. *Journal of Social Psychology, 135*(5), 663–665.

*Straub, C., & Rodgers. R. (1986). Fostering moral development in college women. *Journal of college student personnel, 19,* 430–436.

Strike, K. A. (1982). *Educational policy and the just society.* Chicago: University of Illinois Press.

*Swanson, J. (1990). Moral reasoning among female baccalaureate nursing students. *The Kansas Nurse, 65*(10), 4–5.

*Tan-Willman, C. (1978). A look at the moral reasoning of prospective Canadian teachers. *Psychological Reports, 43,* 172–174.

*Tan-Willman, C., & Gutteridge, G. (1980). Creative thinking and moral reasoning of academically gifted secondary school adolescents. *Gifted Child Quarterly, 25*(4), 149–154.

*Taylor, J., Waters, B., Surbeck, E., & Kelly, M. (1985). Cognitive, psychosocial, and moral development as predictors of pre-service teachers' ability to analyze child behavior. *College Student Journal, 19,* 65–72.

Taylor, S. E., & Crocker, J. (1981). Schematic bases of social information processing. In E. T. Higgins, C. P. Herman, & M. P. Zanna (Eds.), *Social cognition: The Ontario symposium* (Vol. 1, pp. 89–134). Hillsdale, NJ: Lawrence Erlbaum Associates.

*Thies-Sprinthall, L. (1984). Promoting the developmental growth of supervising teachers; Theory, research, programs and implications. *Journal of Teacher Education, 35,* 329–366.

*Thoma, S. J. (1984). Do moral education programs facilitate moral judgment?: A meta-analysis of studies using the Defining Issues Test. *Moral Education Forum, 9*(4), 20–25.

*Thoma, S. J. (1986). Estimating gender differences in the comprehension and preference of moral issues. *Developmental Review, 6,* 165–180.

*Thoma, S. J. (1989). Standardizing the measurement of moral judgments. *Contemporary Psychology, 34,* 533–535.

*Thoma, S. J. (1993). The relationship between political preference and moral judgment development in late adolescence. *Merrill-Palmer Quarterly, 39*(3) 359–374.

*Thoma, S. J. (1994a). Moral judgment and moral action. In J. Rest & D. Narvaez (Eds.), *Moral development in the professions: Psychology and applied ethics* (pp. 199–211). Hillsdale, NJ: Lawrence Erlbaum Associates.

*Thoma, S. J. (1994b). Trends and issues in moral judgment research using the Defining Issues Test. *Moral Education Forum, 19,* 27–39.

Thoma, S. J. (1997). *Formal education, gender and moral decision-making.* Manuscript submitted for publication.

*Thoma, S. J., Barnett, R., Rest, J., & Narvaez, D. (in press). What does the DIT measure? *British Journal of Social Psychology,*

Thoma, S. J., Bebeau, M. J., & Born, D. O. (1997). *The validity and reliability of the Professional Role Inventory.* Manuscript submitted for publication.

*Thoma, S. J., & Davison, M. (1983). Moral reasoning development and graduate education. *Journal of Applied Developmental Psychology, 4,* 227–238.

Thoma, S. J., MaloneBeach, E., & Ladewig, B. (1997). *Moral judgment and adjustment in late adolescence.* Manuscript submitted for publication.

Thoma, S. J., Narvaez, D., & Rest, J. (1997a). *Does the Defining Issues Test measure psychological phenomena distinct from verbal ability? Some relevant data.* Manuscript submitted for publication.

Thoma, S. J., Narvaez, D., & Rest, J. (1997b). *How does moral judgment relate to political attitudes?* Manuscript submitted for publication.

*Thoma, S. J., Narvaez, D., Rest, J., & Derryberry, P. (in press). Does moral judgment development reduce to political attitudes or verbal ability? *Educational Psychology Review,*

*Thoma, S. J., & Rest, J. (1988). Moral judgment and moral sensitivity as predictors of teacher performance. *Moral Education Forum, 13*(3), 15–20.

*Thoma, S. J., & Rest, J. (in press). The relationship between decision-making and patterns of consolidation and transition in moral judgment development. *Developmental Psychology.*

*Thoma, S. J., Rest, J., & Barnett, R. (1986). Moral judgment, behavior, decision making, and attitudes. In J. Rest (Ed.), *Moral development: Advances in research and theory* (pp. 133–175). New York: Praeger.

*Thoma, S. J., Rest, J., & Davison, M. L. (1991). Describing and testing a moderator of the moral judgment and action relationship. *Journal of Personality and Social Psychology, 61,* 659–669.

Thornlindsson, T. (1978). *Social organization, role-taking, elaborated language and moral judgment in an Icelandic setting.* Unpublished doctoral dissertation, University of Iowa.

Thornton, D., & Thornton, S. (1983). Structure, content, and the direction of development in Kohlberg's theory. In H. Weinreich-Haste & D. Locke (Eds.), *Morality in the making: Thought, action, and the social context* (pp. 73–86.) New York: Wiley.

Tillich, P. (1957). *Systematic theology.* Chicago: University of Chicago Press.

Tisak, M. (1995). Domains of social reasoning and beyond. In R. Vista (Ed.), *Annals of child development* (Vol. 11 pp. 95– 130). London: Jessica Kingsley.

Tisak, M., & Turiel, E. (1988). Variation in seriousness of transgressions and children's moral and conventional concepts. *Developmental Psychology, 24,* 352–257.

*Tjosvold, D. N., & Johnson, D. (1977). Effects of controversy on cognitive perspective taking. *Journal of Educational Psychology, 69*(6), 679–685.

Toulmin, S. (1981). The tyranny of principles. *Hastings Center Report, 11,* 31–39.

Triandis, H. C. (1995). *Individualism and collectivism.* San Francisco: Westview.

Tsujimoto, R., & Emmons, K. (1983). Predicting moral conduct: Kohlberg's and Hogan's theories. *The Journal of Psychology, 115*(2), 241– 244.

*Tsuijomoto, R., & Nardi, P. (1977). A comparison of Kohlberg's and Hogan's theories of moral development. *Social Psychology, 41*(3), 235–245.

*Tucker, A. B. (1977). Psychological growth in a liberal arts course: A cross-cultural experience. In G. D. Miller (Ed.), *Developmental theory and its application in guidance programs* (pp. 225–249). St. Paul: Minnesota Department of Education.

Tulving, E., Schacter, D. L., & Stark, H. A. (1982). Priming effects in word-fragment completion are independent of recognition memory. *Journal of Experimental Psychology; Learning, Memory, and Cognition, 8,* 336–342.

Turiel, E. (1966). An experimental test of the sequentiality of developmental stages in the child's moral judgment. *Journal of Personality and Social Psychology, 3,* 611–618.

Turiel, E. (1975). The development of social concepts: Mores, customs, and conventions. In D. J. DePalma & J. M. Foley (Eds.), *Moral development: Current theory and research* (pp. 7–38). Hillsdale, NJ: Lawrence Erlbaum Associates.

Turiel, E. (1978a). The development of concepts of social structure: Social convention. In J. Glick & K.A. Clarke-Stewart (Eds.), *The development of social understanding* (pp. 25–107). New York: Gardner.

Turiel, E. (1978b). Social regulations and domains of social concepts. *New Directions for Child Development, 1,* 45–74.

Turiel, E. (1983). *The development of social knowledge: Morality and convention.* Cambridge, England: Cambridge University Press.

Turiel, E. (1997). The development of morality. In W. Damon (Ed.), *Handbook of child psychology* (5th ed., vol. 3). In N. Eisenberg (Ed.), *Social, emotional, and personality development,* (pp. 863–932). New York: Wiley.

Turiel, E., & Davidson, P. (1986). Heterogeneity, inconsistency, and asynchrony in the development of cognitive structures. In I. Levin (Ed.), *Stage and structure: Reopening the debate* (pp. 106–143). Norwood, NJ: Ablex.

Turiel, E., Killen, M., & Helwig, C. C. (1987). Morality: Its structure, functions, and vagaries. In J. Kagan & S. Lamb (Eds.), *The emergence of morality in young children* (pp. 155– 244). Chicago: University of Chicago Press.

Uleman, J. S., & Bargh, J. A. (1989). *Unintended thought.* New York: Guilford.

U.S. News (1994, August 4). *U.S. News.*

Vine, I. (1986). Moral maturity in socio-cultural perspective: Are Kohlberg's stages universal? In S. Modgil & C. Modgil (Eds.), *Lawrence Kohlberg: Consensus and controversy* (pp. 431–450). Philadelphia: Falmer.

*Wahrman, J. (1981). The relationship of dogmatism, religious affiliation and moral judgment development. *The Journal of Psychology, 108*(2), 151–154.

Wainryb, C. (1997). The mismeasure of diversity: Reflections on the study of cultural differences. In H. D. Saltzstein (Ed.), *Culture as a context for moral development: New perspectives on the particular and the universal, new directions for child development* (pp. 51–68). San Francisco: Jossey-Bass.

*Walker, H., Rowland, G., & Boyes, M. (1991). Personality, personal epistemology, and moral judgment. *Psychological Reports, 68*(3, Pt. 1), 767–772.

Walker, L. J., deVries, B., & Bichard, S. L. (1984). The hierarchical nature of stages of moral development. *Developmental Psychology, 20,* 960–966.

Walker, L. J., deVries, B., & Trevethan, S. D. (1987). Moral stages and moral orientations in real-life and hypothetical dilemmas. *Child Development, 58,* 842–858.

Walker, L. J., Pitts, R. C., Henning, K. H., & Matsuba, M. K. (1995). Reasoning about morality and real-life moral problems. In M. Killen & D. Hart (Eds.), *Morality in everyday life* (pp. 371–408). New York: Cambridge University Press.

Walzer, M. (1983). *Spheres of justice.* New York: Basic.

*Weber, J., & Green, S. (1991). Principled moral reasoning: Is it a viable approach to promote ethical integrity? *Journal of Business Ethics, 10,* 325–333.

Weinreich-Haste, H. (1983). Social and moral cognition. In H. Weinreich-Haste & D. Locke (Eds.), *Morality in the making: Thought, action, and the social context* (pp. 87–110). New York: Wiley.

*Westbrook, T. (1994). Ethics and journalism. In J. R. Rest & D. Narvaez (Eds.), *Moral development in the professions: Psychology and applied ethics.* (pp. 189–198). Hillsdale, NJ: Lawrence Erlbaum Associates.

*Westman, M. (1986). Moral judgment in retrospect. *Scandinavian Journal of Psychology, 27,* 354–362.

Weston, D. R., & Turiel, E. (1980). Act-rule relations: Children's concepts of social rules. *Developmental Psychology, 16,* 417–424.

*Wheaton, W. (1984). An interview and coding instrument for measuring teacher attitudes about educational issues: A developmental approach. *Moral Education Forum, 9*(1), 2–10.

*Whiteley, J. (1980). Evaluation of character development in an undergraduate residential community. In L. Kuhmerker, M. Mentkowski, & V. L. Erickson (Eds.), *Evaluating moral development* (pp. 63–74). Schenectady, NY: Character Research Press.

*Whiteley, J. M. (1986). The principal findings concerning the development of character during the college years. In J. C. Loxley, & J. M. Whiteley (Eds.), *Character development in college students* (Vol. 2, pp. 265–282). New York: Character Research Press.

*Whiteley, J., Bertin, B., Jennings, I., Lee, I., Magana, H., & Resnikoff, A. (1982). *Character Development in college students, vol 1: The freshman year.* New York: Character Research Press.

*Whiteley, J. M., & Loxley, J. C. (1980). A curriculum for the development of character and community in college students. In V. L. Erickson & J. M. Whiteley (Eds.), *Developmental counseling and teaching* (pp. 262–297). Monterey, CA: Brooks/Cole.

*Whiteman, J., Zucker, K., & Grimley, L. (1978). Moral judgment and the others-concept. *Psychological Reports, 42,* 283–289.

*Wilkins, R. (1980a). If the moral reasoning of teachers is deficient, what hope for pupils? *Phi Delta Kappan, 61*(8), 548–549.

*Wilkins, R. (1980b). The moral reasoning of pre-service teachers: are they prepared for the moral education of pupils? *The South Pacific Journal of Teacher Education, 8*(3 & 4), 115–122.

*Willging, T., & Dunn, T. (1982). The moral development of law students. *Journal of Legal Education, 31*(3/5), 306–358.

*Wilmoth, G., & McFarland, S. (1977). A comparison of four measures of moral reasoning. *Journal of Personality Assessment, 41,* 396–401.

*Wilson, F. (1995). The effects of age, gender, and ethnic/cultural background on moral reasoning. *Journal of Social Behavior and Personality, 10*(1), 67–78.

*Wilson, K., & Deemer, D. (1989). Gender, life experiences, and moral judgment development: A process-oriented approach. *Journal of Personality and Social Psychology, 57*(2), 229–238.

*Wilson, K., Rest, J., Boldizar, J., & Deemer, D. (1992). Moral judgment development: The effects of education and occupation. *Social Justice Research, 5*(1), 31–48.

*Wong, J. M. B. (1977). Psychological growth for adult women: An inservice intervention for teachers. In G. D. Miller (Ed.), *Developmental theory and its application in guidance programs* (pp. 265–290). St. Paul: Minnesota Department of Education.

*Wood, J. A., Longenecker, J. G., McKinney, J. A., & Moore, C. W. (1988). Ethical attitudes of students and business professionals: A study of moral reasoning. *Journal of Business Ethics, 7,* 249–257.

Wren, T. (Ed.). (1990). *The moral domain.* Cambridge, MA: MIT Press.

Wyer, R. S., & Srull, T. K. (Eds.). (1994). *Handbook of social cognition* (2 ed.). Hillsdale, NJ: Lawrence Erlbaum Associates.

*Wygant, S. A. (1997). Moral reasoning about real-life dilemmas: Paradox in research using the Defining Issues Test. *Personality and Social Psychology Bulletin, 23*(10), 1022–1033.

*Wygant, S., & Williams, R. (1995). Perceptions of a principled personality: An interpretative examination of the Defining Issues Test. *Journal of Social Behavior and Personality, 10*(1), 53–66.

Wynne, E., & Ryan, K. (1993). *Reclaiming our schools.* New York: Merrill.

*Yeazell, M., & Johnson, S. (1988). Levels of moral judgment of faculty and students in a teacher education program: A micro-study of an institution. *Teacher Education Quarterly, 15*(1), 61–70.

Youniss, J., & Yates, M. (1997). *Community service and social responsibility in youth.* Chicago: University of Chicago Press.

Youniss, J., & Yates, M. (in press). Youth service and moral identity: A case for everyday morality. *Review of Educational Psychology,*

*Yussen, S. (1976). Moral reasoning from the perspective of others. *Child Development, 47,* 551–555.

Zahn-Waxler, C., Radke-Yarrow, M., Wagner, E., & Chapman, M. (1992). Development of concern for others. *Developmental Psychology, 28,* 126–136.

*Zeidner, M. (1988). Moral judgment patterns of university candidates: Some Israeli findings. *Journal of Cross Cultural Psychology, 19*(1), 114–124.

*Zupancic, M., & Svetina, M. (1993). Relations between moral judgment and the concept of human nature: A study of Slovenian young adults. *Studia Psychologica, 35*(4–5), 425–430.

Author Index

Subject Index

About the Authors

❦ ✦ ❧

James Rest (PhD, 1969, University of Chicago) is professor of educational psychology in the Department of Educational Psychology, and research director of the Center for the Study of Ethical Development, College of Education and Human Development, University of Minnesota.

Darcia Narvaez (PhD, 1993, University of Minnesota) is an assistant professor in the Departments of Curriculum and Instruction and Educational Psychology at the University of Minnesota. She is also executive director of the Center for the Study of Ethical Development and faculty associate of the Center for Cognitive Sciences, University of Minnesota.

Muriel J. Bebeau (PhD, 1977, Arizona State University) is professor in the Department of Preventive Science in the School of Dentistry, University of Minnesota. She is also education director of the Center for the Study of Ethical Development, and faculty associate of the Bioethics Center at the University of Minnesota.

Stephen J. Thoma (PhD, 1986, University of Minnesota) is associate professor in the Child Development Center, Department of Human Development and Family Studies, University of Alabama, and a member of the Center for the Study of Ethical Development, University of Minnesota.